enVisionmath 2.0

Volume 2 Topics 8–16

Authors

Randall I. Charles
Professor Emeritus
Department of Mathematics
San Jose State University
San Jose, California

Jennifer Bay-Williams
Professor of Mathematics
Education
College of Education and Human
Development
University of Louisville
Louisville, Kentucky

Robert Q. Berry, III
Associate Professor of
Mathematics Education
Department of Curriculum,
Instruction and Special Education
University of Virginia
Charlottesville, Virginia

Janet H. Caldwell
Professor of Mathematics
Rowan University
Glassboro, New Jersey

Zachary Champagne
Assistant in Research
Florida Center for Research in
Science, Technology, Engineering,
and Mathematics (FCR-STEM)
Jacksonville, Florida

Juanita Copley
Professor Emerita, College
of Education
University of Houston
Houston, Texas

Warren Crown
Professor Emeritus of Mathematics
Education
Graduate School of Education
Rutgers University
New Brunswick, New Jersey

Francis (Skip) Fennell
L. Stanley Bowlsbey Professor
of Education and Graduate and
Professional Studies
McDaniel College
Westminster, Maryland

Karen Karp
Professor of Mathematics
Education
Department of Early Childhood
and Elementary Education
University of Louisville
Louisville, Kentucky

Stuart J. Murphy
Visual Learning Specialist
Boston, Massachusetts

Jane F. Schielack
Professor of Mathematics
Associate Dean for Assessment
and Pre K-12 Education,
College of Science
Texas A&M University
College Station, Texas

Jennifer M. Suh
Associate Professor for
Mathematics Education
George Mason University
Fairfax, Virginia

Jonathan A. Wray
Mathematics Instructional
Facilitator
Howard County Public Schools
Ellicott City, Maryland

SAVVAS
LEARNING COMPANY

Mathematicians

Roger Howe
Professor of Mathematics
Yale University
New Haven, Connecticut

Gary Lippman
Professor of Mathematics and
Computer Science
California State University,
East Bay
Hayward, California

ELL Consultants

Janice R. Corona
Independent Education Consultant
Dallas, Texas

Jim Cummins
Professor
The University of Toronto
Toronto, Canada

ISBN-13: 978-0-328-89112-2
ISBN-10: 0-328-89112-6

11 2022

Digital Resources

You'll be using these digital resources throughout the year!

Go to SavvasRealize.com

 MP
Math Processes Animations to play anytime

 Learn
Visual Learning Animation Plus with animation, interaction, and math tools

 Practice Buddy
Online Personalized Practice for each lesson

 Assessment
Quick Check for each lesson

Games
Math Games to help you learn

ACTIVe-book
Student Edition online for showing your work

 Solve
Solve & Share problems plus math tools

 Glossary
A-Z Animated Glossary in English and Spanish

 Tools
Math Tools to help you understand

 Help
Another Look Homework Video for extra help

 eText
Student Edition online

SAVVAS **realize.** Everything you need for math anytime, anywhere

Contents

Digital Resources at SavvasRealize.com

And remember, your eText is available at SavvasRealize.com!

TOPIC 8 Extend Understanding of Fraction Equivalence and Ordering

*Lesson exclusively for Indiana at the end of this volume

This shows how fraction strips can be used to determine equivalent fractions.

TOPIC 9 Understand Addition and Subtraction of Fractions

This shows how you can use fraction strips to model the addition of fractions.

TOPIC 10 Extend Multiplication Concepts to Fractions

You can use a number line to help multiply fractions and whole numbers.

$$\frac{1}{3} \times 4 = \frac{4}{3}$$

TOPIC 11 Represent and Interpret Data on Line Plots

*Lesson exclusively for Indiana at the end of this volume

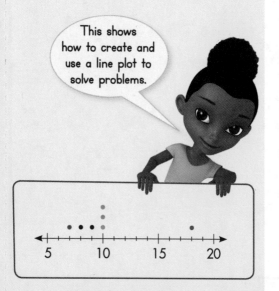

This shows how to create and use a line plot to solve problems.

TOPIC 12 Understand and Compare Decimals

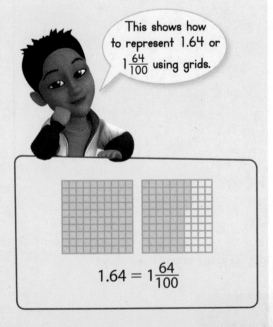

This shows how to represent 1.64 or $1\frac{64}{100}$ using grids.

$$1.64 = 1\frac{64}{100}$$

TOPIC 13 Measurement: Find Equivalence in Units of Measure

*Lesson exclusively for Indiana at the end of this volume

This shows how metric units are related.

DATA

Metric Units of Length
1 m = 1,000 mm
1 cm = 10 mm
1 m = 100 cm
1 km = 1,000 m

TOPIC 14 Algebra: Generate and Analyze Patterns

*Lesson exclusively for Indiana at the end of this volume

This shows how to use a rule to generate a pattern.

Rule: Add 7

TOPIC 15 Geometric Measurement: Understand Concepts of Angles and Angle Measurement

This shows how to measure and draw angles.

TOPIC 16 Lines, Angles, and Shapes

This shows how to draw lines of symmetry in a figure.

STEP UP to Grade 5

These lessons help prepare you for Grade 5.

Problem Solving Handbook

Math processes are ways we think about and do math.

Math processes will help you solve problems.

Math Processes

1 Make sense of problems and persevere in solving them.

2 Reason abstractly and quantitatively.

3 Construct viable arguments and critique the reasoning of others.

4 Model with mathematics.

5 Use appropriate tools strategically.

6 Attend to precision.

7 Look for and make use of structure.

8 Look for and express regularity in repeated reasoning.

There are good Thinking Habits for each of these math processes.

Make sense of problems and persevere in solving them.

Good math thinkers make sense of problems and think of ways to solve them.

If they get stuck, they don't give up.

Here I listed what I know and what I am trying to find.

Mia buys 2 T-shirts for $7 each and a dress that costs $15. She uses a $4 coupon and pays with $40. How much change will Mia get back?

What I Know:
- Mia has $40 and a $4 coupon.
- Mia buys 2 T-shirts for $7 each.
- Mia buys a dress for $15.

What I need to find:
- The amount of change Mia gets.

Thinking Habits

Be a good thinker! These questions can help you.

- What do I need to find?
- What do I know?
- What's my plan for solving the problem?
- What else can I try if I get stuck?
- How can I check that my solution makes sense?

Reason abstractly and quantitatively.

MP

Good math thinkers know how to think about words and numbers to solve problems.

I drew a bar diagram that shows how things in the problem are related.

Sam buys a box of 6 thank you cards that costs $12. How much does each thank you card cost?

cost of box of cards →

6 cards →

$12

| c | c | c | c | c | c |

↑ c cost of each card

$12 ÷ 6 = c

Each card costs $2.

Thinking Habits

Be a good thinker! These questions can help you.

- What do the numbers and symbols in the problem mean?

- How are the numbers or quantities related?

- How can I represent a word problem using pictures, numbers, or equations?

3 Construct viable arguments and critique the reasoning of others.

> Good math thinkers use math to explain why they are right. They can talk about the math that others do, too.

> I wrote a clear argument with words, numbers, and symbols.

Jackie drew a number line and placed a point at $\frac{2}{3}$. Bonnie drew a number line and placed a point at $\frac{2}{3}$ as well. Which student correctly marked the point?

Jackie

$$0 \qquad \frac{1}{3} \qquad \frac{2}{3} \qquad 1$$

Bonnie

$$0 \quad \frac{1}{3} \quad \frac{2}{3} \quad 1$$

$\frac{2}{3}$ is correctly marked on both number lines.
The two number lines are different lengths, but both show three equal parts.

Thinking Habits

Be a good thinker! These questions can help you.

- How can I use numbers, objects, drawings, or actions to justify my argument?

- Am I using numbers and symbols correctly?

- Is my explanation clear and complete?

- What questions can I ask to understand other people's thinking?

- Are there mistakes in other people's thinking?

- Can I improve other people's thinking?

Model with mathematics.

Good math thinkers choose and apply math they know to show and solve problems from everyday life.

I can use what I know about division to solve this problem. I can draw a picture to help.

Josie has a piece of twine that is 45 feet long. She wants to use the twine to tie up plants in her garden. If Josie cuts the twine into 9 equal pieces, how long is each piece?

45 feet

t t t t t t t t t

$45 \div 9 = t$

Each piece of twine is 5 feet long.

Thinking Habits

Be a good thinker! These questions can help you.

- How can I use math I know to help solve this problem?

- How can I use pictures, objects, or an equation to represent the problem?

- How can I use numbers, words, and symbols to solve the problem?

Use appropriate tools strategically.

Good math thinkers know how to pick the right tools to solve math problems.

I decided to use counters because I could make an array to solve the problem.

Hank has $13 in his wallet. He earns $15 more for mowing a lawn. He would like to download movies that cost $7 each. How many movies can Hank download? Choose a tool to represent and solve the problem.

$13 + $15 = $28

$28 ÷ $7 = 4

Hank can download 4 movies.

Thinking Habits

Be a good thinker! These questions can help you.

- Which tools can I use?
- Why should I use this tool to help me solve the problem?
- Is there a different tool I could use?
- Am I using the tool appropriately?

6 Attend to precision.

Good math thinkers are careful about what they write and say, so their ideas about math are clear.

I was precise with my work and the way that I wrote my solution.

Write three clues to describe a square.

Clue 1: I have 4 right angles.

Clue 2: I have four sides that are the same length.

Clue 3: I have 2 sets of sides that are parallel.

A square has 4 right angles, 4 sides with the same length, and 2 sets of parallel sides.

Thinking Habits

Be a good thinker! These questions can help you.

- Am I using numbers, units, and symbols appropriately?

- Am I using the correct definitions?

- Am I calculating accurately?

- Is my answer clear?

MP **7** **Look for and make use of structure.**

Good math thinkers look for relationships in math to help solve problems.

I used what I know about basic facts to solve the problem.

Use <, >, or = to compare the expressions without calculating.

$3 \times 6 \bigcirc 3 \times 9$

$3 \times 6 < 3 \times 9$ because $6 < 9$.

Thinking Habits

Be a good thinker! These questions can help you.

- What patterns can I see and describe?

- How can I use the patterns to solve the problem?

- Can I see expressions and objects in different ways?

Look for and express regularity in repeated reasoning.

Good math thinkers look for things that repeat, and they make generalizations.

I used reasoning to generalize about calculations.

Cathy has arranged some shells in two different ways. One array has 2 rows with 6 shells in each row. The other array has 6 rows with 2 shells in each row. Do both arrays have the same number of shells? Explain.

Yes, both arrays have the same number of counters. The arrays are the same except that the number of shells in the rows and columns are reversed.

Thinking Habits

Be a good thinker! These questions can help you.

- Are any calculations repeated?

- Can I generalize from examples?

- What shortcuts do I notice?

Problem Solving Guide

These questions can help you solve problems.

Make Sense of the Problem

Reason Abstractly and Quantitatively

- What do I need to find?
- What given information can I use?
- How are the quantities related?

Think About Similar Problems

- Have I solved problems like this before?

Persevere in Solving the Problem

Model with Math

- How can I use the math I know?
- How can I represent the problem?
- Is there a pattern or structure I can use?

Use Appropriate Tools Strategically

- What math tools could I use?
- How can I use those tools strategically?

Check the Answer

Make Sense of the Answer

- Is my answer reasonable?

Check for Precision

- Did I check my work?
- Is my answer clear?
- Did I construct a viable argument?
- Did I generalize correctly?

Some Ways to Represent Problems

- Draw a Picture
- Make a Bar Diagram
- Make a Table or Graph
- Write an Equation

Some Math Tools

- Objects
- Grid Paper
- Rulers
- Technology
- Paper and Pencil

Problem Solving Recording Sheet

This sheet helps you organize your work.

Name **Carlos**

Teaching Tool
1

Problem Solving Recording Sheet

Problem

Lynda wants to buy a bike that costs $80. Her father will help by paying for $20. She will earn the rest by walking dogs. She earns $6 for each dog she walks. How many dogs does Lynda need to walk in order to have enough money for the bike?

MAKE SENSE OF THE PROBLEM

Need to Find	Given
Number of dogs to walk	Earns $6 per walk
	Bike costs $80
	Dad's part is $20

PERSEVERE IN SOLVING THE PROBLEM

Some Ways to Represent Problems

- ☐ Draw a Picture
- ☑ Make a Bar Diagram
- ☐ Make a Table or Graph
- ☑ Write an Equation

Some Math Tools

- ☐ Objects
- ☐ Grid Paper
- ☐ Rulers
- ☐ Technology
- ☑ Paper and Pencil

Solution and Answer

```
                $80
  ┌──────────────────────────┐
  │ $20  │    d dollars       │
  └──────┴────────────────────┘
     ↑            ↑
 Dad's money  Lynda's money
```

$20 + d = 80$

Lynda must earn $60.

Money earned →
Dogs walked → 6 d

$$\$60 \div \$6 = 10$$

Lynda must walk 10 dogs.

CHECK THE ANSWER

I used operations that undo each other to check my work.

$10 \times \$6 = \$60$ $\$60 + \$20 = \$80$

My answer is reasonable.

T1

Bar Diagrams

You can draw a **bar diagram** to show how the quantities in a problem are related. Then you can write an equation to solve the problem.

Add To

Draw this **bar diagram** for situations that involve *adding* to a quantity.

Result → 72

| 17 | 55 |

↑ Start   ↑ Change

Change Unknown

Monica bought the used desk below at a yard sale. She also bought a sofa. Monica spent a total of $153. How much did she spend on the sofa?

$42

$153 total spent → $153

| $42 | s |

↑ $42 spent on the desk   ↑ s dollars spent on the sofa

$42 + s = $153

Monica spent $111 on the sofa.

Start Unknown

Avery had some colored pencils. Then his brother gave him the pencils shown below. After that, Avery had 98 pencils. How many colored pencils did Avery start with?

26 colored pencils

98 colored pencils →   98

| p | 26 |

↑ p colored pencils to start   ↑ 26 colored pencils added

$p + 26 = 98$

Avery started with 72 colored pencils.

Bar Diagrams

You can use bar diagrams to make sense of addition and subtraction problems.

Take From

Draw this **bar diagram** for situations that involve *taking* from a quantity.

Start → 186

| 120 | 66 |

↑ Change ↑ Result

Result Unknown

The number of photos on Jenna's phone is shown below. She deleted 128 photos. How many are left?

700 photos

700 photos → 700

| 128 | x |

↑ 128 photos deleted ↑ x photos left

$$700 - 128 = x$$

Jenna has 572 photos left on her phone.

Start Unknown

Alex had a collection of baseball cards. Then he gave the cards below to his brother. Now Alex has 251 cards. How many cards did Alex have before he gave cards to his brother?

24 cards

Trading cards to start → c

| 24 | 251 |

↑ 24 cards given away ↑ 251 cards left

$$c - 24 = 251$$

Alex had 275 baseball cards before he gave the cards to his brother.

The **bar diagrams** on this page can help you make sense of more addition and subtraction situations.

Put Together/Take Apart

Draw this **bar diagram** for situations that involve *putting together* or *taking apart* quantities.

Whole →

428	
145	283

↑ Part   ↑ Part

Whole Unknown

Tanner drove from his home to Providence, Rhode Island, and back over two days. Each way was 27 miles. How far did Tanner drive?

Tanner's house

Providence

m total miles →

m	
27	27

↑ 27 miles to Providence   ↑ 27 miles from Providence

$27 + 27 = m$

Tanner drove a total of 54 miles.

Part Unknown

Mrs. Addy's class collected a total of 128 cans on Tuesday and Wednesday. How many cans were collected on Wednesday?

70 Cans Collected on Tuesday

128 total cans collected →

128	
70	c

↑ 70 cans collected Tuesday   ↑ c cans collected Wednesday

$70 + c = 128$ or $128 - 70 = c$

Mrs. Addy's class collected 58 cans on Wednesday.

Bar Diagrams

Pictures help you understand a problem.

Compare: Addition and Subtraction

Draw this **bar diagram** for *compare* situations involving the difference between two quantities (how many more or fewer.)

Bigger quantity → | 126 |
| 78 | 48 |

Smaller quantity   Difference

Difference Unknown

Perri read the entire book shown below. Jay read 221 facts in the book. How many more facts did Perri read than Jay?

999 facts
Perri read → | 999 |
| 221 | f |

221 facts   f more
Jay read   facts

$221 + f = 999$ or $999 - 221 = f$

Perri read 778 more facts than Jay.

Smaller Unknown

Stanley has 234 fewer songs on his computer than Joanne. Joanne has 362 songs on her computer. How many songs does Stanley have on his computer?

Joanne has
362 songs → | 362 |
| s | 234 |

s songs   234 fewer
Stanley has   songs

$362 - s = 234$ or $s + 234 = 362$

Stanley has 128 songs on his computer.

The **bar diagrams** on this page can help you solve problems involving multiplication and division.

Equal Groups: Multiplication and Division

Draw this **bar diagram** for situations that involve *equal groups*.

Number of Groups Unknown

Malik spent $27 riding the train this week. How many times did Malik ride the train?

Train Ride: $3 each

$r \times 3 = 27$ or $27 \div 3 = r$

Malik rode the train 9 times.

Group Size Unknown

If 36 cookies are packaged equally in the boxes below, how many cookies will be in each box?

$3 \times c = 36$ or $36 \div 3 = c$

Each box will have 12 cookies.

Bar Diagrams

Bar diagrams can be used to show how quantities that are being compared are related.

Compare: Multiplication and Division

Draw this **bar diagram** for *compare* situations involving how many times one quantity is of another quantity.

Bigger Unknown

On Saturday, a deli sold 8 times as many sandwiches as wraps. They sold 14 wraps. How many sandwiches did they sell?

$14 \times 8 = s$

They sold 112 sandwiches.

Multiplier Unknown

Alice ran 300 yards. Uri ran 50 yards. The distance Alice ran is how many times the distance Uri ran?

$r \times 50 = 300$ or $300 \div 50 = r$

Alice ran 6 times the distance Uri ran.

TOPIC 8

Extend Understanding of Fraction Equivalence and Ordering

Essential Questions: What are some ways to name the same part of a whole? How can you compare fractions with unlike denominators?

Digital Resources

Solve   Learn   Glossary   Practice Buddy

Tools   Assessment   Help   Games

Some animals use their senses differently from humans. The entire body of a catfish is covered with taste-sensitive cells.

They use their sense of taste to locate food that is far away in the water.

Lots of animals have special ways of receiving information. Here is a project about senses.

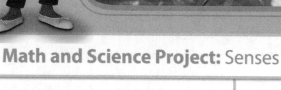

Math and Science Project: Senses

Do Research Use the Internet or other resources to find information about how animals use special senses, such as echolocation, electricity, or magnetism. Include information about where the animal lives and how the special sense is used.

Journal: Write a Report Include what you found. Also in your report:

- Some spiders rely on sight to receive information about food. Spiders can have as many as 8 eyes. Draw a picture of a spider with many eyes, using some shaded circles as eyes and some empty circles as eyes.

- Write a fraction that names shaded spider eyes to total spider eyes. Write three equivalent fractions.

Name _____

Review What You Know

A-Z Vocabulary

Choose the best term from the box.
Write it on the blank.

> • denominator   • numerator
>
> • fraction   • unit fraction

1. A symbol, such as $\frac{2}{3}$ or $\frac{1}{2}$, used to name part of a whole, part of a set, or a location on a number line is called a _____.

2. The number above the fraction bar in a fraction is called the _____.

3. A fraction with a numerator of 1 is called a _____.

Unit Fractions

Write a fraction for each statement.

4. 2 copies of $\frac{1}{6}$ is _____.

5. 3 copies of $\frac{1}{3}$ is _____.

6. 4 copies of $\frac{1}{5}$ is _____.

7. 2 copies of $\frac{1}{10}$ is _____.

8. 7 copies of $\frac{1}{12}$ is _____.

9. 3 copies of $\frac{1}{8}$ is _____.

Fraction Concepts

Write the fraction shown by each figure.

10.

11.

12.

13.

14.

15.

Parts of Wholes

16. **Construct Arguments** Is $\frac{1}{4}$ of the figure below green? Explain.

17. This picture shows a square. Shade in $\frac{3}{4}$ of the square.

My Word Cards

Use the examples for each word on the front of the card to help complete the definitions on the back.

equivalent fractions

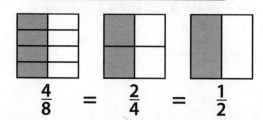

$$\frac{4}{8} = \frac{2}{4} = \frac{1}{2}$$

fraction

of a whole
$\frac{1}{4}$

of a set
$\frac{1}{4}$

on a number line
$\frac{1}{4}$ 0 —————— 1

numerator

$\frac{1}{4}$ ← numerator

denominator

$\frac{1}{4}$ ← denominator

common factor

Common factors are 3 and 1.

6: 6 3 2 1   9: 9 3 1

benchmark fraction

$$\frac{1}{4}, \ \frac{1}{2}, \ \frac{3}{4}$$

My Word Cards

A symbol used to name part of a whole, part of a set, or a location on a number line is called a _____.

Fractions that name the same region, part of a set, or part of a segment are _____.

In a fraction, the number below the fraction bar that represents the total number of equal parts in one whole is the _____.

In a fraction, the number above the fraction bar that represents the part of the whole is the _____.

A known fraction that is commonly used for estimating is called a _____.

A _____ is a number that is a factor of two or more given numbers.

Help Practice Buddy Tools Games

Another Look!

Use an area model to find two fractions equivalent to $\frac{1}{2}$.

Many fractions are equivalent to $\frac{1}{2}$.

The circle is divided into 2 equal parts. The shaded part represents $\frac{1}{2}$.

Divide the circle into 4 equal parts. The shaded part represents $\frac{2}{4}$.

Divide the circle into 8 equal parts. The shaded part represents $\frac{4}{8}$.

$\frac{1}{2}$, $\frac{2}{4}$, and $\frac{4}{8}$ are equivalent fractions.

1. Write a fraction equivalent to $\frac{3}{5}$.

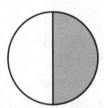

2. Write two fractions equivalent to $\frac{9}{12}$.

For **3–10**, draw an area model or use fraction strips to solve each problem.

3. $\frac{3}{5} = \frac{\square}{10}$

4. $\frac{3}{6} = \frac{\square}{12}$

5. $\frac{4}{10} = \frac{\square}{5}$

6. $\frac{3}{4} = \frac{\square}{8}$

7. $\frac{5}{10} = \frac{1}{\square}$

8. $\frac{4}{6} = \frac{\square}{12}$

9. $\frac{5}{5} = \frac{\square}{10}$

10. $\frac{1}{2} = \frac{6}{\square}$

11. Write two equivalent fractions to describe the portion of the eggs that are brown.

For **12–13**, use the table at the right.

12. The results of an election for mayor are shown at the right. Which candidate received the most votes and which received the least votes?

DATA	Candidate	Number of Votes
	Leonard Hansen	12,409
	Margaret O'Connor	12,926
	Jillian Garcia	12,904

13. How many people voted for the three candidates?

---

14. Reasoning Tell what operations are needed to solve the following problem. Then solve the problem.

The school auditorium has 22 rows with 28 seats each. At a school concert, 19 seats were empty. How many seats were filled?

15. Higher Order Thinking Barbara is tiling her craft room floor with square tiles. She wants $\frac{6}{10}$ of the square tiles to be red. If she uses 18 red tiles, how many square tiles will be used to cover the floor? Draw an area model to help solve.

Assessment ISTEP+ Ready

16. Select all the fractions that are equivalent to $\frac{3}{4}$. Use the area models to help.

- ☐ $\frac{6}{6}$
- ☐ $\frac{2}{8}$
- ☐ $\frac{9}{12}$
- ☐ $\frac{6}{8}$
- ☐ $\frac{1}{2}$

17. Select all the pairs that are equivalent fractions. Use the area models to help.

- ☐ $\frac{1}{6}, \frac{3}{12}$
- ☐ $\frac{2}{6}, \frac{4}{12}$
- ☐ $\frac{3}{6}, \frac{1}{2}$
- ☐ $\frac{1}{6}, \frac{6}{12}$
- ☐ $\frac{6}{6}, \frac{12}{12}$

Another Look!

You can write equivalent fractions for
a point shown on a number line.

Label the number line in two different ways.

The point is at $\frac{4}{6}$.

The point is at $\frac{8}{12}$.

$\frac{4}{6} = \frac{8}{12}$

$\frac{4}{6}$ and $\frac{8}{12}$ are equivalent fractions.

Equivalent fractions
represent the same fractional
amount of the same whole or
same-sized wholes.

For **1–6**, write two fractions for the point on each number line.

1.

2.

3.

4.

5.

6.

7. Are $\frac{3}{8}$ and $\frac{3}{4}$ equivalent fractions?
   Draw a number line to decide.

8. Draw a number line to show $\frac{1}{4}$ and $\frac{2}{8}$
   are equivalent.

9. **Critique Reasoning** Mike says he can find a fraction equivalent to $\frac{1}{10}$, even though $\frac{1}{10}$ is a unit fraction. Is Mike correct? Explain.

10. **Algebra** There are 267 students and 21 adults going on a school trip. An equal number of people will ride on each bus. If there are 9 buses, how many people will ride on each bus? Write and solve equations.

11. Point X is at $\frac{2}{3}$ on a number line. On the same number line, point Y is the same distance from 0 as point X, but has a numerator of 8. What is the denominator of the fraction at point Y? Draw a number line to model the problem.

12. **Higher Order Thinking** A recipe calls for $\frac{1}{4}$ cup of flour. Carter only has a measuring cup that holds $\frac{1}{8}$ cup. How can Carter measure the flour he needs for his recipe?

 Assessment 🖐 (ISTEP+ Ready)

13. Monty is using a number line to find fractions equivalent to $\frac{4}{6}$.

He says he can find an equivalent fraction with a denominator greater than 6 and an equivalent fraction with a denominator less than 6.

0    $\frac{1}{6}$ $\frac{2}{6}$ $\frac{3}{6}$ $\frac{4}{6}$ $\frac{5}{6}$ 1

You can further divide or relabel the number line to find equivalent fractions.

Part A

Write to explain how Monty can use the number line to find an equivalent fraction with a denominator greater than 6.

Part B

Write to explain how Monty can use the number line to find an equivalent fraction with a denominator less than 6.

Name _____

☆ Solve & Share ☆

Wayne bought a box of muffins. Four sixths of the muffins are blueberry. Write a fraction equivalent to $\frac{4}{6}$. **Solve this problem any way you choose.**

I can ...
use multiplication to find equivalent fractions.

Content Standard 4.NS.4
Process Standards PS.2, PS.3, PS.4

What can you draw to model with math to help represent the problem? *Show your work in the space below!*

Look Back! **Reasoning** How are the numerator and denominator of your fraction related to the numerator and denominator of $\frac{4}{6}$?

Essential Question

How Can You Use Multiplication to Find Equivalent Fractions?

A

A librarian said $\frac{1}{2}$ of the books checked out yesterday were nonfiction. What are some fractions equivalent to $\frac{1}{2}$?

To find equivalent fractions, multiply by a fraction equal to one.

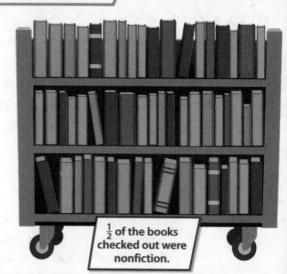

$\frac{1}{2}$ of the books checked out were nonfiction.

B **Multiply by $\frac{2}{2}$.**

Multiply the numerator and the denominator by 2.

$$\frac{1}{2} \times \frac{2}{2} = \frac{2}{4}$$

C **Multiply by $\frac{3}{3}$.**

Multiply the numerator and the denominator by 3.

$$\frac{1}{2} \times \frac{3}{3} = \frac{3}{6}$$

D **Multiply by $\frac{4}{4}$.**

Multiply the numerator and the denominator by 4.

$$\frac{1}{2} \times \frac{4}{4} = \frac{4}{8}$$

$\frac{2}{2}$, $\frac{3}{3}$, and $\frac{4}{4}$ are all equal to 1. Multiplying by 1 gives the same number.

$\frac{1}{2}$, $\frac{2}{4}$, $\frac{3}{6}$, and $\frac{4}{8}$ are equivalent fractions.

Convince Me! **Critique Reasoning** Kevin said, "In each of the examples above, all you are doing is multiplying by one. When you multiply by 1, the value doesn't change." Is Kevin correct? Explain.

☆ Guided Practice*

Do You Understand?

1. Use an area model and multiplication to show why $\frac{5}{6}$ and $\frac{10}{12}$ are equivalent fractions.

2. Reasoning Use multiplication to explain why $\frac{3}{4}$ and $\frac{8}{12}$ are **NOT** equivalent fractions.

Do You Know How?

For **3–7**, multiply to find equivalent fractions.

3.

$\frac{1}{2} = \dfrac{\Box}{\Box}$

4. $\frac{3}{4} = \dfrac{\Box}{12}$ **5.** $\frac{5}{5} = \dfrac{10}{\Box}$

6. $\frac{3}{2} = \dfrac{6}{\Box}$ **7.** $\frac{1}{6} = \dfrac{\Box}{12}$

☆ Independent Practice ☆

Leveled Practice For **8–13**, multiply to find equivalent fractions.

8. $\frac{2}{3} \times \frac{2}{2} = \dfrac{\Box}{\Box}$

9. $\frac{3}{6} \times \frac{2}{2} = \dfrac{\Box}{\Box}$

10. $\frac{1}{5} \times \dfrac{\Box}{\Box} = \dfrac{\Box}{10}$ **11.** $\frac{5}{4} \times \dfrac{\Box}{\Box} = \dfrac{\Box}{100}$ **12.** $\frac{7}{4} \times \dfrac{\Box}{\Box} = \dfrac{\Box}{12}$ **13.** $\frac{3}{4} \times \dfrac{\Box}{\Box} = \dfrac{9}{\Box}$

For **14–21**, write two equivalent fractions for each given fraction.

14. $\frac{1}{10}$ **15.** $\frac{4}{2}$ **16.** $\frac{5}{6}$ **17.** $\frac{1}{3}$

18. $\frac{2}{5}$ **19.** $\frac{3}{4}$ **20.** $\frac{9}{2}$ **21.** $\frac{7}{12}$

Problem Solving

For **22–23**, use the chart at the right.

22. Write three equivalent fractions to describe the portion of the garden planted with carrots.

23. Reasoning Which vegetable takes up the same amount of the garden as the tomatoes? Explain.

Vegetable	Fraction of Garden Planted
Carrots	$\frac{1}{6}$
Tomatoes	$\frac{1}{4}$
Peppers	$\frac{4}{12}$
Beans	$\frac{3}{12}$

24. Jeena has 5 packets of seeds. Each packet has 12 seeds. Jeena wants to divide the seeds evenly among 10 flower pots. How many seeds can she plant in each flower pot?

25. Higher Order Thinking Jenny said, "I'm thinking of a fraction that is equivalent to $\frac{2}{6}$. The numerator is 8 less than the denominator." What fraction is Jenny thinking of?

26. Use each of the fractions from the box once to complete the tables.

$$\frac{2}{8} \qquad \frac{3}{12} \qquad \frac{4}{6} \qquad \frac{8}{12}$$

Fractions Equivalent to $\frac{2}{3}$

Fractions Equivalent to $\frac{1}{4}$

27. Use each of the numbers from the box once to complete the equations.

$$2 \quad 4 \quad 6 \quad 8 \quad 10 \quad 12$$

$$\frac{1}{2} = \frac{\square}{\square}$$

$$\frac{5}{6} = \frac{\square}{\square}$$

$$\frac{3}{4} = \frac{\square}{\square}$$

Another Look!

Find two fractions that are equivalent to $\frac{3}{4}$.

Multiply the given fraction by a fraction equal to one to find equivalent fractions.

$$\frac{3}{4} \times \frac{2}{2} = \frac{6}{8} \qquad \frac{3}{4} \times \frac{3}{3} = \frac{9}{12}$$

$\frac{2}{2}$ and $\frac{3}{3}$ are equal to one.

$\frac{3}{4}$, $\frac{6}{8}$, and $\frac{9}{12}$ are equivalent fractions. So, $\frac{3}{4} = \frac{6}{8} = \frac{9}{12}$.

For **1–6**, multiply to find equivalent fractions.

1. $\frac{5}{6} \times \frac{2}{2} = \dfrac{\square}{\square}$

2. $\frac{2}{2} \times \frac{3}{3} = \dfrac{\square}{\square}$

3. $\frac{3}{5} \times \dfrac{\square}{\square} = \dfrac{\square}{10}$

4. $\frac{1}{6} \times \dfrac{\square}{\square} = \dfrac{2}{\square}$

5. $\frac{1}{4} \times \dfrac{\square}{\square} = \dfrac{\square}{100}$

6. $\frac{2}{3} \times \dfrac{\square}{\square} = \dfrac{8}{\square}$

For **7–14**, write an equivalent fraction for each given fraction.

7. $\frac{10}{2}$

8. $\frac{4}{5}$

9. $\frac{9}{3}$

10. $\frac{3}{12}$

11. $\frac{5}{8}$

12. $\frac{5}{100}$

13. $\frac{7}{12}$

14. $\frac{9}{5}$

For **15–18**, write two equivalent fractions for each given fraction.

15. $\frac{10}{12}$

16. $\frac{4}{10}$

17. $\frac{4}{6}$

18. $\frac{3}{8}$

19. Write three equivalent fractions to describe the portion of the stained-glass window that is gold.

20. Math and Science During winter months, freshwater fish sense the water getting colder and swim to the bottoms of lakes and rivers to find warmer water. If a fish swims $\frac{7}{8}$ of the depth of a 32-foot deep lake, how many feet down did the fish swim?

21. 🄰🅉 **Vocabulary** Use *numerator* and *denominator* to complete the sentences.

A _____ is the number above the fraction bar in a fraction. A _____ is the number below the fraction bar that represents the number of equal parts in the whole.

22. Reasoning Which cost more, 8 printers priced at $145 per printer or 3 laptop computers priced at $439 per computer? Explain.

23. Higher Order Thinking Three eighths of the students in Ms. Mull's class ride the bus. If there are 24 students in the class, how many students ride the bus? Explain how to use equivalent fractions to solve.

Assessment 🄳🄾 (ISTEP+ Ready)

24. Use each of the fractions from the box once to complete the tables.

| $\frac{2}{6}$ | $\frac{4}{12}$ | $\frac{6}{10}$ | $\frac{60}{100}$ |

Fractions Equivalent to $\frac{1}{3}$	Fractions Equivalent to $\frac{3}{5}$

25. Use each of the numbers from the box once to complete the equations.

| 2 | 6 | 8 | 10 | 12 | 18 |

$$\frac{5}{6} = \frac{\square}{\square}$$

$$\frac{1}{3} = \frac{\square}{\square}$$

$$\frac{9}{4} = \frac{\square}{\square}$$

Name _____

☆ ☆
Solve & Share

Sara bought a piece of ribbon. The length of the ribbon is given in tenths. Write the length as two other equivalent fractions. *Solve this problem any way you choose.*

Lesson 8-4

Generate Equivalent Fractions: Division

I can ...
use division to find equivalent fractions.

⊙ **Content Standard** 4.NS.4
Process Standards PS.1, PS.2, PS.3, PS.4, PS.6

Remember to be precise when answering the question. Use appropriate labels.

$\frac{6}{10}$ meter

Look Back! **Make Sense and Persevere** Sara wrote the following equivalent fractions: $\frac{6}{10} = \frac{3}{5}$. What two operations could Sara have used to find her equivalent fractions? Explain.

Essential Question

How Can You Use Division to Find Equivalent Fractions?

A

In early May, Fairbanks, Alaska, has daylight for $\frac{18}{24}$ of the day. What are some fractions equivalent to $\frac{18}{24}$?

Fairbanks

18 hours of daylight in May

To find equivalent fractions, divide the numerator and the denominator by a common factor greater than 1.

A common factor is a factor two or more numbers have in common.

B Two common factors of 18 and 24 are 2 and 3.

5:00 6:00 7:00 8:00 9:00 10:00 11:00 12:00 1:00 2:00 3:00 4:00 5:00 6:00 7:00 8:00 9:00 10:00 11:00 12:00 1:00 2:00 3:00 4:00 5:00

Divide the numerator and denominator by 2.

$$\frac{18}{24} \div \frac{2}{2} = \frac{9}{12}$$

$\frac{18}{24}$ of a day is equal to $\frac{9}{12}$ of a day.

5:00 6:00 7:00 8:00 9:00 10:00 11:00 12:00 1:00 2:00 3:00 4:00 5:00 6:00 7:00 8:00 9:00 10:00 11:00 12:00 1:00 2:00 3:00 4:00 5:00

Divide the numerator and denominator by 3.

$$\frac{18}{24} \div \frac{3}{3} = \frac{6}{8}$$

$\frac{18}{24}$ of a day is equal to $\frac{6}{8}$ of a day.

$\frac{18}{24}$, $\frac{9}{12}$, and $\frac{6}{8}$ are equivalent fractions.

Convince Me! **Model with Math** Draw a number line and label it with equivalent fractions to show $\frac{18}{24} = \frac{9}{12} = \frac{6}{8} = \frac{3}{4}$.

Practice Buddy   Tools   Assessment

☆ Guided Practice *

Do You Understand?

1. Use division to show $\frac{9}{12}$ and $\frac{3}{4}$ are equivalent fractions.

2. **Reasoning** Is there a fraction with a smaller numerator and denominator that is equivalent to $\frac{4}{12}$? Explain.

Do You Know How?

For **3–8**, divide to find equivalent fractions.

3. $\frac{6}{10} = \frac{\square}{\square}$ 4. $\frac{8}{12} = \frac{\square}{\square}$

5. $\frac{8}{12} = \frac{\square}{3}$ 6. $\frac{10}{12} = \frac{5}{\square}$

7. $\frac{2}{10} = \frac{\square}{5}$ 8. $\frac{10}{100} = \frac{\square}{10}$

☆ Independent Practice ☆

Leveled Practice For **9–16**, divide to find equivalent fractions.

9. $\frac{6}{12} \div \frac{6}{6} = \frac{\square}{\square}$

10. $\frac{70}{10} \div \frac{5}{5} = \frac{\square}{\square}$

11. $\frac{2}{6} \div \frac{2}{2} = \frac{\square}{\square}$

12. $\frac{50}{100} \div \frac{10}{10} = \frac{\square}{\square}$

13. $\frac{9}{6} \div \frac{\square}{\square} = \frac{3}{\square}$

14. $\frac{10}{4} \div \frac{\square}{\square} = \frac{\square}{2}$

15. $\frac{4}{12} \div \frac{\square}{\square} = \frac{\square}{6}$

16. $\frac{2}{8} \div \frac{\square}{\square} = \frac{\square}{4}$

For **17–24**, divide to find two equivalent fractions.

17. $\frac{20}{100}$

18. $\frac{40}{10}$

19. $\frac{16}{12}$

20. $\frac{12}{8}$

21. $\frac{24}{12}$

22. $\frac{10}{100}$

23. $\frac{90}{10}$

24. $\frac{80}{100}$

*For another example, see Set B on page 455.

Problem Solving

For **25–27**, use the table at the right.

Animal		Number of Hours Spent Sleeping	Fraction of the Day Spent Sleeping	Equivalent Fraction
Cat		12		
Cow		4		
Squirrel		15		
Tiger		16		

25. Complete the table at the right by writing the fraction of the day each animal sleeps and an equivalent fraction. Remember, there are 24 hours in a day.

26. Suppose the cow slept 4 more hours. What fraction of the day would the cow spend sleeping?

27. How many hours does a tiger sleep in 7 days?

---

28. Make Sense and Persevere Ethan ate $\frac{4}{8}$ of the sandwich. Andy ate $\frac{1}{2}$ of the sandwich. The sandwiches were the same size.

   a. Whose sandwich had more equal parts?

   b. Whose sandwich had larger equal parts?

   c. Who ate more? Explain.

29. Higher Order Thinking If the numerator and denominator of a fraction are both odd numbers, can you write an equivalent fraction with a smaller numerator and denominator? Explain.

  ISTEP+ Ready

30. Which equation is **NOT** true?

   Ⓐ $\frac{12}{10} = \frac{6}{5}$

   Ⓑ $\frac{3}{1} = \frac{30}{10}$

   Ⓒ $\frac{6}{12} = \frac{2}{3}$

   Ⓓ $\frac{8}{6} = \frac{16}{12}$

31. There are 12 students in DeLynn's class. Eight students own pets. Which shows the fraction of the class that owns pets?

   Ⓐ $\frac{8}{12}$

   Ⓑ $\frac{1}{2}$

   Ⓒ $\frac{6}{4}$

   Ⓓ $\frac{12}{8}$

Name _____

Homework & Practice 8-4
Generate Equivalent
Fractions: Division

Another Look!

Use division to find two fractions equivalent to $\frac{8}{12}$.

To find an equivalent fraction, divide the numerator and denominator by any common factor other than 1.

$$\frac{8}{12} \div \frac{2}{2} = \frac{4}{6} \qquad \frac{8}{12} \div \frac{4}{4} = \frac{2}{3}$$

$\frac{8}{12}$, $\frac{4}{6}$, and $\frac{2}{3}$ are equivalent fractions.

For **1–8**, divide to find equivalent fractions.

1. $\frac{5}{10} \div \frac{5}{5} = \frac{\square}{\square}$

2. $\frac{2}{12} \div \frac{2}{2} = \frac{\square}{\square}$

3. $\frac{12}{6} \div \frac{3}{3} = \frac{\square}{\square}$

4. $\frac{40}{100} \div \frac{10}{10} = \frac{\square}{\square}$

5. $\frac{25}{100} \div \frac{\square}{\square} = \frac{\square}{4}$

6. $\frac{8}{12} \div \frac{\square}{\square} = \frac{2}{\square}$

7. $\frac{70}{100} \div \frac{\square}{\square} = \frac{7}{\square}$

8. $\frac{18}{10} \div \frac{\square}{\square} = \frac{9}{\square}$

For **9–16**, find an equivalent fraction for each given fraction.

9. $\frac{75}{100}$

10. $\frac{4}{10}$

11. $\frac{10}{12}$

12. $\frac{200}{100}$

13. $\frac{24}{100}$

14. $\frac{60}{12}$

15. $\frac{84}{100}$

16. $\frac{70}{10}$

For **17–24**, divide to find two equivalent fractions.

17. $\frac{500}{100}$

18. $\frac{4}{12}$

19. $\frac{30}{10}$

20. $\frac{60}{100}$

21. $\frac{50}{10}$

22. $\frac{6}{12}$

23. $\frac{12}{8}$

24. $\frac{18}{6}$

25. What fraction of the game spinner is red? Write two equivalent fractions.

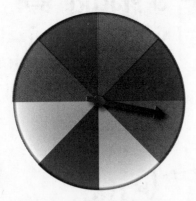

26. Solve this number riddle:
I am an odd number.
I am less than 100.
The sum of my digits is 12.
I am a multiple of 15.

What number am I?

27. It took Bob 55 minutes to clean the garage. How many seconds did it take Bob? There are 60 seconds in one minute.

28. Betty is canning 104 pears and 126 apples separately. Each jar holds 8 pears or 6 apples. How many jars does Betty need?

29. Critique Reasoning Laurie says summer is $\frac{1}{4}$ of the year. Maria says summer is $\frac{3}{12}$ of the year. Who is correct? Explain.

30. Higher Order Thinking Cindy is using division to write a fraction equivalent to $\frac{30}{100}$. She tried to divide the numerator and denominator by 3. She got stuck. What advice would you give her?

Assessment ⊙ — ISTEP+ Ready

31. Which equation is **NOT** true?

Ⓐ $\frac{10}{12} = \frac{5}{6}$

Ⓑ $\frac{69}{100} = \frac{6}{10}$

Ⓒ $\frac{10}{5} = \frac{200}{100}$

Ⓓ $\frac{12}{4} = \frac{6}{2}$

32. There are 100 pieces of fruit in a basket. Twelve of the pieces are apples. Which shows the fraction of the fruit that are apples?

Ⓐ $\frac{12}{12}$

Ⓑ $\frac{12}{100}$

Ⓒ $\frac{100}{12}$

Ⓓ $\frac{100}{100}$

434   **Topic 8** | Lesson 8-4

Name _____

Solve & Share

Color a part of each strip of paper below. Estimate what fraction of each strip is colored. Explain how you made your estimate. *Solve this problem any way you choose.*

I can ...
use benchmarks, area models, and number lines to compare fractions.

Content Standard 4.NS.5
Process Standards PS.1, PS.2, PS.3, PS.8

You can use reasoning. Use $\frac{1}{4}$, $\frac{1}{2}$, and $\frac{3}{4}$ to compare. Did you color more or less than $\frac{1}{2}$ of the strip? $\frac{1}{4}$ of the strip? $\frac{3}{4}$ of the strip?

Look Back! **Generalize** How could you tell if a fraction is greater than, less than, or equal to $\frac{1}{2}$ just by looking at the numerator and the denominator?

How Can You Use Benchmarks to Compare Fractions?

A

Robert needs $\frac{3}{8}$ stick of butter to make muffins and $\frac{2}{3}$ stick of butter to make cookies. Which recipe uses more butter?

You can use benchmark fractions to compare fractions. Benchmark fractions are commonly used fractions such as $\frac{1}{4}$, $\frac{1}{3}$, $\frac{1}{2}$, $\frac{2}{3}$, and $\frac{3}{4}$.

BUTTER

B Compare $\frac{3}{8}$ to the benchmark fraction $\frac{1}{2}$.

Muffins

$\frac{1}{2}$

$\frac{3}{8}$

$$\frac{3}{8} < \frac{1}{2}$$

You can compare these fractions because they refer to the same whole, a stick of butter.

C Compare $\frac{2}{3}$ to the benchmark fraction $\frac{1}{2}$.

Cookies

$\frac{1}{2}$

$\frac{2}{3}$

$$\frac{2}{3} > \frac{1}{2}$$

$\frac{3}{8} < \frac{1}{2}$ and $\frac{2}{3} > \frac{1}{2}$, so $\frac{3}{8} < \frac{2}{3}$.

The cookie recipe uses more butter.

Convince Me! **Critique Reasoning** Ernesto said, "I know $\frac{3}{8}$ is less than $\frac{2}{3}$ because $\frac{3}{8}$ is closer to 0 and $\frac{2}{3}$ is closer to 1." Does Ernesto's reasoning make sense? Draw two number lines to support your answer.

Another Example!

Compare $\frac{9}{10}$ and $\frac{7}{6}$. Use 1 whole as a benchmark.

$\frac{9}{10} < 1$ and $\frac{7}{6} > 1$, so $\frac{9}{10} < \frac{7}{6}$.

☆ Guided Practice *

Do You Understand?

1. **Reasoning** Carl found $\frac{4}{8}$ is equal to $\frac{1}{2}$, and $\frac{1}{3}$ is less than $\frac{1}{2}$. How can Carl compare $\frac{4}{8}$ to $\frac{1}{3}$? Explain.

2. Write a fraction that is closer to 0 than to 1. Write another fraction that is closer to 1 than to 0. Use your fractions to complete the comparison.

$$\frac{\Box}{\Box} < \frac{\Box}{\Box}$$

Do You Know How?

For **3–4**, compare. Write $<$, $>$, or $=$.

3. $\frac{2}{6} \bigcirc \frac{4}{5}$

4. $\frac{11}{12} \bigcirc \frac{9}{8}$

5. Circle the fractions that are less than $\frac{1}{2}$.

$\frac{5}{4}$ $\frac{1}{4}$ $\frac{1}{5}$ $\frac{2}{3}$ $\frac{2}{12}$ $\frac{51}{100}$

6. Circle the fractions that are greater than 1.

$\frac{99}{100}$ $\frac{6}{5}$ $\frac{7}{8}$ $\frac{14}{8}$ $\frac{11}{10}$ $\frac{11}{12}$

Independent Practice ☆

For **7–10**, circle all the fractions that match each statement.

7. Fractions less than $\frac{1}{2}$

$\frac{3}{4}$ $\frac{1}{6}$ $\frac{6}{12}$ $\frac{4}{10}$ $\frac{5}{8}$ $\frac{5}{2}$

8. Fractions greater than $\frac{1}{2}$

$\frac{5}{8}$ $\frac{1}{4}$ $\frac{6}{3}$ $\frac{7}{10}$ $\frac{5}{12}$ $\frac{6}{12}$

9. Fractions greater than 1

$\frac{5}{4}$ $\frac{2}{3}$ $\frac{6}{6}$ $\frac{1}{10}$ $\frac{15}{12}$ $\frac{7}{8}$

10. Fractions closer to 0 than to 1

$\frac{3}{4}$ $\frac{1}{8}$ $\frac{1}{4}$ $\frac{7}{5}$ $\frac{2}{4}$ $\frac{3}{10}$

For **11–18**, compare using benchmark fractions or 1. Then write $>$, $<$, or $=$.

11. $\frac{1}{3} \bigcirc \frac{4}{6}$

12. $\frac{4}{8} \bigcirc \frac{2}{4}$

13. $\frac{7}{5} \bigcirc \frac{7}{8}$

14. $\frac{6}{12} \bigcirc \frac{4}{5}$

15. $\frac{4}{5} \bigcirc \frac{2}{5}$

16. $\frac{6}{6} \bigcirc \frac{13}{12}$

17. $\frac{8}{10} \bigcirc \frac{1}{8}$

18. $\frac{4}{4} \bigcirc \frac{10}{10}$

*For another example, see Set C on page 456.

Problem Solving

19. **Reasoning** Jordan has $\frac{5}{8}$ can of green paint and $\frac{3}{6}$ can of blue paint. If the cans are the same size, does Jordan have more green paint or blue paint? Explain.

20. **Vocabulary** Write two examples of a *benchmark fraction*.

21. Four neighbors each have gardens that are the same size.

    a. Which neighbors planted vegetables in less than half of their gardens?

    b. Who has a larger section of vegetables in their garden, Margaret or Wayne?

Neighbor	Fraction of Garden Planted with Vegetables
James	$\frac{5}{12}$
Margaret	$\frac{5}{10}$
Claudia	$\frac{1}{6}$
Wayne	$\frac{2}{3}$

22. **Make Sense and Persevere** Gavin bought 3 pizzas for a party. Each pizza had 8 slices. There were 8 other people at the party. Everyone ate the same number of slices. What is the greatest number of slices each person ate? How many slices were left over?

23. **Higher Order Thinking** How can you tell just by looking at the numerator and denominator of a fraction if it is closer to 0 or to 1? Give some examples in your explanation.

Assessment ISTEP+ Ready

24. Donna ate $\frac{7}{12}$ box of popcorn. Jack ate $\frac{4}{10}$ box of popcorn. The boxes of popcorn are the same size. Write to explain how to use a benchmark fraction to determine who ate more popcorn.

Name _____

Help Practice Tools Games
      Buddy

Homework
& Practice 8-5

Use Benchmarks to
Compare Fractions

Another Look!

Compare $\frac{6}{8}$ and $\frac{5}{12}$.

One Way

Compare the fractions to $\frac{1}{2}$.

$$\frac{6}{8} > \frac{1}{2} \qquad \frac{5}{12} < \frac{1}{2}$$

$$\frac{6}{8} > \frac{5}{12}$$

Another Way

Compare the fractions to 0 and to 1.

$\frac{6}{8}$ is closer to 1 than to 0.

$\frac{5}{12}$ is closer to 0 than to 1.

$$\frac{6}{8} > \frac{5}{12}$$

Benchmarks can
help you compare
fractions.

For **1–6**, write three fractions that match each statement.

1. Fractions equal to $\frac{1}{2}$

2. Fractions less than $\frac{1}{2}$

3. Fractions greater than 1

4. Fractions closer to 1 than to 0

5. Fractions closer to 0 than to 1

6. Fractions greater than $\frac{1}{2}$

For **7–18**, compare using benchmark fractions or 1.
Then write >, <, or =.

7. $\frac{3}{4} \bigcirc \frac{2}{10}$

8. $\frac{4}{12} \bigcirc \frac{7}{10}$

9. $\frac{5}{10} \bigcirc \frac{1}{2}$

10. $\frac{3}{8} \bigcirc \frac{6}{12}$

11. $\frac{7}{8} \bigcirc \frac{2}{5}$

12. $\frac{15}{12} \bigcirc \frac{5}{6}$

13. $\frac{5}{5} \bigcirc \frac{4}{4}$

14. $\frac{4}{6} \bigcirc \frac{1}{3}$

15. $\frac{8}{10} \bigcirc \frac{3}{5}$

16. $\frac{5}{8} \bigcirc \frac{6}{12}$

17. $\frac{48}{12} \bigcirc \frac{10}{5}$

18. $\frac{9}{12} \bigcirc \frac{5}{6}$

19. Write three fractions that are greater than $\frac{1}{2}$ but less than 1.

20. Critique Reasoning Mary lives $\frac{6}{10}$ mile from school. Thad lives $\frac{9}{8}$ miles from school. Mary says Thad lives farther from school. Is she correct? Explain.

21. Mr. Phillips is mixing paint for his art class. How many 6-ounce bottles can he fill with the quantities of paint shown at the right? Explain.

Paint

64 ounces of blue

12 ounces of yellow

32 ounces of white

22. Sandra used benchmark fractions to describe some insects she collected. She said the ladybug is about $\frac{1}{4}$ inch long, and the cricket is about $\frac{2}{3}$ inch long. Which insect is longer?

23. Higher Order Thinking Austin said, "I know $\frac{1}{4}$ is less than $\frac{1}{2}$, so that means $\frac{3}{12}$ is less than $\frac{1}{2}$." Does Austin's reasoning make sense? Explain.

Assessment ⊶ (**ISTEP+ Ready**)

24. Kiyo and Steven are tiling the floors in an office building. Kiyo tiled $\frac{3}{6}$ of the floor in one office, and Steven tiled $\frac{5}{12}$ of the floor in another office.

Write to explain how to use a benchmark fraction to determine who tiled a greater portion of a floor.

You can compare these fractions because the floors in each office are the same size.

Name _____

Solve & Share

Juan read for $\frac{5}{6}$ of an hour. Larissa read for $\frac{10}{12}$ of an hour. Who read for a longer period of time? Explain. **Solve this problem any way you choose.**

I can ...
use equivalent fractions to compare fractions.

Content Standard 4.NS.5
Process Standards PS.2, PS.3, PS.5

You can select and use appropriate tools such as drawings, number lines, or fraction strips to solve. *Show your work in the space below!*

Look Back! **Reasoning** Carlos read for $\frac{8}{10}$ of a hour. Did Carlos read for more or less time than Juan? Write your answer as a number sentence using $>$, $<$, or $=$.

Essential Question **How Can You Compare Fractions with Unlike Denominators?**

A

Isabella's father is building a model dinosaur with small pieces of wood. Compare the lengths of the pieces of wood. Compare $\frac{1}{4}$ inch and $\frac{5}{6}$ inch. Then, compare $\frac{4}{5}$ inch and $\frac{4}{10}$ inch.

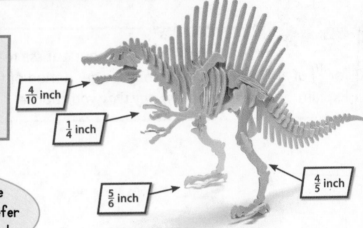

$\frac{4}{10}$ inch

$\frac{1}{4}$ inch

$\frac{4}{5}$ inch

$\frac{5}{6}$ inch

You can compare these fractions because they refer to the same whole, an inch.

B Compare $\frac{1}{4}$ and $\frac{5}{6}$ by renaming each fraction so they both have the same denominator.

$$\frac{1}{4} = \frac{1}{4} \times \frac{3}{3} = \frac{3}{12} \qquad \frac{5}{6} = \frac{5}{6} \times \frac{2}{2} = \frac{10}{12}$$

Compare the numerators of the renamed fractions.

$$\frac{3}{12} < \frac{10}{12}$$

So, $\frac{1}{4} < \frac{5}{6}$.

C Compare $\frac{4}{5}$ and $\frac{4}{10}$ on a number line.

The fraction that is farther to the right on a number line is greater.

So, $\frac{4}{5} > \frac{4}{10}$.

Convince Me! **Critique Reasoning** Kelly looked at the fractions on the right and said, "These are easy to compare. I just think about $\frac{1}{8}$ and $\frac{1}{6}$." Circle the greater fraction. Explain what Kelly was thinking.

$\frac{5}{8}$ $\frac{5}{6}$

Practice Buddy   Tools   Assessment

Another Example!

Compare $\frac{3}{4}$ and $\frac{6}{10}$.

Create an equivalent fraction for $\frac{3}{4}$ that has a numerator of 6.

$$\frac{3}{4} \times \frac{2}{2} = \frac{6}{8}$$

$\frac{6}{8} > \frac{6}{10}$ because 8 equal parts are each larger than one of the 10 equal parts of the same whole.

When two fractions have different denominators but the same numerators, the fraction with the greater denominator is less.

☆ Guided Practice*

Do You Understand?

1. **Critique Reasoning** Mary says $\frac{1}{8}$ is greater than $\frac{1}{4}$ because 8 is greater than 4. Is Mary's reasoning correct? Explain.

Do You Know How?

For **2–5**, write $>$, $<$, or $=$. Use number lines, fraction strips, or equivalent fractions.

2. $\frac{3}{4} \bigcirc \frac{6}{8}$ 3. $\frac{1}{4} \bigcirc \frac{1}{10}$

4. $\frac{3}{5} \bigcirc \frac{5}{10}$ 5. $\frac{1}{2} \bigcirc \frac{4}{5}$

☆ Independent Practice ☆

Leveled Practice For **6–15**, find equivalent fractions to compare. Then write $>$, $<$, or $=$.

6. $\frac{7}{8} \bigcirc \frac{3}{4}$

7. $\frac{5}{6} \bigcirc \frac{10}{12}$

8. $\frac{7}{10} \bigcirc \frac{11}{12}$ 9. $\frac{7}{12} \bigcirc \frac{4}{12}$ 10. $\frac{5}{12} \bigcirc \frac{4}{5}$ 11. $\frac{2}{6} \bigcirc \frac{3}{12}$

12. $\frac{6}{8} \bigcirc \frac{8}{10}$ 13. $\frac{3}{5} \bigcirc \frac{3}{6}$ 14. $\frac{2}{10} \bigcirc \frac{2}{12}$ 15. $\frac{5}{6} \bigcirc \frac{4}{5}$

Problem Solving

16. Felicia drew the pictures at the right to show $\frac{3}{8}$ is greater than $\frac{3}{4}$. What was Felicia's mistake?

17. **Critique Reasoning** Jake said you can compare two fractions with the same denominator by only comparing the numerators. Is Jake correct? Explain.

18. Tina completed $\frac{2}{3}$ of her homework. George completed $\frac{7}{8}$ of his homework. Tina and George have the same amount of homework. Who completed a greater fraction of homework?

19. If $34 \times 2 = 68$, then what does 34×20 equal?

20. What can you conclude about $\frac{3}{5}$ and $\frac{60}{100}$ if you know $\frac{3}{5}$ is equivalent to $\frac{6}{10}$ and $\frac{6}{10}$ is equivalent to $\frac{60}{100}$?

21. Jackson played a video game for $\frac{1}{6}$ hour. Hailey played a video game for $\frac{1}{3}$ hour. Who played the video game for a greater amount of time? Explain.

22. **Higher Order Thinking** Four fourth-grade classes from an elementary school took a trip to the United States Capitol. There were 25 students in each class. At the capitol, a maximum of 40 students were allowed on a tour at one time. What was the least number of tours needed for all students to take the tour?

  ISTEP+ Ready

23. Select all answer choices that show a correct comparison.

- [ ] $\frac{3}{8} > \frac{3}{6}$
- [ ] $\frac{5}{5} > \frac{5}{8}$
- [ ] $\frac{1}{5} < \frac{1}{2}$
- [ ] $\frac{2}{3} < \frac{2}{10}$
- [ ] $\frac{1}{6} > \frac{2}{6}$

24. Select all answer choices that show a correct comparison.

- [ ] $\frac{5}{6} > \frac{7}{12}$
- [ ] $\frac{1}{2} > \frac{10}{10}$
- [ ] $\frac{4}{10} > \frac{2}{6}$
- [ ] $\frac{1}{5} < \frac{2}{3}$
- [ ] $\frac{2}{3} > \frac{9}{12}$

Name _____

Another Look!

Compare $\frac{2}{3}$ and $\frac{1}{2}$.

One Way

Rename one or both fractions so they both have the same denominator.

Rename both $\frac{2}{3}$ and $\frac{1}{2}$.

$\frac{2}{3} = \frac{2}{3} \times \frac{2}{2} = \frac{4}{6}$

$\frac{1}{2} = \frac{1}{2} \times \frac{3}{3} = \frac{3}{6}$

$\frac{4}{6} > \frac{3}{6}$, so $\frac{2}{3} > \frac{1}{2}$.

Another Way

Rename one or both fractions so they both have the same numerator.

Leave $\frac{2}{3}$ alone. Rename $\frac{1}{2}$.

$\frac{1}{2} = \frac{1}{2} \times \frac{2}{2} = \frac{2}{4}$

$\frac{2}{3} > \frac{2}{4}$, so $\frac{2}{3} > \frac{1}{2}$.

You can use fraction strips, number lines, or benchmark fractions to justify your comparisons.

For **1–16**, find equivalent fractions to compare. Then write $>$, $<$, or $=$. Use fraction strips or number lines.

1. $\frac{5}{6} \bigcirc \frac{2}{3}$

2. $\frac{1}{5} \bigcirc \frac{2}{8}$

3. $\frac{9}{10} \bigcirc \frac{6}{8}$

4. $\frac{3}{4} \bigcirc \frac{1}{4}$

5. $\frac{7}{8} \bigcirc \frac{5}{10}$

6. $\frac{2}{5} \bigcirc \frac{2}{6}$

7. $\frac{1}{3} \bigcirc \frac{3}{8}$

8. $\frac{2}{10} \bigcirc \frac{3}{5}$

9. $\frac{8}{10} \bigcirc \frac{3}{4}$

10. $\frac{3}{8} \bigcirc \frac{11}{12}$

11. $\frac{2}{3} \bigcirc \frac{10}{12}$

12. $\frac{7}{8} \bigcirc \frac{1}{6}$

13. $\frac{3}{8} \bigcirc \frac{7}{8}$

14. $\frac{2}{4} \bigcirc \frac{4}{8}$

15. $\frac{6}{8} \bigcirc \frac{8}{12}$

16. $\frac{1}{3} \bigcirc \frac{4}{8}$

For **17–18**, use the table at the right. The same number of students attended school each day.

17. Did more students buy lunch on Tuesday or on Wednesday?

18. Did more students buy lunch on Thursday or on Friday?

DATA	Day	Fraction of Students Buying Lunch
	Monday	$\frac{1}{2}$
	Tuesday	$\frac{2}{5}$
	Wednesday	$\frac{3}{4}$
	Thursday	$\frac{5}{8}$
	Friday	$\frac{4}{6}$

19. Number Sense Explain how you know $\frac{21}{100}$ is greater than $\frac{1}{5}$.

20. An orange was divided into 10 equal sections. Lily ate 4 sections. Manny and Emma ate the remaining sections. What fraction of the orange did Manny and Emma eat?

21. Which is longer, $\frac{1}{4}$ of line A or $\frac{1}{4}$ of line B? Explain.

22. Critique Reasoning James says $\frac{5}{5}$ is greater than $\frac{9}{10}$. Is James correct? Explain.

23. Write 3 fractions with unlike denominators that are greater than the fraction shown below.

24. Ann works at a store in the mall and earns a wage of $8 an hour. She earns $10 an hour if she works on the weekends. Last week she worked 24 hours during the week and 16 hours on the weekend. How much did Ann earn last week?

25. Higher Order Thinking Four friends each ordered individual pizzas at a restaurant. Suzy ate $\frac{3}{8}$ of her pizza. Ethan ate $\frac{3}{5}$ of his pizza. Tenaya ate $\frac{4}{6}$ of her pizza. Sam ate $\frac{1}{3}$ of his pizza. Who ate more than half of their pizza? less than half?

Assessment **ISTEP+ Ready**

26. Select all the answer choices that show a correct comparison.

☐ $\frac{10}{12} > \frac{5}{6}$

☐ $\frac{6}{8} = \frac{3}{4}$

☐ $\frac{1}{8} > \frac{1}{10}$

☐ $\frac{9}{10} < \frac{4}{5}$

☐ $\frac{1}{100} > \frac{1}{10}$

27. Select all the answer choices that show a correct comparison.

☐ $\frac{4}{12} < \frac{2}{5}$

☐ $\frac{6}{10} > \frac{60}{100}$

☐ $\frac{1}{4} < \frac{1}{10}$

☐ $\frac{3}{10} < \frac{1}{2}$

☐ $\frac{3}{5} < \frac{6}{12}$

Name _____

Solve & Share

Sherry and Karl both started their hike with a small bottle filled with water. Tia started her hike with a larger bottle that was $\frac{1}{2}$ full. At the end of the hike, Sherry and Tia's bottles were each half filled with water. Karl's bottle was $\frac{1}{3}$ filled with water. Who has the most water left? Construct a math argument to support your answer.

I can ...
construct math arguments using what I know about fractions.

Process Standards PS.3 Also PS.1, PS.2, PS.5
Content Standard 4.NS.5

Sherry   Karl   Tia

Thinking Habits

Be a good thinker!
These questions can help you.

• How can I use numbers, objects, drawings, or actions to justify my argument?

• Am I using numbers and symbols correctly?

• Is my explanation clear and complete?

Look Back! **Construct Arguments** If Tia's bottle was $\frac{1}{3}$ filled with water at the end of the hike, would you be able to decide who had the most water left? Construct an argument to support your answer.

How Can You Construct Arguments?

A

Erin said $\frac{1}{2}$ is the same amount as $\frac{2}{4}$.

Matt said $\frac{1}{2}$ and $\frac{2}{4}$ can be different amounts.

Which student is correct?

> A good math argument is correct, simple, complete, and easy to understand.

What do you need to do to solve this problem?

I need to construct an argument with what I know about fraction models and ways to show $\frac{1}{2}$ and $\frac{2}{4}$.

B How can I construct an argument?

I can

- use numbers, objects, drawings, or models to justify my arguments.

- use a counterexample in my argument.

- give an explanation of my argument that is clear and complete.

C

> Here's my thinking.

I will use drawings to show which student is correct.

$\frac{1}{2}$ $\frac{2}{4}$

Both wholes are the same size. The $\frac{1}{2}$ and $\frac{2}{4}$ represent the same part of the whole.

$\frac{2}{4}$ $\frac{1}{2}$

These wholes are not the same size. So, $\frac{2}{4}$ of the larger circle represents more than $\frac{1}{2}$ of the smaller circle.

Both students are correct. $\frac{1}{2}$ and $\frac{2}{4}$ of the same-size whole are the same amount. $\frac{1}{2}$ and $\frac{2}{4}$ of different-size wholes are different amounts.

Convince Me! **Critique Reasoning** Erin also said $\frac{3}{6}$ and $\frac{5}{10}$ are **NOT** the same size because the denominators are not factors of each other. Is Erin's argument correct? Explain.

Name _____

☆ Guided Practice *

Construct Arguments

Margie and Parker ordered the same-size burritos. Margie ate $\frac{4}{6}$ of her burrito. Parker ate $\frac{4}{5}$ of his burrito. Margie concluded she ate more than Parker because the fraction of the burrito she ate has a greater denominator.

1. What is Margie's argument? How does she support her argument?

2. Does Margie's conclusion make sense?

Independent Practice ☆

Construct Arguments

In the after-school club, Dena, Shawn, and Amanda knit scarves that are all the same size with yellow, white, and blue yarn. Dena's scarf is $\frac{3}{5}$ yellow, Shawn's scarf is $\frac{2}{5}$ yellow, and Amanda's scarf is $\frac{3}{4}$ yellow. The rest of each scarf has an equal amount of white and blue.

When you construct an argument, you need to make sure your explanation is complete.

3. Describe how Amanda could make the argument that her scarf has the most yellow.

4. How much of Dena's scarf is blue?

5. Dena has a scarf at home that is the same length as the scarf she made in the club. The scarf at home is $\frac{6}{8}$ yellow. Dena said the scarf at home has more yellow. Is she correct?

Snail Race

Mr. Aydin's science class had a snail race to see which snail would crawl the farthest from a starting line in two minutes. The table shows the distances the snails crawled.

DATA	Snail	Slimy	Slinky	Curly	Pod	Stylo	Creeper
	Distance in feet	$\frac{3}{12}$	$\frac{2}{12}$	$\frac{1}{5}$	$\frac{3}{10}$	$\frac{2}{10}$	$\frac{3}{8}$

6. **Use Appropriate Tools** Curly and Stylo traveled the same distance. Justify this conjecture using a number line or fraction strips.

7. **Construct Arguments** Who traveled farther, Slimy or Slinky? Explain.

When I construct arguments, I give a complete explanation.

8. **Reasoning** Who traveled farther, Creeper or Slimy? Explain.

9. **Make Sense and Persevere** Who won the race?

Help Practice Buddy Tools Games

Another Look!

Gina and her brother Don made cornbread in equal-sized pans. Gina ate $\frac{1}{4}$ pan of cornbread. Don ate $\frac{3}{8}$ pan.

Tell how you can construct an argument to justify the conjecture that Don ate more cornbread.

- I can decide if the conjecture makes sense to me.

- I can use drawings and numbers to explain my reasoning.

When you construct arguments, you use drawings and numbers to explain.

One Way

I can draw a picture of two equal-sized wholes to show that Don ate more cornbread.

$\frac{1}{4} < \frac{3}{8}$

Don ate more cornbread.

Another Way

I can use common denominators to compare $\frac{1}{4}$ and $\frac{3}{8}$. $\frac{1}{4}$ is equivalent to $\frac{2}{8}$.

Then I can compare the numerators of $\frac{2}{8}$ and $\frac{3}{8}$. Because the denominators are the same and $\frac{3}{8}$ has the greater numerator, $\frac{3}{8} > \frac{2}{8}$. Don ate more cornbread.

1. **Construct Arguments** A human usually has 20 baby teeth, which are replaced by 32 adult teeth. Raul lost 8 of his baby teeth. Raul said he lost $\frac{4}{10}$ of his baby teeth. Ana said Raul lost $\frac{2}{5}$ of his baby teeth. Which of these conjectures are true? Construct an argument to justify your answer.

Remember, a good argument is correct, simple, complete, and easy to understand.

2. **Construct Arguments** Trip has 15 coins worth 95 cents. Four of the coins are each worth twice as much as the rest. Construct a math argument to justify the conjecture that Trip has 11 nickels and 4 dimes.

Animal Weight and Food
Molly claims when one animal weighs more than another animal, it always eats more than the other animal. She also claims that when one animal weighs less than another, it always eats less. She supports her claims with the information shown in the table.

Animal	Weight	Food Eaten
Caribou	$\frac{3}{5}$ ton	12 pounds a day
Giraffe	$\frac{7}{8}$ ton	100 pounds a day
Panda	$\frac{1}{4}$ ton	301 pounds a week
Siberian Tiger	$\frac{1}{3}$ ton	55 pounds a day

3. **Make Sense and Persevere** Which animal eats the most? Explain.

4. **Reasoning** Does the animal that eats the most weigh more than the other animals? Explain.

5. **Critique Reasoning** Explain whether or not you agree with Molly's claim.

6. **Make Sense and Persevere** Which animal eats the least? Explain.

7. **Reasoning** Does the animal that eats the least weigh less than the other animals? Explain.

Remember, you can use words, objects, drawings, or diagrams when you construct an argument.

Find a partner. Get paper and a pencil. Each partner chooses a different color: light blue or dark blue.

Partner 1 and Partner 2 each point to a black number at the same time. Each partner subtracts the two numbers.

If the answer is on your color, you get a tally mark. Work until one partner has twelve tally marks.

I can ...
subtract multi-digit whole numbers.

Partner 1

510

608

701

850

909

93	362	322	267
714	607	191	421
433	229	213	471
365	530	315	655
131	492	284	413
458	120	22	506

Partner 2

195

243

379

488

417

Tally Marks for Partner 1

Tally Marks for Partner 2

A-Z
Glossary

Word List

- benchmark fraction
- common factor
- denominator
- equivalent fractions
- fraction
- numerator

Understand Vocabulary

Choose the best term from the box. Write it on the blank.

1. A number that names part of a whole, part of a set, or a location on a number line is a(n) _____.

2. A commonly used fraction that helps you understand a different size or amount is called a(n) _____.

3. The number below the fraction bar in a fraction that shows the total number of equal parts is the _____.

4. Fractions that name the same part of a whole or the same location on a number line are called _____.

5. The number above the fraction bar that represents part of the whole is called a(n) _____.

For each of these terms, give an example and a non-example.

	Example	Non-example
6. Fraction	_____	_____
7. Equivalent fractions	_____	_____
8. A fraction with a common factor for its numerator and denominator	_____	_____

Use Vocabulary in Writing

9. Explain how to compare $\frac{5}{8}$ and $\frac{3}{8}$. Use at least 3 terms from the Word List in your explanation.

Set A pages 411–422

Use an area model to write an equivalent fraction for $\frac{1}{2}$.

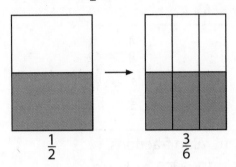

$\frac{1}{2}$ and $\frac{3}{6}$ name the same part of the whole.
$\frac{1}{2}$ and $\frac{3}{6}$ are equivalent fractions.

Use a number line to write an equivalent fraction for $\frac{1}{3}$.

$\frac{1}{3}$ and $\frac{2}{6}$ name the same part of the whole.
$\frac{1}{3}$ and $\frac{2}{6}$ are equivalent fractions.

Remember that equivalent fractions name the same part of a whole.

Reteaching

> Write an equivalent fraction for each fraction given.

1. $\frac{2}{8}$ **2.** $\frac{2}{3}$

3. $\frac{1}{4}$ **4.** $\frac{3}{5}$

> Draw a number line to shown each fraction and an equivalent fraction.

5. $\frac{4}{6}$

6. $\frac{4}{10}$

Set B pages 423–434

Find two equivalent fractions for $\frac{1}{2}$.

$\frac{1}{2} \times \frac{2}{2} = \frac{2}{4}$ $\frac{1}{2} \times \frac{3}{3} = \frac{3}{6}$

$\frac{1}{2}$, $\frac{2}{4}$, and $\frac{3}{6}$ are equivalent fractions.

Find two equivalent fractions for $\frac{8}{12}$.

$\frac{8}{12} \div \frac{2}{2} = \frac{4}{6}$ $\frac{8}{12} \div \frac{4}{4} = \frac{2}{3}$

$\frac{8}{12}$, $\frac{4}{6}$, and $\frac{2}{3}$ are equivalent fractions.

Remember that you can multiply or divide to find equivalent fractions.

> Multiply or divide to find equivalent fractions.

1. $\frac{2}{3} = \frac{8}{\square}$ **2.** $\frac{1}{4} = \frac{\square}{8}$

3. $\frac{1}{6} = \frac{2}{\square}$ **4.** $\frac{3}{5} = \frac{\square}{10}$

5. $\frac{10}{12} = \frac{5}{\square}$ **6.** $\frac{4}{10} = \frac{\square}{5}$

7. $\frac{2}{6} = \frac{1}{\square}$ **8.** $\frac{6}{10} = \frac{\square}{5}$

Compare $\frac{5}{8}$ and $\frac{4}{10}$. Use benchmark fractions.

	$\frac{1}{2}$						
$\frac{1}{8}$	$\frac{1}{8}$	$\frac{1}{8}$	$\frac{1}{8}$	$\frac{1}{8}$			

$\frac{5}{8} > \frac{1}{2}$

	$\frac{1}{2}$						
$\frac{1}{10}$	$\frac{1}{10}$	$\frac{1}{10}$	$\frac{1}{10}$				

$\frac{4}{10} < \frac{1}{2}$

So, $\frac{5}{8} > \frac{4}{10}$.

Compare $\frac{4}{6}$ and $\frac{3}{4}$. Rename each fraction.

$\frac{4}{6} = \frac{4}{6} \times \frac{2}{2} = \frac{8}{12}$ $\frac{3}{4} = \frac{3}{4} \times \frac{3}{3} = \frac{9}{12}$

$\frac{8}{12}$ is less than $\frac{9}{12}$ so, $\frac{4}{6}$ is less than $\frac{3}{4}$.

Remember benchmark fractions are commonly used fractions such as $\frac{1}{4}$, $\frac{1}{2}$, and $\frac{3}{4}$.

> Use benchmark fractions to compare. Write $>$, $<$, or $=$ for each $\bigcirc$.

1. $\frac{5}{5} \bigcirc \frac{4}{6}$ 2. $\frac{4}{8} \bigcirc \frac{1}{2}$

3. $\frac{4}{5} \bigcirc \frac{7}{8}$ 4. $\frac{2}{3} \bigcirc \frac{4}{6}$

> Compare by renaming fractions. Write $>$, $<$, or $=$ for each $\bigcirc$.

5. $\frac{3}{4} \bigcirc \frac{5}{8}$ 6. $\frac{1}{5} \bigcirc \frac{2}{10}$

7. $\frac{2}{5} \bigcirc \frac{1}{4}$ 8. $\frac{3}{6} \bigcirc \frac{3}{4}$

9. $\frac{2}{4} \bigcirc \frac{2}{3}$ 10. $\frac{8}{10} \bigcirc \frac{4}{6}$

Think about these questions to help you **construct arguments**.

Thinking Habits

- How can I use numbers, objects, drawings, or actions to justify my argument?

- Am I using numbers and symbols correctly?

- Is my explanation clear and complete?

Remember when you construct arguments, you use drawings and numbers to explain.

Peter says $\frac{3}{4}$ of a pizza is always the same as $\frac{6}{8}$ of a pizza. Nadia says while $\frac{3}{4}$ and $\frac{6}{8}$ are equivalent fractions, $\frac{3}{4}$ and $\frac{6}{8}$ of a pizza could represent different amounts.

1. Who is correct? Explain. Use a drawing to justify your argument.

2. Use a counterexample to explain who is correct.

Name _____

1. After a bake sale, only $\frac{2}{3}$ pie remains. What fraction is equivalent to $\frac{2}{3}$?

Ⓐ $\frac{1}{3}$

Ⓑ $\frac{3}{3}$

Ⓒ $\frac{2}{6}$

Ⓓ $\frac{4}{6}$

2. Leslie will use more than $\frac{1}{2}$ cup but less than 1 whole cup of flour for a recipe. What fraction of a cup might Leslie use? Explain.

3. Danielle said she read $\frac{1}{2}$ of a book. Select all the fractions that are equivalent to $\frac{1}{2}$.

☐ $\frac{3}{6}$

☐ $\frac{5}{10}$

☐ $\frac{6}{12}$

☐ $\frac{3}{5}$

☐ $\frac{6}{8}$

4. Explain how to use division to find an equivalent fraction for $\frac{9}{12}$.

5. Draw lines to match each fraction on the left to an equivalent fraction on the right.

$\frac{2}{3}$	$\frac{10}{6}$
$\frac{6}{10}$	$\frac{6}{8}$
$\frac{20}{12}$	$\frac{2}{5}$
$\frac{4}{10}$	$\frac{8}{12}$
$\frac{3}{4}$	$\frac{3}{5}$

6. Compare the fractions to $\frac{1}{2}$. Write each fraction in the correct answer space.

Less Than $\frac{1}{2}$	Equal to $\frac{1}{2}$	Greater Than $\frac{1}{2}$

$\frac{5}{4}$	$\frac{5}{10}$	$\frac{2}{12}$
$\frac{6}{12}$	$\frac{3}{8}$	$\frac{2}{3}$

7. For questions 7a–7d, choose Yes or No to tell if the fraction is greater than $\frac{3}{5}$.

7a. $\frac{3}{10}$ ○ Yes ○ No

7b. $\frac{3}{8}$ ○ Yes ○ No

7c. $\frac{5}{3}$ ○ Yes ○ No

7d. $\frac{6}{6}$ ○ Yes ○ No

8. The Sahas were reading a best-selling novel as a family. After the first week, they checked in with each other to see how much of the book each had read.

Fraction Read	
Mr. Saha	$\frac{2}{6}$
Mrs. Saha	$\frac{1}{3}$
Maddie	$\frac{3}{4}$
George	$\frac{2}{3}$

Part A

Who read the greatest fraction of the book?

Part B

Name the two family members that read the same fraction of the book. Explain.

9. Johnny found a fraction equivalent to the one shown by the point on the number line. Which fraction could Johnny have found?

Ⓐ $\frac{1}{4}$ Ⓒ $\frac{1}{2}$

Ⓑ $\frac{1}{3}$ Ⓓ $\frac{2}{3}$

10. Bill and Gina each ate $\frac{1}{2}$ of their own pizza. Bill ate more pizza than Gina. Draw a picture and explain how that is possible.

11. Use multiplication to find an equivalent fraction for $\frac{1}{3}$.

$$\frac{1}{3} \times \frac{\square}{\square} = \frac{\square}{\square}$$

12. Only one of the comparisons below is correct. Which is correct?

Ⓐ $\frac{2}{3} < \frac{1}{2}$

Ⓑ $\frac{1}{2} = \frac{3}{5}$

Ⓒ $\frac{3}{4} < \frac{4}{5}$

Ⓓ $\frac{3}{4} < \frac{2}{3}$

13. Use 1 as a benchmark to compare $\frac{6}{5}$ and $\frac{5}{6}$.

Name _____

Comparing Grasshoppers

Mrs. Rakin's class measured the lengths of some grasshoppers.
The **Grasshopper Lengths** table shows the lengths they found.

1. Mrs. Rakin asked the students to choose two
   grasshoppers and compare their lengths.

Part A

Henry used benchmark fractions to compare
the lengths of grasshoppers A and C. Which
grasshopper is longer? Explain.

Grasshopper Lengths	
Grasshopper	Length (inch)
A	$\frac{5}{8}$
B	$\frac{3}{2}$
C	$\frac{7}{4}$
D	$\frac{7}{8}$
E	$\frac{3}{4}$
F	$\frac{3}{8}$

Part B

Riley used a number line to compare the
lengths of grasshoppers A and E. Which
grasshopper is longer? Use the number line
to show the comparison.

Part C

Jack compared the lengths of grasshoppers D and E. He said
grasshopper D is longer. Is Jack correct? Justify the comparison
using fraction strips.

2. One group of students measured the lengths of grasshoppers in centimeters, instead of inches. The **More Grasshopper Lengths** table shows the lengths they found.

More Grasshopper Lengths	
Grasshopper	**Length (centimeter)**
G	$\frac{7}{10}$
H	$\frac{4}{5}$
I	$\frac{6}{10}$

Part A

Tommy compared the lengths of grasshoppers G and H. Which grasshopper is longer? Explain how to rename the fractions using multiplication so they have the same denominator to compare.

Part B

Venon compared the lengths of grasshoppers H and I. Which grasshopper is longer? Explain how to rename the fractions using division so they have the same denominator to compare.

Part C

Rina wants to determine if grasshopper D is longer or shorter than grasshopper G. Explain how Rina can compare the fractions.

Understand Addition and Subtraction of Fractions

Essential Questions: How do you add and subtract fractions and mixed numbers with like denominators? How can fractions be added and subtracted on a number line?

Digital Resources

Solve   Learn   Glossary   Practice Buddy

Tools   Assessment   Help   Games

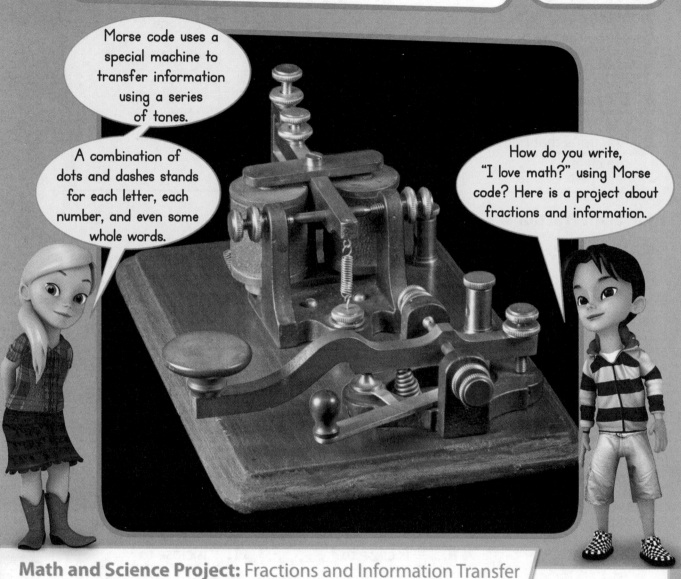

Morse code uses a special machine to transfer information using a series of tones.

A combination of dots and dashes stands for each letter, each number, and even some whole words.

How do you write, "I love math?" using Morse code? Here is a project about fractions and information.

Math and Science Project: Fractions and Information Transfer

Do Research Morse code uses patterns to transfer information. Any word can be written using Morse code. Use the Internet or other sources to find how to write *fourth, grade,* and *school* using Morse code.

Journal: Write a Report Include what you found. Also in your report:

- Write *one* in Morse code. Write a fraction that tells what part of the code for *one* is dashes.

- Write *three* in Morse code. Write a fraction that tells what part of the code for *three* is dots.

- Write and solve an equation to find how much greater the fraction for dots is than the fraction for dashes in the word *three*.

Name _____

Review What You Know

Vocabulary

Choose the best term from the box.
Write it on the blank.

- benchmark fractions
- equivalent fractions
- denominator
- numerator

1. In $\frac{2}{3}$, 2 is the _____ of the fraction and 3 is the _____ of the fraction.

2. Fractions that name the same region, part of a set, or part of a segment are called _____.

Equivalent Fractions

Write the missing values to show pairs of equivalent fractions.

3. $\frac{2}{3} = \frac{\square}{6}$

4. $\frac{\square}{4} = \frac{3}{12}$

5. $\frac{6}{5} = \frac{\square}{10}$

6. $\frac{1}{2} = \frac{50}{\square}$

7. $\frac{1}{5} = \frac{\square}{10}$

8. $\frac{3}{\square} = \frac{30}{100}$

Benchmark Fractions

Use the number line to find a benchmark fraction or whole number for each given fraction.

9. $\frac{7}{8}$ is close to _____.

10. $\frac{8}{12}$ is close to _____.

11. $\frac{2}{6}$ is close to _____.

Problem Solving

12. Adult admission to the dog show is $16. Children's admission is $9. How much would it cost 3 adults and 2 children to enter the dog show?

13. Meg saved coins she found for a year. She found a total of 95 pennies, 13 nickels, 41 dimes, and 11 quarters. She would like to evenly divide the coins into 4 piggy banks. How many coins will go in each piggy bank?

My Word Cards

Use the examples for each word on the front of the card to help complete the definitions on the back.

 decompose

$$\frac{4}{5} = \frac{1}{5} + \frac{2}{5} + \frac{1}{5}$$

 compose

$$\frac{1}{4} + \frac{1}{4} + \frac{1}{4} = \frac{3}{4}$$

mixed number

$$1\frac{1}{3}, \ 4\frac{1}{2}, \ 6\frac{5}{8}$$

My Word Cards

_____ means to combine parts.

_____ means to break into parts.

A number that has a whole number part and a fraction part is a

_____.

Name _____

Solve & Share

Kyle and Jillian are working on a sports banner. They painted $\frac{3}{8}$ of the banner green and $\frac{4}{8}$ purple. How much of the banner have they painted? **Solve this problem any way you choose.**

I can ...
use tools such as fraction strips or area models to add fractions.

Content Standard 4.C.5
Process Standards PS.1, PS.2, PS.3, PS.4, PS.5

You can use appropriate tools. You can use drawings, area models, or fraction strips to solve this problem. *Show your work in the space below!*

Look Back! **Use Appropriate Tools** Kyle says $\frac{1}{8} + \frac{1}{8} + \frac{1}{8} = \frac{3}{8}$. Jillian says $\frac{1}{8} + \frac{1}{8} + \frac{1}{8} = \frac{3}{24}$. Use fraction strips to decide who is correct.

Essential Question **How Can You Use Tools to Add Fractions?**

A

Ten canoeing teams are racing downriver. Five teams have silver canoes and two teams have brown canoes. What fraction of the canoes are either silver or brown?

You can use tools such as fraction strips to add two or more fractions.

B Find $\frac{5}{10} + \frac{2}{10}$. Use five $\frac{1}{10}$ fraction strips to show $\frac{5}{10}$ and two $\frac{1}{10}$ strips to show $\frac{2}{10}$.

Five $\frac{1}{10}$ strips joined with two $\frac{1}{10}$ strips are seven $\frac{1}{10}$ strips.

Add the numerators. Then write the sum over the like denominator.

$$\frac{5}{10} + \frac{2}{10} = \frac{7}{10}$$

C Find $\frac{5}{10} + \frac{2}{10}$. Mark five $\frac{1}{10}$ segments to show $\frac{5}{10}$ and two $\frac{1}{10}$ segments to show $\frac{2}{10}$.

$$\frac{2}{10} = \frac{1}{10} + \frac{1}{10}$$

$$\frac{5}{10} = \frac{1}{10} + \frac{1}{10} + \frac{1}{10} + \frac{1}{10} + \frac{1}{10}$$

Adding $\frac{5}{10}$ and $\frac{2}{10}$ means joining five $\frac{1}{10}$ segments and two $\frac{1}{10}$ segments.

$\frac{7}{10}$ of the canoes are either silver or brown.

Convince Me! **Make Sense and Persevere** What two fractions would you add to find the fraction of the canoes that are either green or brown? What is the sum? How do you know your sum is correct?

Name _____

 ☆ **Guided Practice** *

Practice   Tools   Assessment
Buddy

Do You Understand?

1. Reasoning In the problem on the previous page, why aren't the purple $\frac{1}{10}$ strips the same length as the red strip?

2. What two fractions are being added below? What is the sum?

Do You Know How?

 For **3–4**, find each sum.

3. $\frac{2}{5} + \frac{1}{5}$

4. $\frac{1}{6} + \frac{1}{6}$

Independent Practice ☆

Leveled Practice For **5–16**, find each sum. Use fraction strips or other tools.

5. $\frac{3}{12} + \frac{4}{12}$

6. $\frac{4}{10} + \frac{1}{10}$

7. $\frac{2}{12} + \frac{4}{12}$

8. $\frac{1}{6} + \frac{2}{6} + \frac{3}{6}$

9. $\frac{1}{4} + \frac{2}{4}$

10. $\frac{1}{3} + \frac{1}{3}$

11. $\frac{5}{8} + \frac{1}{8}$

12. $\frac{1}{4} + \frac{3}{4}$

13. $\frac{7}{12} + \frac{2}{12}$

14. $\frac{1}{4} + \frac{1}{4}$

15. $\frac{2}{5} + \frac{2}{5}$

16. $\frac{1}{10} + \frac{2}{10} + \frac{1}{10}$

*For another example, see Set A on page 533.

Topic 9 | Lesson 9-1   **467**

Problem Solving

17. Number Sense Using three different numerators, write an equation in which three fractions, when added, have a sum of 1.

18. Model with Math A rope is divided into 8 equal parts. Draw a picture to show $\frac{1}{8} + \frac{3}{8} = \frac{4}{8}$.

19. A bakery sells about 9 dozen bagels per day. About how many bagels does the bakery sell in a typical week? Explain.

There are 12 bagels in one dozen.

20. What addition problem is shown by the fraction strips below?

21. Higher Order Thinking Terry ran $\frac{1}{10}$ of the distance from school to home. He walked $\frac{3}{10}$ more of the distance and then skipped $\frac{2}{10}$ more of the distance. What fraction of the distance home does Terry still have to go?

Look back to see if you answered the question that was asked.

22. Jackson said, "I am thinking of two fractions that when added have a sum of one." Which fractions could Jackson have been thinking about?

Ⓐ $\frac{5}{3}$ and $\frac{5}{3}$

Ⓑ $\frac{1}{4}$ and $\frac{3}{4}$

Ⓒ $\frac{2}{5}$ and $\frac{4}{5}$

Ⓓ $\frac{3}{8}$ and $\frac{4}{8}$

23. Lindsay has 5 red hats, 2 blue hats, and 3 black hats. Which statement is true?

Ⓐ $\frac{8}{10}$ of the hats are either red or black.

Ⓑ $\frac{5}{3}$ of the hats are either red or black.

Ⓒ $\frac{5}{10}$ of the hats are either red or black.

Ⓓ $\frac{3}{10}$ of the hats are either red or black.

Name _____

Homework & Practice 9-1

Model Addition of Fractions

Another Look!

Eight friends went out to lunch. Four of them had pizza. Two had hamburgers and two had soup. What fraction of the group had either pizza or soup?

You can use a circle fraction model to add fractions.

Divide a circle into eighths to represent each of the 8 people in the group.	Four people had pizza. Shade 4 of the sections to represent $\frac{4}{8}$. Two people had soup. Shade 2 more sections to represent $\frac{2}{8}$. 	Count the number of $\frac{1}{8}$ sections. There are six $\frac{1}{8}$ sections shaded. So, $\frac{6}{8}$ of the group had either pizza or soup. $$\frac{4}{8} + \frac{2}{8} = \frac{6}{8}$$

For **1–12**, find each sum. Use fraction strips or other tools.

1. $\frac{1}{5} + \frac{1}{5}$

2. $\frac{4}{6} + \frac{1}{6}$

3. $\frac{5}{8} + \frac{2}{8}$

4. $\frac{2}{12} + \frac{2}{12}$

5. $\frac{2}{5} + \frac{3}{5}$

6. $\frac{2}{10} + \frac{3}{10}$

7. $\frac{5}{8} + \frac{3}{8}$

8. $\frac{3}{10} + \frac{1}{10}$

9. $\frac{3}{4} + \frac{1}{4}$

10. $\frac{5}{10} + \frac{4}{10}$

11. $\frac{1}{6} + \frac{1}{6} + \frac{1}{6}$

12. $\frac{1}{12} + \frac{5}{12} + \frac{2}{12}$

13. Critique Reasoning When Jared found $\frac{1}{5} + \frac{2}{5}$, he wrote the sum $\frac{3}{10}$. Is Jared correct? Explain.

14. Number Sense Leah wrote 2 different fractions with the same denominator. Both fractions were less than 1. Can their sum equal 1? Can their sum be greater than 1? Explain.

15. Sasha has a box of antique letters. She wants to give an equal number of letters to each of her 5 friends. How many antique letters will each friend receive?

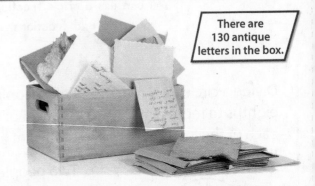

There are 130 antique letters in the box.

16. Model with Math Sandy made 8 friendship bracelets. She gave 1 bracelet to her best friend and 5 bracelets to her friends on the tennis team. Use the model to find the fraction that represents the total number of bracelets Sandy gave away.

17. Higher Order Thinking Julia writes 2 fractions with the same denominator that have numerators 5 and 7. What could the denominator be if the sum is less than 1? Equal to 1? Greater than 1?

Assessment ISTEP+ Ready

18. Billy did $\frac{1}{6}$ of his homework on Friday. He did $\frac{1}{6}$ more on Saturday. Billy still had $\frac{4}{6}$ to finish. How much of his homework did Billy do on Friday and Saturday?

Ⓐ $\frac{2}{6}$ Ⓒ $\frac{4}{6}$

Ⓑ $\frac{3}{6}$ Ⓓ $\frac{5}{6}$

19. Roberto shares a bag of almonds with 2 friends. He shares $\frac{1}{8}$ bag with Jeremy and $\frac{2}{8}$ bag with Emily. He eats $\frac{3}{8}$ of the almonds himself. What fraction of the almonds do Roberto and his friends eat?

Ⓐ $\frac{1}{12}$ Ⓒ $\frac{6}{8}$

Ⓑ $\frac{3}{8}$ Ⓓ $\frac{7}{8}$

Name _____

☆ ☆
Solve & Share

Karyn has $\frac{11}{8}$ pounds of chili to put into three bowls. The amount of chili in each bowl does not have to be the same. How much chili could Karyn put into each bowl? *Solve this problem any way you choose.*

How can you model the amount of chili Karyn puts in each bowl? *Show your work in the space below!*

I can ...
use fraction strips, area models, or drawings to decompose fractions.

Content Standard 4.C.5
Process Standards PS.2, PS.4, PS.5

Look Back! **Use Appropriate Tools** Use a drawing or fraction strips to help write equivalent fractions for the amount of chili in one of the bowls.

How Can You Represent a Fraction in a Variety of Ways?

A

Charlene wants to leave $\frac{1}{6}$ of her garden empty. What are some different ways Charlene can plant the rest of her garden?

$\frac{1}{6}$ empty

Decompose means to break into parts. Compose means to combine parts. The fraction of the garden that Charlene will plant can be decomposed in more than one way.

B **One Way**

Charlene could plant four $\frac{1}{6}$ sections with blue flowers and one $\frac{1}{6}$ section with red peppers.

$\frac{5}{6}$ is $\frac{4}{6}$ and $\frac{1}{6}$.

$\frac{5}{6} = \frac{4}{6} + \frac{1}{6}$

C **Another Way**

Charlene could plant one $\frac{1}{6}$ section with green beans, one $\frac{1}{6}$ section with yellow squash, one $\frac{1}{6}$ section with red peppers, and two $\frac{1}{6}$ sections with blue flowers.

$\frac{5}{6}$ is $\frac{1}{6}$ and $\frac{1}{6}$ and $\frac{1}{6}$ and $\frac{2}{6}$.

$\frac{5}{6} = \frac{1}{6} + \frac{1}{6} + \frac{1}{6} + \frac{2}{6}$

Convince Me! **Use Appropriate Tools** Draw pictures or use fraction strips to show why these equations are true.

$\frac{5}{6} = \frac{3}{6} + \frac{2}{6}$ $\frac{5}{6} = \frac{1}{6} + \frac{2}{6} + \frac{2}{6}$

472 **Topic 9** | Lesson 9-2

Name _____

Another Look!

Shannon wants to use $\frac{5}{8}$ of her garden space to plant petunias and marigolds. How can Shannon use the available space?

1

| $\frac{1}{8}$ | $\frac{1}{8}$ | $\frac{1}{8}$ | $\frac{1}{8}$ | $\frac{1}{8}$ |

There are more than two solutions to this problem.

Write $\frac{5}{8}$ as the sum of fractions in two different ways.

$$\frac{5}{8} = \frac{1}{8} + \frac{4}{8} \qquad \frac{5}{8} = \frac{2}{8} + \frac{3}{8}$$

Shannon could use $\frac{1}{8}$ of the space for petunias and $\frac{4}{8}$ for marigolds, or she could use $\frac{2}{8}$ of the space for petunias and $\frac{3}{8}$ for marigolds.

For **1–8**, decompose each fraction or mixed number in two different ways. Use drawings or fraction strips as needed.

1. $\frac{4}{8} = \dfrac{\square}{\square} + \dfrac{\square}{\square}$

$\frac{4}{8} = \dfrac{\square}{\square} + \dfrac{\square}{\square} + \dfrac{\square}{\square}$

2. $\frac{7}{10} = \dfrac{\square}{\square} + \dfrac{\square}{\square}$

$\frac{7}{10} = \dfrac{\square}{\square} + \dfrac{\square}{\square} + \dfrac{\square}{\square}$

3. $\frac{4}{5} =$

$\frac{4}{5} =$

4. $\frac{3}{10} =$

$\frac{3}{10} =$

5. $1\frac{1}{4} =$

$1\frac{1}{4} =$

6. $2\frac{2}{3} =$

$2\frac{2}{3} =$

Challenge yourself! Include ways that break a fraction or mixed number into more than two parts.

7. $1\frac{3}{5} =$

$1\frac{3}{5} =$

8. $1\frac{1}{2} =$

$1\frac{1}{2} =$

9. Yvonne ran $\frac{3}{8}$ of the race before stopping for water. She wants to stop for water one more time before finishing the race. List two ways Yvonne can do this.

$\frac{1}{8}$	$\frac{1}{8}$	$\frac{1}{8}$	$\frac{1}{8}$	$\frac{1}{8}$	$\frac{1}{8}$	$\frac{1}{8}$	$\frac{1}{8}$

10. Reasoning A teacher noticed $\frac{5}{8}$ of the students were wearing either blue shorts or white shorts. Write two different ways this could be done.

11. Connie made $1\frac{1}{3}$ pounds of trail mix for a hike. Is there a way Connie can break up the trail mix into four bags? Explain.

12. Jo's Donut Express earned $4,378 at a festival by selling chocolate or vanilla donuts for $2 each. If they sold 978 chocolate donuts, how many vanilla donuts did they sell?

13. Higher Order Thinking Mark said he can decompose $\frac{5}{6}$ into three fractions with three different numerators and the same denominator. Is this possible? Explain. Remember, you can use equivalent fractions.

Assessment ⊙ (**ISTEP+ Ready**)

14. Mrs. Evans asked the class to decompose $1\frac{3}{4}$. Which of the following are **NOT** ways to decompose $1\frac{3}{4}$? Select all that apply. Use area models if needed.

☐ $1 + \frac{3}{4}$

☐ $\frac{1}{4} + \frac{1}{4} + \frac{1}{4} + \frac{1}{4} + \frac{1}{4} + \frac{1}{4} + \frac{1}{4}$

☐ $\frac{4}{4} + \frac{3}{4}$

☐ $\frac{3}{4} + \frac{5}{4}$

☐ $1 + \frac{1}{2} + \frac{2}{2}$

15. Ms. Anderson showed her class how to decompose $1\frac{3}{8}$. Select all the ways Ms. Anderson could have decomposed $1\frac{3}{8}$. Use fraction strips if needed.

☐ $\frac{3}{8} + \frac{3}{8} + \frac{3}{8} + \frac{2}{8}$

☐ $1 + \frac{3}{8}$

☐ $\frac{8}{8} + \frac{3}{8}$

☐ $\frac{5}{8} + \frac{5}{8} + \frac{1}{8}$

☐ $1 + \frac{1}{4} + \frac{2}{4}$

Name _____

Solve & Share

Jonas is making nachos and tacos for a family party. He uses $\frac{2}{5}$ bag of shredded cheese for the nachos and $\frac{1}{5}$ bag for the tacos. How much of the bag of shredded cheese does Jonas use? **Solve this problem any way you choose.**

I can ...
use my understanding of addition as joining parts of the same whole to add fractions with like denominators.

Content Standards 4.C.5, 4.AT.5
Process Standards PS.1, PS.3, PS.4, PS.7

You can model with math. What equation can you write to represent this problem?

Look Back! **Look for Relationships** What do you notice about the denominators in your equation?

Learn Glossary

Essential Question

How Can You Add Fractions with Like Denominators?

A

The table shows the results of a fourth-grade Pets Club survey. What fraction of the club members chose a hamster or a dog as their favorite pet?

Add the fractions for hamsters and dogs to find the result.

Favorite Pet	
cat	$\frac{5}{12}$
dog	$\frac{4}{12}$
hamster	$\frac{2}{12}$
parrot	$\frac{1}{12}$

B Find $\frac{2}{12} + \frac{4}{12}$ using a model.

$$\frac{4}{12} = \frac{1}{12} + \frac{1}{12} + \frac{1}{12} + \frac{1}{12}$$

0 ——————————— 1

$$\frac{2}{12} = \frac{1}{12} + \frac{1}{12}$$

$$\frac{2}{12} + \frac{4}{12} = \frac{1}{12} + \frac{1}{12} + \frac{1}{12} + \frac{1}{12} + \frac{1}{12} + \frac{1}{12} = \frac{6}{12}$$

C Find $\frac{2}{12} + \frac{4}{12}$ by joining parts.

Add the numerators. Write the sum over the like denominator.

$$\frac{2}{12} + \frac{4}{12} = \frac{6}{12}$$

$\frac{6}{12}$ is equivalent to $\frac{1}{2}$. One half of the club members chose a hamster or a dog as their favorite pet.

Convince Me! Critique Reasoning Frank solved the problem above and found $\frac{2}{12} + \frac{4}{12} = \frac{6}{24}$. What error did Frank make? Explain.

Name _____

Another Example!

Find $\frac{4}{5} + \frac{3}{5}$.

$$\overbrace{\quad\quad}^{4} \quad \overbrace{\quad}^{3}$$

$$\frac{4}{5} + \frac{3}{5} = \frac{1}{5} + \frac{1}{5} + \frac{1}{5} + \frac{1}{5} + \frac{1}{5} + \frac{1}{5} + \frac{1}{5} = \frac{7}{5}$$

Write the fraction as a mixed number. $\quad \frac{7}{5} = \frac{5}{5} + \frac{2}{5} = 1\frac{2}{5}$

You can write the sum as a fraction or a mixed number.

☆ Guided Practice*

Do You Understand?

1. Using the survey on the previous page, what fraction of the club members chose either a bird or a cat?

2. **Critique Reasoning** Greg found $\frac{1}{3} + \frac{2}{3} = \frac{3}{6}$. What error did Greg make?

Do You Know How?

For **3–6**, find each sum. Use drawings or fraction strips as needed.

3. $\frac{2}{4} + \frac{1}{4}$ 4. $\frac{1}{3} + \frac{2}{3}$

5. $\frac{2}{12} + \frac{11}{12}$ 6. $\frac{1}{10} + \frac{4}{10}$

☆ Independent Practice ☆

For **7–18**, find each sum. Use drawings or fraction strips as needed.

7. $\frac{2}{8} + \frac{1}{8}$

8. $\frac{3}{6} + \frac{2}{6}$

9. $\frac{1}{8} + \frac{4}{8}$

10. $\frac{3}{10} + \frac{2}{10}$

11. $\frac{3}{10} + \frac{5}{10}$

12. $\frac{5}{12} + \frac{4}{12}$

13. $\frac{4}{5} + \frac{3}{5} + \frac{2}{5}$

14. $\frac{3}{10} + \frac{2}{10} + \frac{6}{10}$

15. $\frac{2}{6} + \frac{5}{6}$

16. $\frac{3}{6} + \frac{9}{6}$

17. $\frac{11}{10} + \frac{11}{10}$

18. $\frac{7}{8} + \frac{1}{8}$

*For another example, see Set A on page 533.   **Topic 9** | Lesson 9-3   **479**

Problem Solving

For 19–21, use the table at the right.

19. What fraction of the set is either triangles or rectangles?

20. Which two shapes make up $\frac{7}{10}$ of the shapes in the set?

21. Which two shapes make up half of the set? Find two possible answers.

Shapes in the Set

▲	$\frac{2}{10}$
▭	$\frac{4}{10}$
⬡	$\frac{1}{10}$
●	$\frac{3}{10}$

22. **Make Sense and Persevere** There are 64 crayons in each box. A school bought 25 boxes of crayons for the art classes. If the crayons are shared equally among 5 classes, how many crayons will each class receive? Explain.

23. **Higher Order Thinking** Three-tenths of Ken's buttons are blue, $\frac{4}{10}$ are green, and the rest are black. What fraction of Ken's buttons are black?

  Assessment **ISTEP+ Ready**

24. Draw lines connecting each fraction or mixed number on the left with the correct expression on the right.

$\frac{3}{4}$	$\frac{3}{8} + \frac{2}{8} + \frac{32}{8}$
$4\frac{5}{8}$	$\frac{2}{6} + \frac{4}{6}$
$\frac{7}{6}$	$\frac{2}{4} + \frac{1}{4}$
1	$\frac{6}{6} + \frac{1}{6}$

25. Draw lines connecting each fraction or mixed number on the left with the correct expression on the right.

$1\frac{1}{10}$	$\frac{1}{4} + \frac{2}{4} + \frac{8}{4}$
2	$\frac{1}{10} + \frac{0}{10} + \frac{10}{10}$
$\frac{6}{12}$	$\frac{3}{12} + \frac{3}{12}$
$2\frac{3}{4}$	$\frac{5}{4} + \frac{3}{4}$

Name _____

Homework & Practice 9-3

Add Fractions with Like Denominators

Another Look!

Find $\frac{4}{8} + \frac{2}{8}$.

> When you add fractions with like denominators, add the numerators and keep the denominators the same.

$\frac{4}{8} = \frac{1}{8} + \frac{1}{8} + \frac{1}{8} + \frac{1}{8}$ $\frac{2}{8} = \frac{1}{8} + \frac{1}{8}$

$\frac{4}{8} + \frac{2}{8} = \frac{6}{8}$

For **1–18**, find each sum. Use drawings or fraction strips as needed.

1. $\frac{1}{3} + \frac{1}{3}$

2. $\frac{3}{10} + \frac{6}{10}$

3. $\frac{5}{12} + \frac{2}{12}$

4. $\frac{3}{12} + \frac{7}{12}$

5. $\frac{5}{10} + \frac{3}{10}$

6. $\frac{2}{8} + \frac{4}{8}$

7. $\frac{7}{10} + \frac{3}{10}$

8. $\frac{1}{8} + \frac{6}{8}$

9. $\frac{1}{10} + \frac{5}{10}$

10. $\frac{4}{5} + \frac{1}{5}$

11. $\frac{2}{8} + \frac{6}{8}$

12. $\frac{6}{10} + 0$

13. $\frac{1}{5} + \frac{2}{5} + \frac{4}{5}$

14. $\frac{2}{8} + \frac{1}{8} + \frac{12}{8}$

15. $\frac{2}{6} + \frac{10}{6}$

16. $\frac{20}{100} + \frac{25}{100} + \frac{25}{100}$

17. $\frac{2}{10} + \frac{6}{10} + \frac{1}{10}$

18. $\frac{10}{10} + \frac{10}{10} + \frac{10}{10}$

For **19–21**, use the table at the right.

19. What fraction of the students voted for fruit juice or soda?

20. Which two beverages have a sum of $\frac{5}{8}$ of the student votes?

21. What combination of beverages makes up $\frac{6}{8}$ of the student votes?

Favorite Beverage	Fraction of Student Votes
Iced Tea	$\frac{3}{8}$
Fruit Juice	$\frac{2}{8}$
Water	$\frac{1}{8}$
Soda	$\frac{2}{8}$

22. **Make Sense and Persevere** A bus traveled 336 miles in 7 hours. It traveled the same number of miles each hour. If the bus continues at the same number of miles per hour, how many miles will the bus travel in 15 hours? Explain.

23. **Higher Order Thinking** How can you add $\frac{3}{10}$ and $\frac{2}{5}$? Explain.

Think about how you can rewrite fractions so they have like denominators.

24. In Martha's pet store, $\frac{6}{6}$ of the hamsters are brown, $\frac{3}{6}$ of the mice are white, $\frac{2}{6}$ of the fish are blue, and $\frac{5}{6}$ of the birds are yellow. Draw lines connecting each fraction with the correct expression.

$\frac{6}{6}$		$\frac{2}{6} + \frac{0}{6}$
$\frac{3}{6}$		$\frac{3}{6} + \frac{1}{6} + \frac{1}{6}$
$\frac{2}{6}$		$\frac{2}{6} + \frac{1}{6}$
$\frac{5}{6}$		$\frac{1}{6} + \frac{1}{6} + \frac{1}{6} + \frac{3}{6}$

25. In Fred's catering order, $\frac{5}{12}$ of the lunches are sandwiches, $\frac{2}{12}$ are salads, $\frac{4}{12}$ are pastas, and $\frac{1}{12}$ are soups. Draw lines connecting each fraction with the correct expression.

$\frac{5}{12}$		$\frac{0}{12} + \frac{1}{12}$
$\frac{2}{12}$		$\frac{1}{12} + \frac{2}{12} + \frac{1}{12}$
$\frac{4}{12}$		$\frac{3}{12} + \frac{2}{12}$
$\frac{1}{12}$		$\frac{1}{12} + \frac{1}{12}$

Name _____

☆ ☆
Solve & Share

Mr. Yetkin uses $\frac{4}{6}$ of a sheet of plywood to board up a window. How much of the plywood is left? *Solve this problem any way you choose.*

You can select tools such as fraction strips, drawings, or area models to solve this problem. *Show your work in the space below!*

Lesson 9-4
Model Subtraction of Fractions

I can ...
use tools such as fractions strips or area models to subtract fractions with like denominators.

Content Standards 4.C.5, 4.AT.5
Process Standards PS.1, PS.2, PS.4, PS.5, PS.6

Look Back! **Be Precise** Explain why $\frac{4}{6}$ is subtracted from $\frac{6}{6}$ to find how much of the plywood is left.

How Can You Use Tools to Subtract Fractions?

A

A flower garden is divided into eighths. If $\frac{2}{8}$ of the garden is used to grow yellow roses, what fraction is left to grow other flowers?

> You can use tools such as fraction strips to represent subtraction.

B **One Way**

Find $\frac{8}{8} - \frac{2}{8}$.

$\frac{8}{8} = \frac{1}{8} + \frac{1}{8} + \frac{1}{8} + \frac{1}{8} + \frac{1}{8} + \frac{1}{8} + \frac{1}{8} + \frac{1}{8}$

$\frac{2}{8} = \frac{1}{8} + \frac{1}{8}$

Separating the $\frac{2}{8}$ from $\frac{8}{8}$ leaves $\frac{6}{8}$.

$\frac{8}{8} - \frac{2}{8} = \frac{1}{8} + \frac{1}{8} + \frac{1}{8} + \frac{1}{8} + \frac{1}{8} + \frac{1}{8} + \cancel{\frac{1}{8}} + \cancel{\frac{1}{8}} = \frac{6}{8}$

C **Another Way**

Find $\frac{8}{8} - \frac{2}{8}$.

$\frac{8}{8} = \frac{1}{8} + \frac{1}{8} + \frac{1}{8} + \frac{1}{8} + \frac{1}{8} + \frac{1}{8} + \frac{1}{8} + \frac{1}{8}$

$\overbrace{\hspace{2cm}}$

0 ————————————————— 1

$\frac{2}{8} = \frac{1}{8} + \frac{1}{8}$

Separating the $\frac{2}{8}$ from $\frac{8}{8}$ leaves $\frac{6}{8}$.

$\frac{8}{8} - \frac{2}{8} = \frac{1}{8} + \frac{1}{8} + \frac{1}{8} + \frac{1}{8} + \frac{1}{8}$

$+ \frac{1}{8} + \cancel{\frac{1}{8}} + \cancel{\frac{1}{8}} = \frac{6}{8}$

> Six eighths of the garden is left to grow other flowers.

Convince Me! **Use Appropriate Tools** In the problem above, suppose six sections of the garden are used for yellow roses and two other sections are used for petunias. How much more of the garden is used for yellow roses than is used for petunias? Use fraction strips or another tool to help. Write your answer as a fraction.

Another Example!

Find $\frac{11}{8} - \frac{2}{8}$.

Use eleven $\frac{1}{8}$-fraction strips to show $\frac{11}{8}$. Take 2 strips away.

$\frac{11}{8} - \frac{2}{8} = \frac{9}{8}$

$\frac{9}{8} = \frac{8}{8} + \frac{1}{8} = 1\frac{1}{8}$

You can write the difference as a fraction or a mixed number.

Guided Practice *

Do You Understand?

1. **Reasoning** In the problem at the top of the previous page, suppose one other $\frac{1}{8}$ section was used to grow peonies. What fraction of the garden is now available for flowers?

Do You Know How?

For **2–5**, use fraction strips or other tools to subtract.

2. $\frac{1}{3} - \frac{1}{3}$

3. $\frac{5}{5} - \frac{2}{5}$

4. $\frac{7}{12} - \frac{3}{12}$

5. $\frac{7}{8} - \frac{1}{8}$

Independent Practice

Leveled Practice For **6–14**, find each difference. Use fraction strips or other tools as needed.

6. $\frac{11}{12} - \frac{5}{12}$

7. $\frac{2}{2} - \frac{1}{2}$ $\frac{2}{2} = \frac{1}{2} + \frac{1}{2}$

8. $\frac{2}{3} - \frac{1}{3}$

9. $\frac{4}{5} - \frac{2}{5}$

10. $\frac{17}{10} - \frac{3}{10}$

11. $\frac{8}{6} - \frac{2}{6}$

12. $\frac{9}{6} - \frac{1}{6}$

13. $\frac{21}{10} - \frac{1}{10}$

14. $\frac{1}{5} - \frac{1}{5}$

Problem Solving

15. Model with Math What subtraction problem did Miles show using the fraction strips below?

16. Using only odd numbers for numerators, write two different subtraction problems that have a difference of $\frac{1}{2}$. Remember, you can find equivalent fractions for $\frac{1}{2}$.

17. In Kayla's class, some of the students are wearing blue shirts. $\frac{6}{8}$ of the students are **NOT** wearing blue shirts. What fraction of the students are wearing blue shirts? Show your work.

18. Reasoning In Exercise 17, what number represents the whole class? How do you know what fraction to use to represent this number?

19. Rick shared his bag of grapes with friends. He gave $\frac{2}{10}$ of the bag to Melissa and $\frac{4}{10}$ of the bag to Ryan. What fraction of the bag of grapes does Rick have left? Show your work.

20. Higher Order Thinking Teresa gave away 8 baseball cards and has 4 baseball cards left. Write a subtraction problem to show the fraction of the baseball cards Teresa has left.

 Assessment ISTEP+ Ready

21. Audry wrote a subtraction problem that has a difference of $\frac{1}{3}$. Which problem did Audry write?

 Ⓐ $\frac{2}{2} - \frac{1}{2}$

 Ⓑ $\frac{5}{3} - \frac{3}{3}$

 Ⓒ $\frac{4}{3} - \frac{3}{3}$

 Ⓓ $\frac{5}{3} - \frac{1}{3}$

22. Kinsey wrote a subtraction problem that has a difference of $\frac{10}{8}$. What problem did Kinsey write?

 Ⓐ $\frac{20}{8} - \frac{10}{8}$

 Ⓑ $\frac{8}{10} + \frac{2}{10}$

 Ⓒ $\frac{10}{8} - \frac{4}{8}$

 Ⓓ $\frac{6}{8} - \frac{1}{4}$

Help   Practice   Tools   Games
        Buddy

Another Look!

Kimberly cut a pizza into 10 equal slices. She ate two of the slices. What fraction of the pizza is left? Remember, $\frac{10}{10}$ = 1 whole pizza.

Step 1

Divide a circle into tenths to show the pizza cut into 10 slices.

Step 2

Take away the 2 slices or $\frac{2}{10}$ of the pizza that Kimberly ate.

Step 3

Count the remaining slices and write the subtraction.

$$\frac{10}{10} - \frac{2}{10} = \frac{8}{10}$$

$\frac{8}{10}$ of the pizza is left.

For **1–12**, find each difference. Use fraction strips or other tools as needed.

1. $\frac{3}{5} - \frac{2}{5}$

$\frac{3}{5} = \frac{1}{5} + \frac{1}{5} + \frac{1}{5}$

0   1

$\frac{2}{5} = \frac{1}{5} + \frac{1}{5}$

2. $\frac{7}{10} - \frac{3}{10}$

3. $\frac{4}{4} - \frac{2}{4}$

4. $\frac{8}{10} - \frac{5}{10}$

5. $\frac{6}{6} - \frac{3}{6}$

6. $\frac{11}{12} - \frac{7}{12}$

7. $\frac{5}{6} - \frac{2}{6}$

8. $\frac{4}{8} - \frac{2}{8}$

9. $\frac{11}{12} - \frac{8}{12}$

10. $\frac{9}{8} - \frac{2}{8}$

11. $\frac{24}{4} - \frac{18}{4}$

12. $\frac{30}{10} - \frac{20}{10}$

13. Eddie noticed that out of 10 students, one student was wearing brown shoes, and seven students were wearing black shoes. What fraction of students were **NOT** wearing brown or black shoes?

14. Make Sense and Persevere A marathon is a race that covers about 26 miles. Cindy ran 5 miles before taking her first water break. Then she ran another 7 miles to get to her next water break. After 6 more miles, she took her last water break. About how much farther does Cindy have until she reaches the finish line?

15. Algebra Jeffrey has already run $\frac{3}{8}$ of the race. What fraction of the race does Jeffrey have left? Write and solve an equation.

16. Higher Order Thinking Rob's tablet is fully charged. He uses $\frac{1}{12}$ of the charge playing games, $\frac{5}{12}$ of the charge reading, and $\frac{3}{12}$ completing homework. What fraction of the charge remains on Rob's tablet?

You can use fraction strips to help solve the problem.

17. Roger found he had $\frac{2}{5}$ of his quarters left to use at the arcade. Which of the following subtraction problems could **NOT** be used to find the fraction of quarters Roger had left?

Ⓐ $\frac{4}{5} - \frac{2}{5}$

Ⓑ $\frac{3}{6} - \frac{1}{2}$

Ⓒ $\frac{3}{5} - \frac{1}{5}$

Ⓓ $\frac{5}{5} - \frac{3}{5}$

18. Krys has $\frac{2}{3}$ of her homework finished. Which of the following does **NOT** have a difference of $\frac{2}{3}$?

Ⓐ $\frac{7}{3} - \frac{3}{3}$

Ⓑ $\frac{4}{3} - \frac{2}{3}$

Ⓒ $\frac{3}{3} - \frac{1}{3}$

Ⓓ $\frac{9}{3} - \frac{7}{3}$

Name _____

Solve

☆ ☆
Solve & Share

Leah and Josh live the same direction from school and on the same side of Forest Road. Leah's house is $\frac{8}{10}$ mile from school. Josh's house is $\frac{5}{10}$ mile from school. How much farther does Leah have to walk home when she reaches Josh's house? *Solve this problem any way you choose.*

I can ...
use my understanding of subtraction as separating parts of the same whole to subtract fractions with like denominators.

Content Standards 4.C.5, 4.AT.5
Process Standards PS.2, PS.3, PS.4

You can model with math. What expression can you use to represent this problem?

Look Back! **Critique Reasoning** Sarah wrote the expression $\frac{8}{10} - \frac{5}{10}$ to solve the problem. Jared wrote the expressions $\frac{10}{10} - \frac{8}{10}$, $\frac{10}{10} - \frac{5}{10}$, and $\frac{5}{10} - \frac{2}{10}$ to solve the problem. Who is correct? Explain.

  How Can You Subtract Fractions with Like Denominators?

A

Tania is squeezing lemons to make lemonade. The recipe calls for $\frac{5}{8}$ cup of lemon juice. The amount Tania has squeezed is shown at the right. What fraction of a cup of lemon juice does Tania still need to squeeze?

Subtract the fractions to find the difference.

B **One Way**

Find $\frac{5}{8} - \frac{3}{8}$ using the relationship between addition and subtraction.

$$\frac{2}{8} = \frac{1}{8} + \frac{1}{8}$$

$$\frac{3}{8} = \frac{1}{8} + \frac{1}{8} + \frac{1}{8}$$

Break $\frac{5}{8}$ apart.
Write a related addition equation:
$$\frac{5}{8} = \frac{2}{8} + \frac{3}{8}$$

Write a related subtraction equation:
$$\frac{5}{8} - \frac{3}{8} = \frac{2}{8}$$

C **Another Way**

Find $\frac{5}{8} - \frac{3}{8}$ using a general method.

$$\frac{5}{8} - \frac{3}{8} = n$$

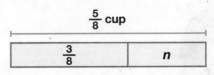

Subtract the numerators. Write the difference over the like denominator.

$$\frac{5}{8} - \frac{3}{8} = \frac{5 - 3}{8} = \frac{2}{8}$$

$\frac{2}{8}$ is equivalent to $\frac{1}{4}$.
Tania needs to squeeze $\frac{1}{4}$ cup more lemon juice.

Convince Me! **Reasoning** In the problem above, suppose Tania decided to double the amount of lemonade she wants to make. Then how much more lemon juice would Tania need to squeeze?

490   **Topic 9** | Lesson 9-5   Copyright © Savvas Learning Company LLC. All Rights Reserved.

Name _____

☆ Guided Practice ☆

Do You Understand?

1. Critique Reasoning Jesse has a bottle that contains $\frac{7}{10}$ liter of water. He drinks $\frac{2}{10}$ liter. Jesse says he has $\frac{1}{2}$ liter left. Is he correct? Explain.

2. Subtract $\frac{4}{10}$ from $\frac{9}{10}$. What addition sentence can you use to check your answer?

Do You Know How?

For **3–10**, subtract the fractions.

3. $\frac{2}{3} - \frac{1}{3}$

4. $\frac{3}{4} - \frac{2}{4}$

5. $\frac{5}{6} - \frac{2}{6}$

6. $\frac{9}{12} - \frac{3}{12}$

7. $\frac{9}{8} - \frac{3}{8}$

8. $\frac{17}{10} - \frac{9}{10}$

9. $\frac{4}{8} - \frac{1}{8}$

10. $\frac{1}{2} - \frac{1}{2}$

☆ Independent Practice ☆

Leveled Practice For **11–18**, subtract the fractions.

11. $\frac{5}{6} - \frac{1}{6}$

12. $\frac{8}{100} - \frac{3}{100}$

13. $\frac{3}{4} - \frac{1}{4}$

14. $\frac{6}{8} - \frac{4}{8}$

15. $\frac{5}{6} - \frac{4}{6}$

16. $\frac{40}{10} - \frac{20}{10}$

17. $\frac{80}{100} - \frac{40}{100}$

18. $\frac{19}{10} - \frac{8}{10}$

Problem Solving

19. Joey ran $\frac{1}{4}$ mile in the morning and $\frac{1}{4}$ mile farther than in the morning in the afternoon. If he wants to run a full mile, how much more does Joey have to run? Write equations to explain.

20. Reasoning Write to explain how subtracting $\frac{4}{5} - \frac{3}{5}$ is similar to subtracting $4 - 3$.

21. Higher Order Thinking The flags of all 5 Nordic countries are displayed. What fraction describes how many more of the flags displayed are 2-color flags than are 3-color flags?

Finland

Denmark

Norway

Iceland

Sweden

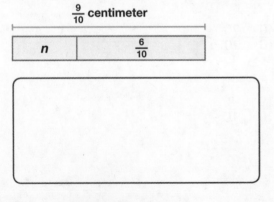

First find how many flags in all, then find how many 2-color and 3-color flags.

22. A piece of chalk is $\frac{9}{10}$ centimeter long. Brian breaks off a piece $\frac{6}{10}$ centimeter long. How long is the piece of chalk that is left? Write and solve an equation.

$\frac{9}{10}$ centimeter

n	$\frac{6}{10}$

23. Marietta baked a chicken pot pie. She serves $\frac{2}{3}$ of the pie at dinner. How much of the pie remains? Write and solve an equation.

$\frac{3}{3}$

$\frac{2}{3}$	n

Name _____

Help Practice Tools Games
         Buddy

**Subtract Fractions
with Like
Denominators**

Another Look!

Flora needs an additional $\frac{2}{8}$ cup flour to make
her dough. The dough recipe calls for $\frac{6}{8}$ cup flour.
How many cups of flour does Flora have?

$\frac{6}{8}$

| $\frac{2}{8}$ | n |

Bar diagrams can
help you represent
the problem.

Subtract the numerators. Write the difference over
the like denominator.

$\frac{6}{8} - \frac{2}{8} = \frac{4}{8}$

Flora has $\frac{4}{8}$ cup flour.

For **1–10**, subtract the fractions.

1. $\frac{6}{8} - \frac{3}{8}$

$\frac{6}{8}$

| $\frac{3}{8}$ | n |

2. $\frac{4}{6} - \frac{1}{6}$

$\frac{4}{6}$

| $\frac{1}{6}$ | n |

3. $\frac{4}{5} - \frac{3}{5}$

$\frac{4}{5}$

| $\frac{3}{5}$ | n |

4. $\frac{3}{6} - \frac{1}{6}$

$\frac{3}{6}$

| $\frac{1}{6}$ | n |

5. $\frac{97}{100} - \frac{40}{100}$

6. $\frac{5}{8} - \frac{1}{8}$

7. $\frac{10}{10} - \frac{9}{10}$

8. $\frac{17}{12} - \frac{5}{12}$

9. $\frac{33}{100} - \frac{4}{100}$

10. $\frac{50}{100} - \frac{10}{100}$

11. **Model with Math** An engineer was supposed to draw a line exactly $\frac{7}{10}$ centimeter long. An error was made, and he drew the line $\frac{9}{10}$ centimeter long. How much longer than needed was the line the engineer drew? Write an equation.

$\frac{9}{10}$ centimeter	
n	$\frac{7}{10}$

12. A mosaic wall is divided into 100 equal sections. If 30 sections are reserved for orange tiles and 40 sections are reserved for blue tiles, what fraction of the mosaic wall is left for other colors?

13. **Number Sense** Jonah is thinking of a 2-digit number. It is a multiple of 6 and 12. It is a factor of 108. The sum of its digits is 9. What number is Jonah thinking of?

14. In a bag of 100 balloons, 12 are red and 13 are green. What fraction of the balloons in the bag are **NOT** red or green?

15. **Math and Science** Morse code is a way to transmit text using a series of dots or dashes. The Morse code for "Add" is shown. What fraction of the shapes are dots in the Morse code for "Add?"

16. **Higher Order Thinking** Diego compared the differences for $\frac{10}{10} - \frac{1}{10}$ and $\frac{100}{100} - \frac{10}{100}$. He said the differences both equal $\frac{9}{10}$. Is Diego correct? Explain.

17. $\frac{5}{8}$ of Marie's marbles are red and $\frac{2}{8}$ are blue. The rest of the marbles are white. Draw a model to represent Marie's marbles. Write and solve equations to find the fraction of the marbles that are white.

Help Practice Tools Games
Buddy

Another Look!

There were 7 slices remaining of an apple pie divided into eighths. Katie and her 3 friends each ate a slice of the remaining pie. Calculate $\frac{7}{8} - \frac{4}{8}$ to find how much of the apple pie is now left.

Subtract to find how much of the pie is left.

What You Show

$$0 \qquad \frac{3}{8} \qquad \frac{7}{8} \quad 1$$

What You Write

$$\frac{7}{8} - \frac{4}{8} = \frac{3}{8}$$

$\frac{3}{8}$ of the pie is left.

For **1–4**, write the equation shown by each number line.

1.

2.

3.

4.

For **5–13**, add or subtract the fractions. Use a number line if needed.

5. $\frac{2}{6} + \frac{1}{6}$

6. $\frac{7}{12} - \frac{2}{12}$

7. $\frac{1}{8} + \frac{5}{8}$

8. $\frac{1}{4} + \frac{3}{4}$

9. $\frac{9}{10} - \frac{3}{10}$

10. $\frac{2}{3} + \frac{3}{3}$

11. $\frac{4}{5} + \frac{3}{5}$

12. $\frac{9}{8} - \frac{6}{8}$

13. $\frac{1}{3} + \frac{5}{3}$

14. Robbie drew the number line below to find $\frac{4}{5} - \frac{1}{5}$. Explain why Robbie is incorrect.

0    $\frac{1}{5}$ $\frac{4}{5}$ 1

15. Reasoning Kayla used $\frac{4}{10}$ of her allowance to buy yogurt and $\frac{5}{10}$ to go skating. What fraction of her allowance does Kayla have left? Explain.

16. Which child drank the most juice? How much juice did that child drink?

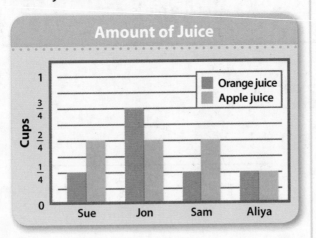

Amount of Juice

Cups

1

$\frac{3}{4}$

$\frac{2}{4}$

$\frac{1}{4}$

0

Sue   Jon   Sam   Aliya

■ Orange juice
■ Apple juice

17. Higher Order Thinking Sofia bought bananas, cereal, and milk at the store. She spent all of her money. She spent $\frac{3}{10}$ of her money on bananas and $\frac{4}{10}$ on cereal. What fraction of her money did Sofia spend on milk? Write and solve equations.

18. Val's construction team was supposed to build a frame $\frac{7}{10}$ meter long. They ended up building the frame $\frac{2}{10}$ meter too long. How long was the frame Val's team built? Use each fraction from the box once to fill in the missing numbers on the number line.

0   $\frac{1}{10}$ $\frac{2}{10}$ $\frac{3}{10}$ $\frac{4}{10}$ $\frac{5}{10}$ $\frac{6}{10}$ $\frac{8}{10}$ 1

Start

| $\frac{2}{10}$ | $\frac{7}{10}$ | $\frac{9}{10}$ |

19. Corinne ran $\frac{5}{6}$ mile from the start of the trail, turned around and ran $\frac{3}{6}$ mile back. How far is Corinne from the start of the trail? Use each fraction from the box once to fill in the missing numbers on the number line.

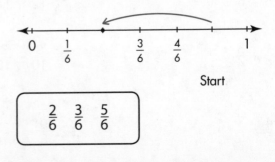

0    $\frac{1}{6}$ $\frac{3}{6}$ $\frac{4}{6}$ 1

Start

| $\frac{2}{6}$ | $\frac{3}{6}$ | $\frac{5}{6}$ |

Name _____

Solve & Share

For **1–2**, use the number lines to decide if each sum is greater than or less than 1. Tell how you decided.

For **3–4**, use the number lines to decide if each difference is less than $\frac{1}{2}$ or greater than $\frac{1}{2}$. Tell how you decided.

I can ...
use number lines and benchmark fractions to estimate fraction sums and differences.

Content Standards 4.C.5, 4.AT.5
Process Standards PS.1, PS.2, PS.3, PS.4, PS.8

1. $\frac{5}{8} + \frac{8}{10}$

2. $\frac{1}{8} + \frac{1}{5} + \frac{1}{10}$

3. $\frac{7}{8} - \frac{1}{10}$

4. $\frac{9}{10} - \frac{5}{8}$

You can use reasoning to think about how fractions relate to 0, $\frac{1}{2}$, and 1.

Look Back! **Generalize** Which fraction in the exercises above is close to $\frac{1}{2}$? How can you use whole numbers and benchmark fractions such as $\frac{1}{2}$ to estimate fraction sums and differences?

Essential Question **How Can You Decide if a Fraction Sum or Difference Is Reasonable?**

A

Are the following statements reasonable?

Together, Randy and Martha bought about 1 pound of nuts. Fana bought about $\frac{1}{4}$ pound less than Chuck.

Randy
$\frac{2}{3}$ lb

Martha
$\frac{1}{5}$ lb

Chuck
$\frac{9}{10}$ lb

Fana
$\frac{1}{4}$ lb

You can use whole numbers and benchmark fractions such as $\frac{1}{4}$ and $\frac{1}{2}$ to decide if a fraction sum or difference is reasonable.

B Is $\frac{2}{3} + \frac{1}{5}$ about 1?

$\frac{2}{3}$ ← Close to $\frac{3}{4}$

0    $\frac{1}{4}$ $\frac{1}{2}$ $\frac{3}{4}$ 1

Think: $\frac{2}{3}$ is close to but less than $\frac{3}{4}$.

Close to $\frac{1}{4}$ → $\frac{1}{5}$

0    $\frac{1}{4}$ $\frac{1}{2}$ $\frac{3}{4}$ 1

Think: $\frac{1}{5}$ is close to but less than $\frac{1}{4}$.

$$\frac{3}{4} + \frac{1}{4} = \frac{4}{4} \text{ or } 1$$

So, $\frac{2}{3} + \frac{1}{5}$ is close to but less than 1. The statement is reasonable.

C Is $\frac{9}{10} - \frac{1}{4}$ about $\frac{1}{4}$?

$\frac{9}{10}$ ← Close to 1

0    $\frac{1}{4}$ $\frac{1}{2}$ $\frac{3}{4}$ 1

Think: $\frac{9}{10}$ is close to but less than 1.

$\frac{1}{4}$

0    $\frac{1}{4}$ $\frac{1}{2}$ $\frac{3}{4}$ 1

Think: $\frac{1}{4}$ is a benchmark fraction.

$$\frac{4}{4} - \frac{1}{4} = \frac{3}{4}$$

So, $\frac{9}{10} - \frac{1}{4}$ is close to but less than $\frac{3}{4}$. The statement is **NOT** reasonable.

Convince Me! **Critique Reasoning** Cammy said, "Each of these pies is about $\frac{1}{2}$. So if I put them together, I have about 1 whole pie." Do you agree with this reasoning? Explain.

Name _____

☆ Guided Practice *

Do You Understand?

1. **Construct Arguments** Use benchmark fractions to estimate $\frac{4}{10} + \frac{3}{8}$. Explain.

2. **Critique Reasoning** Charlie said $\frac{8}{10} - \frac{1}{5}$ is about $\frac{1}{4}$. Do you agree? Explain.

Do You Know How?

For **3–6**, use < or > to complete each equation. Use the number lines as needed.

3. $\frac{1}{3} + \frac{1}{2} \bigcirc 1$ 4. $\frac{5}{4} + \frac{2}{4} \bigcirc 2$

5. $\frac{3}{4} - \frac{1}{8} \bigcirc \frac{1}{2}$ 6. $\frac{3}{2} - \frac{1}{4} \bigcirc \frac{1}{2}$

☆ Independent Practice ☆

For **7–12**, estimate whether each sum or difference is reasonable. If it is **NOT** reasonable, estimate the sum or difference.

7. $\frac{1}{10} + \frac{3}{5}$ is about 1.

8. $\frac{7}{10} - \frac{2}{5}$ is about $\frac{1}{4}$.

9. $\frac{1}{2} + \frac{2}{3} > 1$

10. $\frac{7}{10} + \frac{2}{3} > 1$

11. $\frac{9}{10} - \frac{1}{8} < \frac{1}{2}$

12. $\frac{4}{5} - \frac{2}{3} < \frac{1}{2}$

> Draw number lines to identify benchmark fractions as needed.

*For another example, see Set D on page 534.

Problem Solving

13. Lucy ate $\frac{2}{8}$ of a watermelon, Lily ate $\frac{1}{10}$, and Madelyn ate $\frac{1}{5}$. Estimate how much of the watermelon they ate. Explain.

14. Gavin, Olivia, and Michael are writing a report together. Gavin has written $\frac{2}{5}$ of the report, Olivia has written $\frac{1}{8}$, and Michael has written $\frac{2}{10}$. Use number lines or benchmark fractions to estimate if they have more or less than $\frac{1}{2}$ of their report left to write.

15. Make Sense and Persevere Last year the Levitz family sold 16 boxes of nuts for $6 a box. This year, they only have 8 boxes to sell. How much should they charge per box to have the same income selling nuts as last year? Explain.

16. Higher Order Thinking Choose two fractions from the list that meet each condition.

$$\frac{5}{8} \qquad \frac{1}{10} \qquad \frac{3}{4} \qquad \frac{1}{5}$$

   a. Their sum is greater than 1.
   b. Their difference is close to 0.
   c. Their sum is between $\frac{1}{2}$ and 1.

Use benchmark fractions. You can draw number lines to help.

Assessment 🔵 **ISTEP+ Ready**

17. Harry filled $\frac{1}{5}$ of a pitcher with water. Then he filled another $\frac{6}{10}$ of the pitcher with water. Estimate what fraction of the pitcher is filled with water. Use the number lines to explain.

Help Practice Tools Games
      Buddy

Homework & Practice 9-7

Estimate Fraction Sums and Differences

Another Look!

Jake ran $\frac{1}{10}$ of the distance to the school and walked $\frac{2}{6}$ of the distance. Estimate what fraction of the distance Jake still needs to travel to get to school.

Use the benchmark fractions on the number lines to help you.

Think: $\frac{1}{10}$ is close to but greater than 0.

$\frac{2}{6}$ is close to but greater than $\frac{1}{4}$.

$\frac{1}{10} + \frac{2}{6}$ is close to but greater than $0 + \frac{1}{4} = \frac{1}{4}$.

The whole distance to school is $\frac{4}{4}$ or 1.

$\frac{4}{4} - \frac{1}{4} = \frac{3}{4}$

Jake still needs to travel close to, but less than $\frac{3}{4}$ of the distance to get to school.

For **1–8**, estimate whether each sum or difference is reasonable. If it is **NOT** reasonable, estimate the sum or difference.

1. $\frac{1}{5} + \frac{5}{8}$ is about $\frac{3}{4}$.

2. $\frac{9}{10} - \frac{2}{5}$ is about $\frac{1}{4}$.

3. $\frac{1}{5} + \frac{1}{2} > 1$

4. $\frac{2}{5} + \frac{2}{3} > 1$

5. $\frac{3}{3} + \frac{4}{3} < 2$

6. $\frac{7}{10} - \frac{2}{5} < \frac{1}{2}$

7. $\frac{9}{10} - \frac{1}{3} < \frac{1}{2}$

8. $\frac{7}{6} - \frac{1}{2} > 1$

9. **Model with Math** Elena ate $\frac{2}{8}$ of a pizza and Dylan ate $\frac{1}{5}$. Use the number lines and benchmark fractions to estimate how much of the pizza they ate. Explain.

10. Kara's grandmother is knitting a baby cap. She knitted $\frac{1}{5}$ of the cap yesterday morning. By evening, she had knitted $\frac{7}{10}$ of the cap. Estimate how much of the cap she knitted during the afternoon.

11. **Math and Science** Drums can be used to communicate. If a drummer beats his drum 240 times in a message, how many drum beats will be made if he plays the message twice.

12. In a beaded necklace, $\frac{3}{12}$ of the beads are blue and $\frac{1}{3}$ are green. Use benchmark fractions to estimate about what fraction of the beads are blue or green. Explain.

13. **Higher Order Thinking** Jonathan spends $\frac{2}{8}$ of his money on food, $\frac{1}{5}$ of his money on fuel, and $\frac{2}{10}$ of his money on clothes. Estimate what fraction of his money Jonathan has left. Explain.

14. Margaret's bottle of shampoo is $\frac{7}{8}$ full. She uses $\frac{1}{3}$ of the shampoo in the bottle to wash the dog. Estimate what fraction of the shampoo is left. Use whole numbers and benchmark fractions to explain.

You can draw a number line to find benchmark fractions.

Name _____

Another Look!

You can use fraction strips or number lines to show the addition and subtraction of mixed numbers.

Use a number line to find $1\frac{7}{8} + 2\frac{3}{8}$.

Use a number line for eighths. Start at $1\frac{7}{8}$.

To add, move $2\frac{3}{8}$ to the right.

Write the sum as a fraction or a mixed number.

So, $1\frac{7}{8} + 2\frac{3}{8} = 4\frac{2}{8}$.

Use fraction strips to find $2\frac{1}{5} - 1\frac{2}{5}$.

Model the number you are subtracting from, $2\frac{1}{5}$.

Rename $2\frac{1}{5}$ as $1\frac{6}{5}$. Cross out one whole and $\frac{2}{5}$ to show subtracting $1\frac{2}{5}$.

Write the difference as a fraction.

So, $2\frac{1}{5} - 1\frac{2}{5} = \frac{4}{5}$.

For **1–9**, use fraction strips or number lines to find each sum or difference.

1. $3\frac{1}{2} + 1\frac{1}{2}$

2. $3\frac{3}{4} - 2\frac{1}{4}$

3. $1\frac{3}{4} + 1\frac{3}{4}$

4. $3\frac{4}{5} - 1\frac{2}{5}$

5. $5\frac{2}{6} + 3\frac{5}{6}$

6. $10\frac{2}{8} - 7\frac{5}{8}$

7. $2\frac{5}{12} + 4\frac{3}{12}$

8. $12\frac{1}{3} - 5\frac{2}{3}$

9. $2\frac{2}{4} + 6\frac{3}{4}$

For **10–12**, use the table at the right.

10. How many inches longer is a Hercules beetle than a ladybug?

11. What is the difference between the largest and the smallest stag beetles?

12. How long are a Hercules beetle and a ladybug combined?

DATA

Beetles by Length	
Beetle	**Length in Inches**
Hercules beetle	$6\frac{3}{4}$
Ladybug	$\frac{1}{4}$
Stag beetle	$1\frac{1}{8}$ to $2\frac{4}{8}$

13. Stan needs 90 points to get a passing grade in class. He already has 6 points. If each book report is worth 7 points, what is the fewest number of book reports Stan can do and still pass the class?

Points to pass

7   *b* book reports

Points for each book report

14. **Higher Order Thinking** Nicole, Tasha, Maria, and Joan each walk to school from home. Nicole walks $1\frac{11}{12}$ miles. Tasha walks $2\frac{1}{12}$ miles. Maria walks $1\frac{7}{12}$ miles. Joan walks $2\frac{2}{12}$ miles. How can you find how much farther Joan walks to school than Maria?

Assessment ⊙ (**ISTEP+ Ready**)

15. Alyssa used $1\frac{2}{3}$ gallons of white paint for the ceiling of her kitchen and $1\frac{2}{3}$ gallons of white paint for her bedroom. She used $3\frac{2}{3}$ gallons of green paint for the walls of her kitchen and $1\frac{2}{3}$ gallons of yellow paint for the walls of her bedroom. How much more green paint did Alyssa use than white paint?

Ⓐ $\frac{1}{3}$ gallon

Ⓑ $\frac{2}{3}$ gallon

Ⓒ 1 gallon

Ⓓ 2 gallons

16. Jerome's rain gauge showed $13\frac{9}{10}$ centimeters of rain fell last month. This month, the rain gauge measured $15\frac{3}{10}$ centimeters. How many more centimeters of rain fell this month than last month?

Ⓐ $29\frac{1}{5}$ centimeters

Ⓑ $15\frac{3}{10}$ centimeters

Ⓒ $2\frac{2}{5}$ centimeters

Ⓓ $1\frac{4}{10}$ centimeters

512   **Topic 9** | Lesson 9-8

Name _____

☆ Solve & Share ☆

Joaquin used $1\frac{3}{6}$ cups of apple juice and $1\frac{4}{6}$ cups of orange juice in a recipe for punch. How much juice did Joaquin use? *Solve this problem any way you choose.*

I can ...
use equivalent fractions and properties of operations to add mixed numbers with like denominators.

Content Standards 4.C.6, 4.AT.5
Process Standards PS.1, PS.2, PS.3, PS.8

$1\frac{3}{6}$ cups apple juice

$1\frac{4}{6}$ cups orange juice

Generalize. You can use what you know about adding fractions to solve this problem.

Look Back! **Reasoning** Without solving the problem, use reasoning to estimate the sum. Will the sum be more or less than 3? How much more or less? Explain.

How Can You Add Mixed Numbers?

A

Brenda mixes sand with $2\frac{7}{8}$ cups of potting mixture to prepare soil for her plant. After mixing them together, how many cups of soil does Brenda have?

$1\frac{3}{8}$ cups sand

You can use properties of operations to add mixed numbers. When you break apart a mixed number to add, you are using the Commutative and the Associative Properties.

B Find $2\frac{7}{8} + 1\frac{3}{8}$ by breaking up mixed numbers.

$$2\frac{7}{8} + 1\frac{3}{8} = (2 + 1) + \left(\frac{7}{8} + \frac{3}{8}\right)$$

Add the fractions.	Then add whole numbers.
$2\frac{7}{8}$	$2\frac{7}{8}$
$+ 1\frac{3}{8}$	$+ 1\frac{3}{8}$
$\frac{10}{8}$	$3\frac{10}{8}$

Write the fraction as a mixed number.

$$3\frac{10}{8} = 3 + \frac{8}{8} + \frac{2}{8} = 4\frac{2}{8}$$

C Find $2\frac{7}{8} + 1\frac{3}{8}$ by adding equivalent fractions.

$$2\frac{7}{8} = 2 + \frac{7}{8} = \frac{16}{8} + \frac{7}{8} = \frac{23}{8}$$

$$1\frac{3}{8} = 1 + \frac{3}{8} = \frac{8}{8} + \frac{3}{8} = \frac{11}{8}$$

$$\frac{23}{8} + \frac{11}{8} = \frac{34}{8}$$

Write $\frac{34}{8}$ as a mixed number.

$$\frac{34}{8} = \frac{8}{8} + \frac{8}{8} + \frac{8}{8} + \frac{8}{8} + \frac{2}{8} = 4\frac{2}{8}$$

Brenda has $4\frac{2}{8}$ cups of soil.

Convince Me! **Reasoning** How is adding mixed numbers like adding fractions and whole numbers?

Name _____

☆ Guided Practice *

Do You Understand?

1. Brenda adds $1\frac{1}{8}$ cups of peat moss to her soil in the problem on the previous page. How much soil does Brenda now have? Explain.

2. **Make Sense and Persevere** Use another strategy to find the sum of $4\frac{2}{8} + 1\frac{1}{8}$.

Do You Know How?

For **3–8**, find each sum.

3. $1\frac{7}{8}$
   $+ 1\frac{2}{8}$
   $\overline{}$

4. $2\frac{4}{10}$
   $+ 5\frac{5}{10}$
   $\overline{}$

5. $4\frac{2}{3} + 1\frac{2}{3}$

6. $6\frac{5}{12} + 4\frac{11}{12}$

7. $2\frac{1}{3} + 2\frac{1}{3}$

8. $8\frac{9}{12} + 5\frac{5}{12}$

☆ Independent Practice ☆

Leveled Practice For **9–22**, find each sum by adding mixed numbers or by adding equivalent fractions.

9. **a.** Add the fractions.
   b. Add the whole numbers.
   c. Write the fraction as a mixed number.

   $1\frac{3}{6}$
   $+ 2\frac{4}{6}$
   $\overline{}$
   $\boxed{} = \boxed{}$

10. **a.** Write the mixed numbers as fractions.
    b. Add the fractions.
    c. Write the fraction as a mixed number.

    $2\frac{1}{4} = \boxed{}$
    $+ 3\frac{2}{4} = + \boxed{}$
    $\overline{}$
    $\boxed{} = \boxed{}$

11. $2\frac{5}{6}$
    $+ 5\frac{4}{6}$
    $\overline{}$

12. $11\frac{7}{10}$
    $+ 10\frac{9}{10}$
    $\overline{}$

13. $9\frac{7}{8}$
    $+ 7\frac{5}{8}$
    $\overline{}$

14. $5\frac{7}{8}$
    $+ 8\frac{1}{8}$
    $\overline{}$

15. $4\frac{1}{10} + 6\frac{5}{10}$

16. $9\frac{7}{12} + 4\frac{9}{12}$

17. $5 + 3\frac{1}{8}$

18. $8\frac{3}{4} + 7\frac{3}{4}$

19. $2\frac{4}{5} + 7\frac{3}{5}$

20. $3\frac{2}{6} + 8\frac{5}{6}$

21. $1\frac{7}{12} + 2\frac{10}{12}$

22. $3\frac{6}{8} + 9\frac{3}{8}$

Problem Solving

For **23**, use the map at the right.

23. a. Find the distance from the start of the trail to the end of the trail.

START   BIRD LOOKOUT   END

$3\frac{7}{8}$ miles $2\frac{7}{8}$ miles

b. Linda walked from the start of the trail to the bird lookout and back. Did Linda walk more or less than if she had walked from the start of the trail to the end?

24. Joe biked $1\frac{9}{12}$ miles from home to the lake, then went some miles around the lake, and then back home. Joe biked a total of $4\frac{9}{12}$ miles. How many miles did Joe bike around the lake?

25. Reasoning The bus took $4\frac{3}{5}$ hours to get from the station to Portland and $3\frac{4}{5}$ hours to get from Portland to Seattle. How long did the bus take to get from the station to Seattle?

26. Higher Order Thinking A male Parson's chameleon can be up to $23\frac{3}{4}$ inches long. It can extend its tongue up to $35\frac{1}{4}$ inches. What are 3 possible lengths for the chameleon when its tongue is extended?

Tongue can extend up to $35\frac{1}{4}$ inches.

Assessment ⊙ ISTEP+ Ready

27. How long an extension cord can Julie make by attaching a $22\frac{3}{8}$ foot and a $26\frac{6}{8}$ foot cord together? Select all the possible sums.

☐ $22\frac{3}{8} + 26\frac{6}{8} = \frac{393}{8}$

☐ $22\frac{3}{8} + 26\frac{6}{8} = 49\frac{9}{12}$

☐ $22\frac{3}{8} + 26\frac{6}{8} = 49\frac{1}{8}$

☐ $22\frac{3}{8} + 26\frac{6}{8} = 48\frac{9}{8}$

☐ $22\frac{3}{8} + 26\frac{6}{8} = 48$

28. Mary skips $22\frac{1}{3}$ yards down a trail, then hops another $15\frac{2}{3}$ yards. How far is Mary down the trail? Select all the possible sums.

☐ $22\frac{1}{3} + 15\frac{2}{3} = 37$

☐ $22\frac{1}{3} + 15\frac{2}{3} = 37\frac{3}{3}$

☐ $22\frac{1}{3} + 15\frac{2}{3} = 38$

☐ $22\frac{1}{3} - 15\frac{2}{3} = 6\frac{2}{3}$

☐ $22\frac{1}{3} + 15\frac{2}{3} = \frac{114}{3}$

Name _____

Another Look!

Randy played basketball for $2\frac{5}{6}$ hours on Saturday. He played for $1\frac{3}{6}$ hours on Sunday. How many hours did Randy play basketball on the weekend?

Add Mixed Numbers

a. Add the fractions.

b. Add the whole numbers.

c. Write the fraction as a mixed number.

$$\begin{array}{r} 2\frac{5}{6} \\ +\ 1\frac{3}{6} \\ \hline 3\frac{8}{6} = 4\frac{2}{6} \end{array}$$

Randy played basketball for $4\frac{2}{6}$ hours on the weekend.

Add Fractions

a. Write the mixed numbers as fractions.

b. Add the fractions.

c. Write the fraction as a mixed number.

$$\begin{array}{r} 2\frac{5}{6} = \frac{17}{6} \\ +\ 1\frac{3}{6} = +\frac{9}{6} \\ \hline \frac{26}{6} = 4\frac{2}{6} \end{array}$$

> You can add mixed numbers with like denominators using properties of operations.

For **1–12**, find each sum by adding mixed numbers or adding equivalent fractions.

1. $\begin{array}{r} 2\frac{10}{12} \\ +\ 3\frac{3}{12} \\ \hline \end{array}$

2. $\begin{array}{r} 1\frac{3}{8} \\ +\ 6\frac{6}{8} \\ \hline \end{array}$

3. $\begin{array}{r} 5\frac{4}{10} \\ +\ 4\frac{2}{10} \\ \hline \end{array}$

4. $\begin{array}{r} 10\frac{2}{6} \\ +\ \frac{3}{6} \\ \hline \end{array}$

5. $3\frac{3}{12} + 6\frac{8}{12}$

6. $1\frac{2}{5} + 3\frac{1}{5}$

7. $2\frac{10}{12} + 3\frac{9}{12}$

8. $7\frac{2}{6} + 8\frac{5}{6}$

9. $4\frac{3}{4} + 2\frac{2}{4}$

10. $11\frac{9}{10} + 3\frac{2}{10}$

11. $5\frac{8}{12} + 3\frac{5}{12}$

12. $21\frac{11}{12} + 17\frac{5}{12}$

13. 🅐🅩 **Vocabulary** Use the vocabulary words *mixed number* and *fractions* to complete the sentence.

When adding mixed numbers, you first add the _____, then add the whole numbers. Finally, you write the _____.

14. Critique Reasoning Alan used 9 as an estimate for $3\frac{7}{10} + 5\frac{4}{10}$. He added and got $9\frac{1}{10}$ for the actual sum. Is Alan's answer reasonable?

15. Ruth needs $2\frac{1}{4}$ cups of flour for one cake recipe and $2\frac{3}{4}$ cups of flour for another cake recipe. If she makes both cakes, how much flour will Ruth need altogether?

16. A "stone" is an old unit of weight used in Ireland and England to measure potatoes. A stone is 14 pounds and 80 stones make up half of a "long ton." How many pounds is half of a long ton?

17. Higher Order Thinking Tirzah wants to put a fence around her garden. She has 22 yards of fence material. Does Tirzah have enough to go all the way around the garden?

$6\frac{9}{12}$ yards

$4\frac{8}{12}$ yards

18. Pookie weighs $12\frac{7}{8}$ pounds. Rascal weighs $13\frac{3}{8}$ pounds. What is the total weight of both cats? Select all the possible sums.

☐ $26\frac{2}{8}$ pounds

☐ $26\frac{1}{4}$ pounds

☐ $\frac{210}{8}$ pounds

☐ $13\frac{3}{8}$ pounds

☐ $12\frac{7}{8}$ pounds

19. Rex weighs $30\frac{1}{4}$ pounds. Buckey weighs $50\frac{2}{4}$ pounds. What is the total weight of both dogs? Select all possible sums.

☐ $20\frac{1}{4}$ pounds

☐ 80 pounds

☐ $80\frac{3}{4}$ pounds

☐ $\frac{323}{4}$ pounds

☐ 81 pounds

Name _____

☆ Solve & Share ☆

Evan is walking $2\frac{1}{8}$ miles to his aunt's house. He has already walked $\frac{6}{8}$ mile. How much farther does Evan have to go? *Solve this problem any way you choose.*

Generalize. You can use what you know about subtracting fractions to solve this problem.

Lesson 9-10
Subtract Mixed Numbers

I can ...
use equivalent fractions, properties of operations, and the relationship between addition and subtraction to subtract mixed numbers with like denominators.

Content Standards 4.C.6, 4.AT.5
Process Standards PS.1, PS.2, PS.3, PS.8

$2\frac{1}{8}$ miles

$\frac{6}{8}$ mile m

Home   Aunt's House

Look Back! **Critique Reasoning** Sarah found Evan has $2\frac{7}{8}$ miles left to walk. Is Sarah's answer reasonable? Use estimation to explain.

How Can You Subtract Mixed Numbers?

A

A golf ball measures about $1\frac{4}{6}$ inches across the center. What is the difference between the distances across the centers of a tennis ball and a golf ball?

$2\frac{3}{6}$ inches

You can use properties of operations and the relationship between addition and subtraction to help subtract mixed numbers.

B Find $2\frac{3}{6} - 1\frac{4}{6}$ by subtracting mixed numbers.

To subtract $\frac{4}{6}$ from $\frac{3}{6}$, rename $2\frac{3}{6}$.
Remember, $1 = \frac{6}{6}$.

$2\frac{3}{6} = 1\frac{9}{6}$

$$\begin{array}{r} 2\frac{3}{6} = 1\frac{9}{6} \\ -\ 1\frac{4}{6} = 1\frac{4}{6} \\ \hline \frac{5}{6} \end{array}$$

$2\frac{3}{6} = 2 + \frac{3}{6} = 1 + \frac{6}{6} + \frac{3}{6} = 1\frac{9}{6}$

The tennis ball is $\frac{5}{6}$ inch wider than the golf ball.

C Find $2\frac{3}{6} - 1\frac{4}{6}$ by subtracting equivalent fractions.

$2\frac{3}{6} = 2 + \frac{3}{6} = \frac{12}{6} + \frac{3}{6} = \frac{15}{6}$

$1\frac{4}{6} = 1 + \frac{4}{6} = \frac{6}{6} + \frac{4}{6} = \frac{10}{6}$

$\frac{15}{6} - \frac{10}{6} = \frac{5}{6}$

You can count up to check your work!
$1\frac{4}{6} + \frac{2}{6} = 2$ and $2 + \frac{3}{6} = 2\frac{3}{6}$
$\frac{2}{6} + \frac{3}{6} = \frac{5}{6}$

Convince Me! **Reasoning** Explain why you rename $4\frac{1}{4}$ to find $4\frac{1}{4} - \frac{3}{4}$.

Name _____

Another Look!

Janet grew a pumpkin that weighs $13\frac{3}{4}$ pounds and a melon that weighs $8\frac{2}{4}$ pounds. How much heavier is the pumpkin than the melon?

Subtract Mixed Numbers

$$\begin{array}{r} 13\frac{3}{4} \\ -\ 8\frac{2}{4} \\ \hline 5\frac{1}{4} \end{array}$$

a. Subtract the fractions. Rename whole numbers as fractions as needed.

b. Subtract the whole numbers.

Subtract Fractions

a. Write the mixed numbers as fractions.

b. Subtract the fractions.

c. Write the fraction as a mixed number.

$$\begin{array}{r} 13\frac{3}{4} = \frac{55}{4} \\ -\ 8\frac{2}{4} = -\frac{34}{4} \\ \hline \frac{21}{4} = 5\frac{1}{4} \end{array}$$

The pumpkin is $5\frac{1}{4}$ pounds heavier than the melon.

You can subtract mixed numbers with like denominators using properties of operations.

For **1–16**, find each difference by subtracting mixed numbers or subtracting equivalent fractions.

1. $\begin{array}{r} 10\frac{3}{4} \\ -\ 7\frac{1}{4} \\ \hline \end{array}$

2. $\begin{array}{r} 7\frac{4}{6} \\ -\ 2\frac{3}{6} \\ \hline \end{array}$

3. $\begin{array}{r} 3 \\ -\ 2\frac{2}{3} \\ \hline \end{array}$

4. $\begin{array}{r} 17\frac{8}{12} \\ -\ 12\frac{3}{12} \\ \hline \end{array}$

5. $9\frac{2}{6} - 6\frac{5}{6}$

6. $4\frac{1}{5} - 2\frac{3}{5}$

7. $6\frac{3}{12} - 3\frac{4}{12}$

8. $5\frac{2}{8} - 3\frac{7}{8}$

9. $8\frac{1}{4} - 7\frac{3}{4}$

10. $2\frac{9}{10} - 2\frac{5}{10}$

11. $6\frac{5}{6} - 5\frac{4}{6}$

12. $3 - 1\frac{3}{4}$

13. $11 - 2\frac{1}{2}$

14. $42\frac{6}{10} - 10$

15. $18\frac{1}{5} - 2\frac{2}{5}$

16. $27\frac{2}{6} - 12\frac{1}{6}$

17. A-Z Vocabulary Use a vocabulary word to complete the sentence.

A number that has a whole number part and a fraction part is a called a(n) _____.

18. Some of the world's smallest horses include Thumbelina who stands $17\frac{1}{4}$ inches tall, Black Beauty who stands $18\frac{2}{4}$ inches tall, and Einstein who stands 14 inches tall.

a. How much taller is Black Beauty than Thumbelina?

b. How much taller is Thumbelina than Einstein?

19. Reasoning If Carol hangs a picture using $\frac{3}{8}$ yard of a wire that is $1\frac{1}{8}$ yards long, how much wire will Carol have left?

20. Write 6,219 in expanded form.

21. Higher Order Thinking Some of the largest insects in the world include the Rhinoceros Beetle, the Giant Walking Stick, and the Giant Weta Beetle. How much longer is the Giant Walking Stick than the Rhinoceros Beetle and the Giant Weta Beetle combined?

Rhinoceros Beetle
$16\frac{7}{10}$ cm

Giant Walking Stick
Length $53\frac{3}{10}$ cm

Giant Weta Beetle
$8\frac{5}{10}$ cm

Assessment 🔲◎ ISTEP+ Ready

22. Jessie needs a board $7\frac{9}{12}$ feet long. She has a board $9\frac{1}{12}$ feet long. How much of the length does Jessie need to cut from the board? Use equivalent fractions to solve.

Ⓐ $1\frac{1}{3}$ feet

Ⓑ $2\frac{8}{12}$ feet

Ⓒ $2\frac{2}{3}$ feet

Ⓓ $16\frac{10}{12}$ feet

23. Robyn ran $5\frac{3}{4}$ miles last week. She ran $4\frac{1}{4}$ miles this week. How many more miles did Robyn run last week? Use equivalent fractions to solve.

Ⓐ $1\frac{1}{4}$ miles

Ⓑ $1\frac{1}{2}$ miles

Ⓒ $1\frac{3}{4}$ miles

Ⓓ 10 miles

Name _____

Solve & Share

The table shows how long Jamie studied for a math test over 3 days. How much more time did Jamie spend studying on Tuesday and Wednesday than on Thursday?

I can ...
use math I know to represent and solve problems.

 Process Standards PS.4 Also PS.1, PS.2, PS.5
Content Standard 4.AT.5

Day of the Week	Time Jamie Studied
Tuesday	$1\frac{3}{4}$ hours
Wednesday	$\frac{3}{4}$ hour
Thursday	$\frac{2}{4}$ hour

DATA

Thinking Habits

Be a good thinker!
These questions can help you.

- How can I use math I know to help solve this problem?

- How can I use pictures, objects, or an equation to represent the problem?

- How can I use numbers, words, and symbols to solve the problem?

Look Back! **Model with Math** What representations can you use to help solve this problem?

Essential Question **How Can You Use Math to Model Problems?**

A

Brad and his father hiked the Gadsen Trail and the Rosebriar Trail on Saturday. They hiked the Eureka Trail on Sunday. How much farther did they hike on Saturday than on Sunday?

Gadsen Trail
$1\frac{9}{10}$ mile

Rosebriar Trail
$\frac{5}{10}$ mile

Eureka Trail
$\frac{6}{10}$ mile

What do you need to find?

I need to find how far Brad and his father hiked on Saturday and much farther they hiked on Saturday than on Sunday.

$2\frac{4}{10}$ miles on Saturday

$1\frac{9}{10}$	$\frac{5}{10}$

B

How can I model with math?

I can

- use previously learned concepts and skills.

- use bar diagrams and equations to represent and solve this problem.

- decide if my results make sense.

C Here's my thinking.

Find $2\frac{4}{10} - \frac{6}{10}$.

Use a bar diagram and write an equation to solve.

$2\frac{4}{10}$ miles	
$\frac{6}{10}$	d

$2\frac{4}{10} - \frac{6}{10} = d$ $d = 1\frac{8}{10}$

Brad and his father hiked $1\frac{8}{10}$ miles farther on Saturday than on Sunday.

Convince Me! **Model with Math** How do the bar diagrams help you decide if your answer makes sense?

Name _____

☆ Guided Practice *

Model with Math

Alisa hiked a trail that was $\frac{9}{10}$ mile and Joseph hiked a trail that was $\frac{5}{10}$ mile. How much farther did Alisa hike than Joseph?

When you model with math, you use math to represent and solve a problem.

1. Draw a bar diagram to represent the problem and show the relationships among the quantities.

2. What equation can you write to represent the problem?

3. How much farther did Alisa hike than Joseph?

Independent Practice ☆

Model with Math

The smallest female spider measures about $\frac{3}{5}$ millimeter in length. The smallest male spider measures about $\frac{1}{5}$ millimeter in length. How much longer is the smallest female spider than the smallest male spider? Use Exercises 4–6 to answer the question.

4. Draw a picture and write an equation to represent the problem.

5. What previously learned math can you use to solve the problem?

6. How much longer is the smallest female spider than the smallest male spider?

*For another example, see Set F on page 534.

Problem Solving

On Safari

Sandra and Ron traveled in a safari car while they were in Tanzania. The diagram shows the distances in miles they traveled from start to finish. How far did Sandra and Ron travel from the leopards to the elephants?

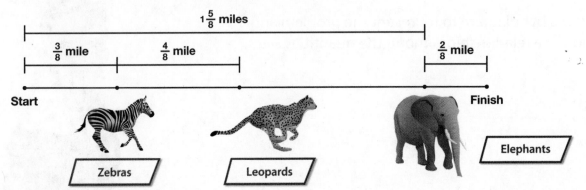

$1\frac{5}{8}$ miles

$\frac{3}{8}$ mile $\frac{4}{8}$ mile $\frac{2}{8}$ mile

Start   Finish

Zebras   Leopards   Elephants

7. **Reasoning** What quantities are given in the problem and what do they mean?

8. **Make Sense and Persevere** What is a good plan for solving the problem?

When you model with math, you use a picture, which shows how the quantities in the problem are related.

9. **Model with Math** Draw pictures and write and solve equations to find how far Sandra and Ron travel from the leopards to the elephants.

Help Practice Tools Games
       Buddy

**Homework
& Practice** 9-11
Model with
Math

Another Look!

Tina built $\frac{1}{8}$ of a model airplane on Saturday and $\frac{4}{8}$ on Sunday. She built $\frac{3}{8}$ more on Monday. How much more of the model airplane did she build on the weekend than on the weekday?

Tell how you can use math to model the problem.

- I can use previously learned concepts and skills.

- I can use bar diagrams and equations to represent and solve this problem.

- I can decide if my results make sense.

Draw a bar diagram and write and solve equations.

$\frac{1}{8} + \frac{4}{8} = \frac{5}{8}$ on the weekend

$\frac{5}{8} - \frac{3}{8} = n$

$n = \frac{2}{8}$

When you model with math, you use previously learned math to solve a problem.

$\frac{5}{8}$	
$\frac{3}{8}$	n

Tina built $\frac{2}{8}$ more of the model airplane on the weekend than on the weekday.

Model with Math

On Nick's playlist, $\frac{5}{12}$ of the songs are pop. What fraction of the songs are **NOT** pop? Use Exercises 1–3 to answer the question.

1. How can you draw a picture and write an equation to represent the problem?

2. What previously learned math can you use to solve the problem?

3. What fraction of the songs on Nick's playlist are **NOT** pop?

Ian and Rachel each made a trail mix. The amounts of ingredients they have are shown. Ian used all of the coconut, dried cranberries, and dried bananas to make his trail mix. Rachel made 2 cups of trail mix containing all of the almonds, pumpkin seeds, and granola. How much trail mix did Ian make? How much more trail mix did Rachel make than Ian?

Trail Mix Ingredients
$\frac{3}{4}$ cup almonds
$\frac{1}{4}$ cup pumpkin seeds
$\frac{2}{4}$ cup coconut
$\frac{3}{4}$ cup dried cranberries
$1\frac{2}{4}$ cup walnuts
1 cup granola
$\frac{2}{4}$ cup dried bananas

4. **Make Sense and Persevere** What do you know, and what do you need to find?

5. **Use Appropriate Tools** What tools could you use to help solve this problem?

6. **Reasoning** How can you use a bar diagram to show how the quantities are related?

When you model with math, you represent the relationships in the problem.

7. **Make Sense and Persevere** Write and solve an equation to find how much trail mix Ian made.

8. **Reasoning** Explain how you were able to calculate how much more trail mix Rachel made than Ian.

Name _____

Find a Match

Work with a partner. Point to a clue. Read the clue.

Look below the clues to find a match. Write the clue letter in the box next to the match.

Find a match for every clue.

I can ...
add and subtract multi-digit whole numbers.

Clues

A The sum is exactly 1,000.

B The sum is exactly 1,001.

C The difference is exactly 371.

D The difference is between 40 and 45.

E The difference is exactly 437.

F The difference is between 150 and 160.

G The sum is between 995 and 1,000.

H The sum is exactly 1,899.

409 − 252	900 − 529	909 + 990	506 + 494
580 + 417	560 − 123	601 − 560	309 + 692

Word List

- decompose
- denominator
- equivalent fractions
- fraction
- like denominators
- mixed number
- numerator
- whole number

Understand Vocabulary

1. Circle the label that best describes $\frac{1}{2}$.

   fraction   mixed number   whole number

2. Circle the label that best describes $1\frac{1}{3}$.

   fraction   mixed number   whole number

3. Circle the label that best describes 4.

   fraction   mixed number   whole number

4. Draw a line from each term to its example.

decompose	$\frac{1}{2} = \frac{5}{10}$
denominator	$\frac{2}{3} = \frac{1}{3} + \frac{1}{3}$
equivalent fractions	$\frac{5}{6}$
like denominators	$\frac{1}{3} + \frac{2}{3} = \frac{3}{3}$
numerator	$\frac{7}{8}$

Use Vocabulary in Writing

5. Find $1\frac{1}{3} + 2\frac{2}{3}$. Use at least 3 terms from the Word List to describe how to find the sum.

Name _____

Set A | pages 465–482

Find $\frac{5}{8} + \frac{2}{8}$.

$\frac{5}{8} = \frac{1}{8} + \frac{1}{8} + \frac{1}{8} + \frac{1}{8} + \frac{1}{8}$ $\frac{2}{8} = \frac{1}{8} + \frac{1}{8}$

Add the numerators.
Keep the like denominator.

$\frac{5}{8} + \frac{2}{8} = \frac{7}{8}$

Remember you can decompose fractions and use properties of operations to help add.

1. $\frac{2}{5} + \frac{2}{5}$
2. $\frac{2}{4} + \frac{1}{4} + \frac{1}{4}$
3. $\frac{3}{8} + \frac{4}{8}$
4. $\frac{4}{10} + \frac{2}{10} + \frac{3}{10}$
5. $\frac{4}{10} + \frac{3}{10}$
6. $\frac{7}{12} + \frac{2}{12}$

Set B | pages 483–494

Find $\frac{5}{8} - \frac{2}{8}$.

Subtract the numerators.
Keep the like denominator.

$\frac{5}{8} - \frac{2}{8} = \frac{3}{8}$

Remember you can use fraction strips and number lines to show how to subtract fractions.

1. $\frac{3}{3} - \frac{1}{3}$
2. $\frac{5}{6} - \frac{2}{6}$
3. $\frac{6}{8} - \frac{3}{8}$
4. $\frac{4}{10} - \frac{3}{10}$
5. $\frac{5}{5} - \frac{3}{5}$
6. $\frac{4}{6} - \frac{2}{6}$

Set C | pages 495–500

Find the sum or difference shown on each number line.

$\frac{2}{10} + \frac{4}{10} = \frac{6}{10}$

$\frac{7}{8} - \frac{3}{8} = \frac{4}{8}$

Remember that when adding or subtracting fractions with like denominators on a number line, the denominator does not change.

Write and solve the equation shown by each number line.

1.

2.

Estimate $\frac{1}{5} + \frac{7}{10}$.

$\frac{1}{5}$ is close to but less than $\frac{1}{4}$.　　$\frac{7}{10}$ is close to but less than $\frac{3}{4}$.

Since $\frac{1}{4} + \frac{3}{4} = 1$, $\frac{1}{5} + \frac{7}{10}$ is close to but less than 1.

Remember to use benchmark fractions to estimate.

1. Is $\frac{2}{5} + \frac{1}{2}$ about 1? Explain.

2. Is $\frac{7}{8} - \frac{2}{5}$ about 1? Explain.

3. Is $\frac{3}{4} + \frac{1}{3}$ about 1? Explain.

Find $5\frac{1}{5} - 3\frac{3}{5}$.　　　Find $1\frac{7}{8} + 2\frac{3}{8}$.

$$5\frac{1}{5} = 4\frac{6}{5}$$
$$-3\frac{3}{5} = 3\frac{3}{5}$$
$$\overline{\qquad 1\frac{3}{5}}$$

$$1\frac{7}{8}$$
$$+2\frac{3}{8}$$
$$\overline{3\frac{10}{8} = 4\frac{2}{8}}$$

Remember you can use fraction strips and number lines to help add and subtract mixed numbers.

1. $5\frac{4}{8} + 2\frac{1}{8}$　　　2. $3\frac{3}{6} + 1\frac{5}{6}$

3. $5\frac{7}{10} + 4\frac{4}{10}$　　　4. $9 - 3\frac{3}{8}$

Think about these questions to help you **model with math.**

Thinking Habits

- How can I use math I know to help solve this problem?

- How can I use pictures, objects, or an equation to represent the problem?

- How can I use numbers, words, and symbols to solve the problem?

Remember to draw a bar diagram to help write an equation.

Bonnie ran $\frac{1}{4}$ mile, Olga ran $\frac{3}{4}$ mile, Gracie ran $\frac{5}{4}$ miles, and Maria ran $\frac{2}{4}$ mile.

1. How much farther did Olga run than Bonnie?

2. How far did Bonnie, Olga, and Maria run altogether?

TOPIC 10

Extend Multiplication Concepts to Fractions

Essential Questions: How can you describe a fraction using a unit fraction? How can you multiply a whole number by a mixed number?

Digital Resources

Solve Learn Glossary Practice Buddy

Tools Assessment Help Games

Light reflecting off of objects enters the eye and makes them visible.

Different kinds of flowers reflect different kinds of light, allowing them to be seen in color.

I could look at flowers all day! Here is a project about light and multiplication.

Math and Science Project: Light and Multiplication

Do Research Use the Internet or other sources to research the words *transparent, translucent,* and *opaque.* Write a definition for each word.

Journal: Write a Report Include what you found. Also in your report:

- List 3 examples of items that are transparent, translucent, or opaque.

- Suppose one third of each of 5 same-sized posters is covered with opaque paper. What fraction of the posters are **NOT** covered by opaque paper? Explain how to use multiplication to find what part of the posters are **NOT** covered by opaque paper.

Name _____

Review What You Know

A-Z Vocabulary

Choose the best term from the box.
Write it on the blank.

• equivalent fractions   • mixed number
• fraction   • whole number

1. A _____ has a whole number and a fraction.

2. Fractions that name the same region, part of a set, or part of a segment are called _____ .

3. A _____ has a numerator and a denominator.

Identifying Fractions

Write the fraction shown by each model.

4.   **5.**   **6.**

7.   **8.**   **9.**

Unit Fractions

Write a fraction for each statement.

10. 3 copies of $\frac{1}{6}$ is ____.   **11.** 9 copies of $\frac{1}{12}$ is ____.   **12.** 5 copies of $\frac{1}{5}$ is ____.

13. 3 copies of $\frac{1}{10}$ is ____.   **14.** 6 copies of $\frac{1}{8}$ is ____.   **15.** 7 copies of $\frac{1}{10}$ is ____.

Equivalent Fractions

16. Draw a rectangle that shows 8 equal parts. Shade more than $\frac{3}{8}$ of the rectangle but less than $\frac{5}{8}$. What fraction did you model? Use multiplication and division to write two equivalent fractions for your model.

Use the examples for each word on the front of the card to help complete the definitions on the back.

unit fraction

$$\frac{1}{2}, \ \frac{1}{3}, \ \frac{1}{5}, \ \frac{1}{10}, \ \frac{1}{12}, \cdots$$

My Word Cards

Complete each definition. Extend learning by writing your own definitions.

A fraction with a numerator of 1 is a

_____

Name _____

Solve & Share

Kalil and Mara were working on their math homework. Mara wrote $\frac{4}{5}$ as $\frac{1}{5} + \frac{1}{5} + \frac{1}{5} + \frac{1}{5}$. Kalil looked at Mara's work and said, "I think you could use multiplication to rewrite your equation." Is Kalil's observation correct? Explain.

Lesson 10-1
Fractions as Multiples of Unit Fractions: Use Models

I can ...
use fraction strips or number lines to understand a fraction as a multiple of a unit fraction.

Content Standard Extends 4.C.5
Process Standards PS.2, PS.4, PS.7

You can use reasoning to compare Mara's work and Kalil's observation.

$\frac{1}{5}$	$\frac{1}{5}$	$\frac{1}{5}$	$\frac{1}{5}$

$$\frac{1}{5} + \frac{1}{5} + \frac{1}{5} + \frac{1}{5} = \frac{4}{5}$$

Look Back! **Model with Math** Write an equation to show the relationship between Mara's work and Kalil's observation.

How Can You Describe a Fraction Using a Unit Fraction?

A

Courtney ran $\frac{3}{4}$ of the way to school. Describe $\frac{3}{4}$ using unit fractions.

A unit fraction is a fraction that describes one part of the whole. Unit fractions always contain the numerator 1.

B

When a whole is divided into four equal parts, each part is described as $\frac{1}{4}$.

Three of those parts are described as $\frac{3}{4}$.

$\frac{3}{4} = 3 \times \frac{1}{4}$, or three $\frac{1}{4}$ parts.

C

Three $\frac{1}{4}$ parts make $\frac{3}{4}$.

$$3 \times \frac{1}{4} = \frac{1}{4} + \frac{1}{4} + \frac{1}{4}$$
$$= \frac{3 \times 1}{4}$$
$$= \frac{3}{4}$$

So, $\frac{3}{4}$ is a multiple of $\frac{1}{4}$.

Remember, a multiple is the result of multiplying a number by a whole number.

Convince Me! **Reasoning** What number in $\frac{5}{8}$ tells you how many equal parts are in one whole? What number tells you how many equal parts are described? How many $\frac{1}{8}$ parts are there in $\frac{5}{8}$?

Another Example!

Describe $\frac{5}{4}$ as a multiple of a unit fraction.

$\frac{5}{4}$ is five $\frac{1}{4}$ parts.

Some fractions are greater than 1.

$$5 \times \frac{1}{4} = \frac{1}{4} + \frac{1}{4} + \frac{1}{4} + \frac{1}{4} + \frac{1}{4}$$
$$= \frac{5 \times 1}{4}$$
$$= \frac{5}{4}$$

☆ Guided Practice*

Do You Understand?

1. **Model with Math** Draw a picture to explain why $\frac{3}{5} = 3 \times \frac{1}{5}$.

2. Write a multiplication equation to show each part of the following story. Mark's family ate $\frac{7}{4}$ chicken pot pies for dinner. There are 7 people in Mark's family. Each family member ate $\frac{1}{4}$ of a pie.

Do You Know How?

For **3–6**, write each fraction as a multiple of a unit fraction. Use fraction strips or number lines to help.

3. $\frac{2}{3} = \square \times \frac{1}{3}$

4. $\frac{5}{6} = 5 \times \frac{1}{\square}$

5. $\frac{4}{2}$

6. $\frac{6}{5}$

☆ Independent Practice ☆

Leveled Practice For **7–18**, write each fraction as a multiple of a unit fraction. Use fraction strips or number lines to help.

7. $\frac{3}{4} = \square \times \frac{1}{4}$

8. $\frac{3}{6} = 3 \times \frac{1}{\square}$

9. $\frac{2}{5} = \square \times \frac{1}{5}$

10. $\frac{7}{10} = 7 \times \frac{\square}{10}$

11. $\frac{8}{8} = \square \times \frac{1}{8}$

12. $\frac{5}{12} = 5 \times \frac{1}{\square}$

13. $\frac{6}{4}$

14. $\frac{9}{6}$

15. $\frac{8}{5}$

16. $\frac{7}{8}$

17. $\frac{9}{4}$

18. $\frac{8}{6}$

Problem Solving

19. Mark is slicing a tomato for 4 members of his family. Each person will get $\frac{1}{6}$ of the tomato. What fraction of the tomato will Mark slice? Use fraction strips as needed.

20. Delia flew 2,416 miles the first year on the job. She flew 3,719 miles the second year. Delia flew 2,076 more miles the third year than the first and second years combined. How many miles did Delia fly the third year?

21. **Model with Math** Write a multiplication equation that describes the picture of the half pears below. Use a unit fraction as a factor in your equation.

22. Look at the picture below. Write and solve a problem for the picture. Show your answer as a multiplication equation with $\frac{1}{2}$ as a factor.

23. **Math and Science** Light travels at a speed of about 186,000 miles per second. How far does light travel in 5 seconds? Use repeated addition to solve.

24. **Higher Order Thinking** Kobe drinks $\frac{1}{3}$ cup of juice each day. He has $2\frac{1}{3}$ cups of juice left. For how many days will it last? Show your answer as a multiplication equation with $\frac{1}{3}$ as a factor. Remember, you can write $2\frac{1}{3}$ as a fraction.

25. Which multiplication equation describes the fraction plotted on the number line?

Ⓐ $6 = \frac{6}{3} \times \frac{1}{8}$ Ⓒ $\frac{1}{8} = \frac{1}{8} \times 6$

Ⓑ $\frac{6}{8} = 6 \times \frac{1}{8}$ Ⓓ $\frac{1}{8} + 6 = \frac{6}{8}$

26. Which multiplication equation describes the picture below?

Ⓐ $\frac{3}{3} = 3 \times 1$ Ⓒ $\frac{3}{1} = 3 \times 1\frac{1}{2}$

Ⓑ $\frac{9}{2} = 3 \times 1\frac{1}{2}$ Ⓓ $\frac{3}{2} = 3 \times \frac{1}{2}$

Name _____

Another Look!

Use fraction strips to show $\frac{5}{8}$ as a multiple of a unit fraction.

Write an equation.

$\frac{5}{8} = \frac{1}{8} + \frac{1}{8} + \frac{1}{8} + \frac{1}{8} + \frac{1}{8}$

$\frac{5}{8} = 5 \times \frac{1}{8}$

You can write any fraction as a multiple of a unit fraction.

For **1–21**, write each fraction as a multiple of a unit fraction. Use fraction strips or number lines to help.

1. $\frac{2}{4} = 2 \times \frac{\square}{4}$

2. $\frac{2}{6} = \square \times \frac{1}{6}$

3. $\frac{2}{5} = 2 \times \frac{1}{\square}$

4. $\frac{3}{3} = 3 \times \frac{1}{\square}$

5. $\frac{10}{8} = 10 \times \frac{\square}{8}$

6. $\frac{5}{2} = \square \times \frac{1}{2}$

7. $\frac{1}{6}$

8. $\frac{9}{5}$

9. $\frac{8}{3}$

10. $\frac{9}{10}$

11. $\frac{9}{12}$

12. $\frac{8}{10}$

13. $\frac{6}{3}$

14. $\frac{6}{8}$

15. $\frac{4}{12}$

16. $\frac{99}{100}$

17. $\frac{8}{12}$

18. $\frac{6}{6}$

19. $\frac{9}{8}$

20. $\frac{35}{100}$

21. $\frac{101}{100}$

22. Kevin is baking cookies. Each batch of cookies uses $\frac{1}{8}$ pound of butter. Kevin has $\frac{11}{8}$ pounds of butter. How many batches of cookies can Kevin make? Show your answer as a multiplication equation with $\frac{1}{8}$ as a factor.

23. Students are painting a mural. So far, the mural is painted $\frac{1}{4}$ blue, $\frac{2}{8}$ red, and $\frac{3}{12}$ green. Use fraction strips to determine how much of the mural has been painted. Tell the fractions you use to solve.

24. 🔤 **Vocabulary** How can you tell if a fraction is a *unit fraction*?

25. **Algebra** How many $\frac{1}{6}$ parts are in $\frac{10}{6}$? Write and solve a multiplication equation with $\frac{1}{6}$ as a factor. Use p for parts.

26. **Look for Relationships** Mari packs the same number of oranges in each bag. How many oranges does Mari need to pack 9 bags? How can you determine the number of oranges Mari needs for 13 bags?

Number of Bags	3	5	7	9	11
Number of Oranges	9	15	21		33

27. **Higher Order Thinking** Katarina uses fraction strips to show how many thirds are in $\frac{4}{6}$. Is Katarina's model correct? Explain.

28. Which multiplication expression describes the fraction plotted on the number line?

Ⓐ $\frac{5}{8} + \frac{6}{8}$

Ⓑ $4 \times \frac{1}{8}$

Ⓒ $\frac{1}{8} + \frac{2}{8} + \frac{3}{8} + \frac{4}{8}$

Ⓓ $4 \times \frac{4}{8}$

29. Which multiplication expression describes the fraction strips below?

Ⓐ $\frac{1}{10} + \frac{1}{10} + \frac{1}{10} + \frac{1}{10} + \frac{1}{10} + \frac{1}{10}$

Ⓑ $6 \times \frac{6}{10}$

Ⓒ $\frac{1}{10} \times \frac{1}{10} \times \frac{1}{10} \times \frac{1}{10} \times \frac{1}{10} \times \frac{1}{10}$

Ⓓ $6 \times \frac{1}{10}$

Name _____

Solve & Share

How much tomato juice is needed for a group of 4 people if each person gets $\frac{1}{3}$ cup of juice? How much tomato juice is needed if they each get $\frac{2}{3}$ cup of juice? *Solve these problems any way you choose.*

You can use drawings or write equations to model with math. *Show your work in the space below!*

Lesson 10-2
Multiply a Fraction by a Whole Number: Use Models

I can ...
use drawings, area models, or number lines to multiply fractions by whole numbers.

Content Standard Extends 4.C.5
Process Standards PS.2, PS.4, PS.7, PS.8

Look Back! **Reasoning** How is multiplying $4 \times \frac{2}{3}$ cup of juice related to multiplying $8 \times \frac{1}{3}$ cup of juice?

Essential Question **How Can You Find the Product of a Fraction Multiplied by a Whole Number?**

A

Dori lives $\frac{1}{4}$ mile from school. If she walks to and from school each day, how far does Dori walk during a school week?

DATA

	Distance Walked (in miles)				
	Mon	**Tues**	**Wed**	**Thurs**	**Fri**
To School	$\frac{1}{4}$	$\frac{1}{4}$	$\frac{1}{4}$	$\frac{1}{4}$	$\frac{1}{4}$
From School	$\frac{1}{4}$	$\frac{1}{4}$	$\frac{1}{4}$	$\frac{1}{4}$	$\frac{1}{4}$

You can use addition or multiplication to solve this problem.

B **One Way**

Draw a picture to show the distance Dori walks.

$\frac{1}{4} + \frac{1}{4} + \frac{1}{4} + \frac{1}{4} + \frac{1}{4} + \frac{1}{4} + \frac{1}{4} + \frac{1}{4} + \frac{1}{4} + \frac{1}{4} = \frac{10}{4}$

Write $\frac{10}{4}$ as a mixed number.

$\frac{10}{4} = 2\frac{2}{4}$

C **Another Way**

Draw a number line to show the distance Dori walks.

$10 \times \frac{1}{4} = \frac{10 \times 1}{4} = \frac{10}{4}$

Write $\frac{10}{4}$ as a mixed number.

$\frac{10}{4} = 2\frac{2}{4}$

$2\frac{2}{4}$ is equivalent to $2\frac{1}{2}$. Dori walks $2\frac{1}{2}$ miles to and from school each week.

Convince Me! **Generalize** Why can both addition and multiplication be used represent the problem above? Write an equation to explain.

Another Example!

Calculate $4 \times \frac{3}{5}$ to determine how far Jess bikes to and from work in 4 days.

$12 \times \frac{1}{5} = 4 \times \frac{3}{5}$

| $\frac{1}{5}$ | $\frac{1}{5}$ | $\frac{1}{5}$ | $\frac{1}{5}$ | $\frac{1}{5}$ | $\frac{1}{5}$ | $\frac{1}{5}$ | $\frac{1}{5}$ | $\frac{1}{5}$ | $\frac{1}{5}$ | $\frac{1}{5}$ | $\frac{1}{5}$ |

$\frac{3}{5}$ $\frac{3}{5}$ $\frac{3}{5}$ $\frac{3}{5}$

Use addition.

$\frac{3}{5} + \frac{3}{5} + \frac{3}{5} + \frac{3}{5} = \frac{12}{5}$ or $2\frac{2}{5}$

Jess bikes $2\frac{2}{5}$ miles.

Use multiplication.

$4 \times \frac{3}{5} = \frac{4 \times 3}{5} = \frac{12}{5}$ or $2\frac{2}{5}$

Jess bikes $2\frac{2}{5}$ miles.

☆ Guided Practice*

Do You Understand?

1. **Use Structure** Draw a picture to explain why $3 \times \frac{2}{5} = 6 \times \frac{1}{5}$.

Do You Know How?

For **2–3**, write and solve a multiplication equation.

2.

3.

Number line from 0 to 3, marked $0, \frac{1}{3}, \frac{2}{3}, 1, 1\frac{1}{3}, 1\frac{2}{3}, 2, 2\frac{1}{3}, 2\frac{2}{3}, 3$

☆ Independent Practice ☆

For **4–7**, write and solve a multiplication equation. Use drawings or number lines as needed.

4.
| $\frac{1}{8}$ mi | $\frac{1}{8}$ mi | $\frac{1}{8}$ mi | $\frac{1}{8}$ mi | $\frac{1}{8}$ mi |

5.

$\frac{2}{10}$ $\frac{2}{10}$ $\frac{2}{10}$

6. Calculate the distance Margo rides her bike if she rides $\frac{7}{8}$ mile each day for 8 days.

7. Calculate the distance Tom rides his bike if he rides $\frac{5}{6}$ mile each day for 5 days.

Problem Solving

8. Kiona fills a measuring cup with $\frac{3}{4}$ cup of juice 3 times to make punch. Write and solve a multiplication equation with a whole number and a fraction to show the total amount of juice Kiona uses.

9. **Reasoning** Each lap around a track is $\frac{3}{10}$ kilometer. Eliot walked around the track 4 times. How far did Eliot walk?

10. Margo bought 4 concert tickets for $38 each, 1 concert T-shirt for $56, and 2 buckets of popcorn for $6 each. How much did Margo spend?

11. A pan of lasagna is cut into 6 equal pieces. The chef serves 5 pieces of the lasagna. Write and solve a multiplication equation to show how much of the lasagna is served.

12. Wendy sliced a loaf of bread into 12 equal slices. She used 4 of the slices to make sandwiches. What fraction of the loaf of bread was left?

13. **Higher Order Thinking** A baker uses $\frac{2}{3}$ cup of rye flour in each loaf of bread. How many cups of rye flour will the baker use in 3 loaves? in 7 loaves? in 10 loaves?

Assessment ⓘ◎ (ISTEP+ Ready)

14. Select all the expressions that represent the following story. Elaine jogged $\frac{4}{5}$ mile each day for 7 days. Use drawings or number lines as needed.

- ☐ $7 \times \frac{4}{5}$
- ☐ $\frac{4}{5} + \frac{4}{5} + \frac{4}{5} + \frac{4}{5} + \frac{4}{5} + \frac{4}{5} + \frac{4}{5}$
- ☐ $14 \times \frac{2}{5}$
- ☐ $7 \times \frac{1}{5}$
- ☐ $7 \times \frac{2}{5}$

15. Select all the expressions that represent the following story. Freddie skated $\frac{1}{2}$ mile each day for 6 days. Use drawings or number lines as needed.

- ☐ $\frac{1}{2} + \frac{1}{2} + \frac{1}{2} + \frac{1}{2} + \frac{1}{2} + \frac{1}{2}$
- ☐ $6 \times \frac{1}{2}$
- ☐ 3×2
- ☐ $6 + 2 \times \frac{1}{2}$
- ☐ 6×3

Name _____

Help Practice Tools Games
      Buddy

Homework
& Practice 10-2
Multiply a Fraction
by a Whole Number:
Use Models

Another Look!

Georgie walked $\frac{2}{3}$ mile to and from the gym. How many miles did Georgie walk?

Find $2 \times \frac{2}{3}$.

You can use a number line to help multiply fractions and whole numbers.

$$\frac{0}{3} \quad \frac{1}{3} \quad \frac{2}{3} \quad \frac{3}{3} \quad \frac{4}{3} \quad \frac{5}{3} \quad \frac{6}{3}$$
$$0 \qquad\qquad\qquad 1 \qquad\qquad\qquad 2$$

$$2 \times \frac{2}{3} = \frac{2 \times 2}{3}$$
$$= \frac{4}{3}$$

Georgie walked $\frac{4}{3}$ or $1\frac{1}{3}$ miles.

For **1–8**, write and solve a multiplication equation. Use drawings or number lines as needed.

1.

| $\frac{1}{6}$ | $\frac{1}{6}$ | $\frac{1}{6}$ | $\frac{1}{6}$ | $\frac{1}{6}$ | $\frac{1}{6}$ | $\frac{1}{6}$ | $\frac{1}{6}$ | $\frac{1}{6}$ | $\frac{1}{6}$ |

$\underbrace{\qquad}_{\frac{5}{6}} \underbrace{\qquad}_{\frac{5}{6}}$

2.
$$0 \qquad 1 \qquad 2 \qquad 3 \qquad 4$$
$$\frac{3}{4} \quad \frac{3}{4} \quad \frac{3}{4} \quad \frac{3}{4} \quad \frac{3}{4}$$

3.

$\frac{3}{10} \qquad \frac{3}{10} \qquad \frac{3}{10}$

4.

| $\frac{4}{12}$ | $\frac{4}{12}$ | $\frac{4}{12}$ | $\frac{4}{12}$ | $\frac{4}{12}$ |

5. Calculate the distance Penny rides her bicycle if she rides $\frac{1}{4}$ mile each day for 5 days.

6. Calculate the distance Benjamin rides his scooter if he rides $\frac{3}{5}$ mile each day for 10 days.

7. Calculate the distance Derek rows his boat if he rows $\frac{5}{6}$ mile each day for 11 days.

8. Calculate the distance Kinsey jogs if she jogs $\frac{7}{8}$ mile each day for 9 days.

9. At a play, 211 guests are seated on the main floor and 142 guests are seated in the balcony. If tickets for the main floor cost $7 and tickets for the balcony cost $5, how much was earned in ticket sales?

10. Audrey uses $\frac{5}{8}$ cup of fruit in each smoothie she makes. She makes 6 smoothies to share with her friends. How many cups of fruit does Audrey use?

$\frac{5}{8}$	$\frac{5}{8}$	$\frac{5}{8}$	$\frac{5}{8}$	$\frac{5}{8}$	$\frac{5}{8}$

11. Gabe is making 5 capes. He uses $\frac{2}{3}$ yard of fabric for each cape he makes. What is the total amount of fabric Gabe needs?

$\frac{2}{3}$	$\frac{2}{3}$	$\frac{2}{3}$	$\frac{2}{3}$	$\frac{2}{3}$

12. Use Structure Explain why $4 \times \frac{3}{5} = 12 \times \frac{1}{5}$. Draw a picture.

13. Higher Order Thinking Mark is training for a mini triathlon. He rode his bike $\frac{3}{4}$ mile, ran $\frac{5}{6}$ mile, and swam $\frac{10}{12}$ mile each day for 7 days. What combined distance did Mark exercise during the week?

Find equivalent fractions and add the fractions first.

14. Select all the expressions that represent the following story. Ronald rode the rollercoaster 3 times. The rollercoaster track is $\frac{1}{4}$ mile in length. Use drawings or number lines as needed.

☐ $\frac{1}{4} + \frac{1}{4} + \frac{1}{4}$

☐ $3 \times \frac{1}{4}$

☐ 3×4

☐ $4 + 3 \times \frac{1}{4}$

☐ $\frac{3}{4}$

15. Select all the expressions that represent the following story. Kurt swam across the lake and back. The lake is $\frac{4}{8}$ mile across. Use drawings or number lines as needed.

☐ $2 \times \frac{4}{8}$

☐ $\frac{4}{8} + \frac{4}{8}$

☐ $4 \times \frac{2}{8}$

☐ $8 \times \frac{4}{8}$

☐ $2 + \frac{4}{8}$

Name _____

Lesson 10-3
Multiply a Fraction by a Whole Number: Use Symbols

⭐ **Solve & Share**

A recipe for 1 gallon of fruit punch calls for $\frac{3}{4}$ cup of orange juice. How many cups of orange juice are needed to make 8 gallons of fruit punch? **Solve this problem any way you choose.**

I can ...
use patterns and equations to multiply a fraction by a whole number.

You can use a drawing, bar diagram, area model, or equation to model with math. *Show your work in the space below!*

Content Standard Extends 4.C.5
Process Standards PS.2, PS.4, PS.6, PS.7

Look Back! **Be Precise** Look back at your solution. What units should you use to label your answer?

Essential Question: When Can You Use the Product of a Fraction and a Whole Number to Solve a Problem?

A

Stanley makes ice cream sundaes. Today Stanley made 2 ice cream sundaes. How much ice cream did Stanley use? Find $2 \times \frac{3}{4}$.

$\frac{3}{4}$ pint of ice cream in each sundae

You can use structure when multiplying a fraction and a whole number.

B One Way

$2 \times \frac{3}{4} = 2 \times \left(3 \times \frac{1}{4}\right)$ $\frac{3}{4}$ is 3 copies of $\frac{1}{4}$ or $3 \times \frac{1}{4}$.

$= (2 \times 3) \times \frac{1}{4}$ Associative Property of Multiplication

$= 6 \times \frac{1}{4}$

$= \frac{6 \times 1}{4}$ Multiply the whole number and the numerator.

$= \frac{6}{4}$

$2 \times \frac{3}{4} = \frac{6}{4}$ or $1\frac{2}{4}$

C Another Way

$2 \times \frac{3}{4} = \frac{2 \times 3}{4}$ Multiply the whole number and the numerator.

$= \frac{6}{4}$

$2 \times \frac{3}{4} = \frac{6}{4}$ or $1\frac{2}{4}$

Stanley used $1\frac{2}{4}$ pints of ice cream to make 2 sundaes.

Convince Me! **Use Structure** Use properties of operations to calculate $3 \times \frac{3}{6}$. Show your work.

Practice Buddy   Tools   Assessment

☆ Guided Practice *

Do You Understand?

1. Sarah has $\frac{1}{2}$ of a granola bar. Her friend has 5 times as many granola bars. How many granola bars does Sarah's friend have?

2. **Model with Math** Sue needs $\frac{5}{6}$ cup of cocoa to make one batch of chocolate pudding. She wants to make 4 batches of pudding to take to a party. Use properties of operations to help write and solve an equation to show how many cups of cocoa Sue will need for all 4 batches of pudding.

Do You Know How?

For **3–4**, multiply.

3. $8 \times \frac{1}{2}$ 4. $13 \times \frac{3}{4}$

For **5–6**, write and solve a multiplication equation.

5. Calculate the amount of medicine taken in 10 days if the dose is $\frac{3}{4}$ fluid ounce per day.

6. Calculate the total length needed to decorate 9 boxes if each box uses $\frac{2}{3}$ yard of ribbon.

☆ Independent Practice ☆

For **7–15**, multiply.

7. $4 \times \frac{1}{3}$

8. $6 \times \frac{3}{8}$

9. $8 \times \frac{2}{5}$

10. $12 \times \frac{5}{6}$

11. $11 \times \frac{2}{3}$

12. $5 \times \frac{7}{8}$

13. $7 \times \frac{3}{4}$

14. $9 \times \frac{3}{5}$

15. $4 \times \frac{5}{8}$

For **16–17**, write and solve a multiplication equation.

16. Calculate the total distance Mary runs in one week if she runs $\frac{7}{8}$ mile each day.

17. Calculate the length of 5 pieces of ribbon laid end to end if each piece is $\frac{2}{3}$ yard long.

Problem Solving

18. A baseball team bought 8 boxes of baseballs. If the team spent a total of $1,696, what was the cost of 1 box of baseballs?

19. Oscar wants to make 4 chicken pot pies. The recipe requires $\frac{2}{3}$ pound of potatoes for each pot pie. How many pounds of potatoes will Oscar need?

20. It takes Mario $\frac{1}{4}$ hour to mow Mr. Harris's lawn. It takes him 3 times as long to mow Mrs. Carter's lawn. How long does it take Mario to mow Mrs. Carter's lawn? Write your answer as a fraction of an hour, then as minutes.

$\frac{1}{4}$ hour is 15 minutes.

21. **A-Z Vocabulary** Use *numerator, denominator,* and *whole number.*

When you multiply a fraction by a whole number, the _____ in the product is the same as the denominator of the fraction. The _____ in the product is the product of the _____ and the numerator of the fraction.

22. **Model with Math** Malik swims $\frac{9}{10}$ mile each day. How many miles will Malik swim in 8 days? Write and solve an equation.

23. **Higher Order Thinking** Sam is making 7 fruit tarts. Each tart needs $\frac{3}{4}$ cup of strawberries and $\frac{1}{4}$ cup of blueberries. What is the total amount of fruit that Sam needs for his tarts? Use properties of operations to solve.

Assessment ⑤○─(ISTEP+ Ready)

24. Sean is making picture frames. Each frame uses $\frac{4}{5}$ yard of wood. What is the total length of wood Sean will need to make 12 frames? Use each of the numbers from the box once to complete and solve the equation.

$12 \times \frac{4}{5} = \dfrac{\boxed{}\boxed{} \times 4}{5} = \dfrac{\boxed{}\boxed{}}{5}$ or $9\frac{\boxed{}}{5}$ yards

| 1 | 2 | 3 | 4 | 8 |

25. Ellen is making plant boxes. Each box uses $\frac{3}{6}$ yard of wood. What is the total length of wood Ellen will need to make 7 plant boxes? Use each of the numbers from the box once to complete and solve the equation.

$7 \times \frac{3}{6} = \dfrac{\boxed{} \times 3}{6} = \dfrac{\boxed{}\boxed{}}{\boxed{}}$ or $\boxed{}\frac{3}{6}$ yards

| 1 | 2 | 3 | 6 | 7 |

Name _____

Help Practice Tools Games
      Buddy

Homework & Practice 10-3

Multiply a Fraction
by a Whole Number:
Use Symbols

Another Look!

Maria swims $\frac{3}{5}$ mile across the lake and another $\frac{3}{5}$ mile back.
How far did Maria swim?

1						1	

$\frac{1}{5}$	$\frac{1}{5}$	$\frac{1}{5}$	$\frac{1}{5}$	$\frac{1}{5}$	$\frac{1}{5}$

Find $2 \times \frac{3}{5}$.

$2 \times \frac{3}{5} = \frac{2 \times 3}{5} = \frac{6}{5}$ or $1\frac{1}{5}$

Maria swims $1\frac{1}{5}$ miles.

When all the groups are
the same size, you can multiply
to find the total.

For **1–12**, multiply.

1. $8 \times \frac{5}{12}$

2. $9 \times \frac{1}{4}$

3. $5 \times \frac{3}{5}$

4. $10 \times \frac{5}{6}$

5. $9 \times \frac{3}{10}$

6. $7 \times \frac{1}{3}$

7. $12 \times \frac{1}{5}$

8. $11 \times \frac{7}{8}$

9. $4 \times \frac{2}{3}$

10. $5 \times \frac{7}{8}$

11. $8 \times \frac{5}{6}$

12. $2 \times \frac{2}{8}$

For **13–16**, write and solve a multiplication equation.

13. Calculate the length of a scarf with 5 sections if each section is $\frac{1}{2}$ foot long.

14. Calculate the distance Kris walks in 8 days if she walks $\frac{7}{8}$ mile each day.

15. Calculate the distance Nathan rides his bike if he rides $\frac{9}{12}$ mile each day for 3 days.

16. Calculate the distance Tarryn drives if she drives $\frac{7}{8}$ mile each way to and from work, 5 days a week.

17. **Reasoning** Xander has 10 pieces of twine that he is using for a project. If each piece of twine is $\frac{1}{3}$ yard long, how many yards of twine does Xander have? Use properties of operations to solve.

18. The Portman's kitchen table is rectangular. The table is 4 feet wide and 8 feet long. Mrs. Portman bought a tablecloth that will cover 56 square feet. Is the tablecloth large enough to cover the table? Explain.

19. **Number Sense** Olivia is doing her math homework. For each problem, she uses $\frac{3}{4}$ sheet of paper. How many sheets of paper will Olivia need to complete 20 math problems? Use estimation to check if your answer is reasonable.

20. **Math and Science** There are 6 pure spectral colors: red, orange, yellow, green, blue, and violet. Some animals cannot see all of these colors. Bees cannot see orange or red. What fraction of the pure spectral colors can bees see?

21. Write a problem to go along with the multiplication sentence $3 \times \frac{3}{10}$. Then solve your problem.

22. **Higher Order Thinking** Lydia is making 4 loaves of rye bread and 3 loaves of wheat bread. Each loaf takes $\frac{3}{4}$ cup of sugar. How many cups of sugar will Lydia need? Explain.

Assessment ISTEP+ Ready

23. Camille walks $\frac{3}{4}$ mile each day for 8 days. How far does Camille walk? Use each of the numbers from the box once to complete and solve the equation.

$$8 \times \frac{3}{4} = \frac{\square \times \square}{4} = \frac{\square\square}{4} = \square \text{ miles}$$

| 2 | 3 | 4 | 6 | 8 |

24. Corinne has cheer practice $\frac{5}{6}$ hour each day, Monday through Friday. How long does Corinne practice each week? Use each of the numbers from the box to complete and solve the equation.

$$5 \times \frac{5}{6} = \frac{5 \times 5}{6} = \frac{\square\square}{\square} = \square\frac{\square}{6}$$

| 1 | 2 | 4 | 5 | 6 |

Name _____

Lesson 10-4
Multiply a Whole Number and a Mixed Number

Jerry is filling his sand pail and pouring the sand into a large bucket. Can the bucket hold 8 of Jerry's pails full of sand? **Solve this problem any way you choose.**

I can ...

use area models, drawings, and equations to represent and solve problems involving multiplying a whole number and a mixed number.

Content Standard Extends 4.C.5
Process Standards PS.1, PS.2, PS.3, PS.7

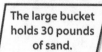

Jerry's pail holds $2\frac{3}{4}$ pounds of sand.

The large bucket holds 30 pounds of sand.

You can use structure. Use what you know about multiplying whole numbers to solve this problem.

Look Back! **Make Sense and Persevere** How do you know you need to multiply to solve this problem?

Essential Question: How Can You Multiply a Whole Number and a Mixed Number?

A

Ellie wants to make 5 blankets as gifts for her friends. It takes $2\frac{2}{3}$ yards of fabric to make each blanket. How many yards of fabric does Ellie need?

You can use appropriate tools such as bar diagrams or fraction strips to help solve the problem.

y				
$2\frac{2}{3}$	$2\frac{2}{3}$	$2\frac{2}{3}$	$2\frac{2}{3}$	$2\frac{2}{3}$

Find $5 \times 2\frac{2}{3}$.

B ## One Way

1	1	$\frac{1}{3}$	$\frac{1}{3}$	
1	1	$\frac{1}{3}$	$\frac{1}{3}$	
1	1	$\frac{1}{3}$	$\frac{1}{3}$	
1	1	$\frac{1}{3}$	$\frac{1}{3}$	
1	1	$\frac{1}{3}$	$\frac{1}{3}$	

5×2 $5 \times \frac{2}{3}$ $5 \times 2\frac{2}{3}$

$5 \times 2\frac{2}{3} = (5 \times 2) + \left(5 \times \frac{2}{3}\right)$

$= 10 + \frac{10}{3}$

$= 10 + 3\frac{1}{3}$

$= 13\frac{1}{3}$

C ## Another Way

$5 \times 2\frac{2}{3} = 5 \times \frac{8}{3}$ Change the mixed number to a fraction.

$= \frac{5 \times 8}{3}$

$= \frac{40}{3}$

$= 13\frac{1}{3}$

Ellie needs $13\frac{1}{3}$ yards of fabric.

Convince Me! **Use Structure** In the example above, what property of operations is shown by the fraction strips? Explain how the model shows the property.

☆ Guided Practice*

Do You Understand?

1. **Use Structure** In the problem on the previous page, how much fabric would Ellie need if she wanted to make 6 blankets? Explain.

2. Find $3 \times 1\frac{1}{3}$ using the two methods shown on the previous page.

Do You Know How?

For **3–4**, find each product.

3. $2 \times 2\frac{1}{4}$

n	
$2\frac{1}{4}$	$2\frac{1}{4}$

4. $2 \times 1\frac{1}{2}$

| 1 | $\frac{1}{2}$ | |
| 1 | $\frac{1}{2}$ | |

☆ Independent Practice ☆

Leveled Practice For **5–18**, find each product.

You can use fraction strips or bar diagrams to show multiplication.

5. $2 \times 3\frac{1}{2}$

6. $2 \times 1\frac{2}{5}$

| 1 | $\frac{1}{5}$ | $\frac{1}{5}$ | | | |
| 1 | $\frac{1}{5}$ | $\frac{1}{5}$ | | | |

7. $3 \times 1\frac{5}{6}$

8. $4 \times 2\frac{3}{8}$

9. $8 \times 2\frac{3}{4}$

10. $10 \times 3\frac{3}{5}$

11. $3 \times 2\frac{4}{5}$

12. $3 \times 4\frac{7}{10}$

13. $7 \times 4\frac{1}{2}$

14. $9 \times 5\frac{3}{4}$

15. $11 \times 1\frac{2}{3}$

16. $4 \times 1\frac{7}{12}$

17. $3 \times 2\frac{1}{5}$

18. $8 \times 9\frac{1}{2}$

Problem Solving

19. Make Sense and Persevere Joel needs 24 apples for bobbing at his party. How many pounds of apples does Joel need? Explain.

8 apples weigh $3\frac{3}{4}$ pounds

20. Critique Reasoning Which student, Lisa or Anthony, correctly found $3 \times 2\frac{1}{4}$? Explain.

Lisa
$$3 \times 2\frac{1}{4} = 3 \times \frac{9}{4}$$
$$= \frac{27}{4}$$
$$= \frac{24}{4} + \frac{3}{4}$$
$$= 6 + \frac{3}{4}$$
$$= 6\frac{3}{4}$$

Anthony
$$3 \times 2\frac{1}{4} = 3 \times (2 + \frac{1}{4})$$
$$= (3 \times 2) + (3 \times \frac{1}{4})$$
$$= 6 + \frac{3}{4}$$
$$= 6\frac{3}{4}$$

21. The stadium contains 8,217 blue seats and 7,236 red seats. There are 1,211 more green seats than red seats. How many seats are in the stadium?

You can estimate to check if your solution is reasonable.

22. Higher Order Thinking Calculate $8 \times 7\frac{3}{4}$ with Lisa's method and then with Anthony's method above. Which method do you find easier? Explain.

Assessment · **ISTEP+ Ready**

23. Which expression can be used to solve the following problem? Seth has 7 cans of tuna. Each can holds $5\frac{9}{10}$ ounces of tuna. How many ounces of tuna does Seth have?

Ⓐ $(7 \times 9) + \left(7 \times \frac{5}{10}\right)$

Ⓑ $(7 \times 59) + \left(7 \times \frac{1}{10}\right)$

Ⓒ $(7 \times 5) + \left(7 \times \frac{9}{10}\right)$

Ⓓ $(7 \times 5) + \frac{9}{10}$

24. Which expression can be used to solve the following problem? Sarah has 6 copies of the same book. If each book weighs $3\frac{5}{8}$ pounds, how many pounds do all 6 books weigh?

Ⓐ $18 + 3\frac{5}{8}$

Ⓑ $18 + 3\frac{6}{8}$

Ⓒ $30 + 1\frac{7}{8}$

Ⓓ $30 + 2\frac{1}{8}$

Another Look!

How much flour does it take to make 3 dozen rolls if 1 dozen rolls uses $1\frac{3}{8}$ cups of flour?

Find $3 \times 1\frac{3}{8}$.

3×1 $3 \times \frac{3}{8}$

$$3 \times 1\frac{3}{8} = 3 \times \left(1 + \frac{3}{8}\right)$$
$$= (3 \times 1) + \left(3 \times \frac{3}{8}\right)$$
$$= 3 + \frac{9}{8}$$
$$= 3 + 1\frac{1}{8}$$
$$= 4\frac{1}{8}$$

You can use the Distributive Property to multiply whole numbers and mixed numbers.

It takes $4\frac{1}{8}$ cups of flour to make 3 dozen rolls.

For **1–14**, find each product. Use fraction strips or bar diagrams if needed.

1. $2 \times 1\frac{1}{4}$

| 1 | $\frac{1}{4}$ | | | |
| 1 | $\frac{1}{4}$ | | | |

2. $2 \times 3\frac{7}{10}$

n

| $3\frac{7}{10}$ | $3\frac{7}{10}$ |

3. $4 \times 2\frac{5}{8}$

4. $3 \times 2\frac{5}{6}$

5. $8 \times 1\frac{2}{3}$

6. $2 \times 5\frac{4}{5}$

7. $3 \times 1\frac{1}{2}$

8. $6 \times 2\frac{2}{3}$

9. $4 \times 2\frac{3}{4}$

10. $7 \times 3\frac{1}{5}$

1. $4 \times 1\frac{5}{6}$

12. $9 \times 3\frac{5}{8}$

13. $12 \times 1\frac{6}{10}$

14. $8 \times 2\frac{3}{12}$

For **15–16**, use the table at the right. Remember, 60 minutes = 1 hour.

15. How many students slept 540 or more minutes at night?

16. How many students slept 540 or less minutes at night?

How Many Hours We Sleep at Night

Number of Hours Slept / Number of Students

17. Make Sense and Persevere Meg runs $1\frac{1}{2}$ miles and walks $2\frac{1}{4}$ miles each day of the week. How far does Meg run and walk in all each week? Explain. Remember, you can write an equivalent fraction for $1\frac{1}{2}$.

18. Higher Order Thinking Which do you think is greater, $4 \times 3\frac{2}{5}$ or $3 \times 4\frac{2}{5}$? How can you tell without multiplying? Explain

Assessment | ISTEP+ Ready

19. Tamika swims $2\frac{7}{10}$ kilometers a day, 4 days a week. How far does she swim each week? Find $4 \times 2\frac{7}{10}$.

n

$2\frac{7}{10}$	$2\frac{7}{10}$	$2\frac{7}{10}$	$2\frac{7}{10}$

Ⓐ $10\frac{8}{10}$ kilometers

Ⓑ $10\frac{4}{10}$ kilometers

Ⓒ $9\frac{8}{10}$ kilometers

Ⓓ $8\frac{8}{10}$ kilometers

20. Mary has 3 packages of hamburger that weigh $1\frac{3}{4}$ pounds each. What is the total weight of the hamburger?

1		$\frac{1}{4}$	$\frac{1}{4}$	$\frac{1}{4}$	
1		$\frac{1}{4}$	$\frac{1}{4}$	$\frac{1}{4}$	
1		$\frac{1}{4}$	$\frac{1}{4}$	$\frac{1}{4}$	

Ⓐ $2\frac{1}{4}$ pounds

Ⓑ $3\frac{3}{4}$ pounds

Ⓒ $4\frac{1}{2}$ pounds

Ⓓ $5\frac{1}{4}$ pounds

Name _____

Solve & Share

The Big Sur International Marathon is run on the California coast each spring. Sean's mother was the women's overall winner. How much less time did it take Sean's mother than the women's winner in the Ages 65–69 group? Tell how you decided. **Solve this problem any way you choose.**

I can ...
use addition, subtraction, multiplication, or division to solve problems involving time.

Content Standard Extends 4.C.5
Process Standards PS.1, PS.2, PS.4, PS.5

You can use appropriate tools such as bar diagrams or number lines to solve problems involving time.

DATA	Men	Women
Overall	2 hours 23 minutes	2 hours 50 minutes
Ages 65–69	3 hours 34 minutes	3 hours 58 minutes
Ages 70–74	4 hours 20 minutes	4 hours 34 minutes

Look Back! **Reasoning** Was the difference in the overall men's winner and the men's winner in the Ages 70–74 group more or less than 2 hours? Explain.

Essential Question **How Can You Use Multiplication and Division to Solve Problems Involving Time?**

A

Krystal is training for a race. She trains every day for 8 days. How many hours does Krystal train?

Krystal spends an equal amount of time sprinting, walking, and jogging. How many minutes does Krystal spend on each activity during her 8 days of training?

You can use properties of operations to help solve these problems.

Krystal trains $2\frac{3}{4}$ hours per day.

B Find how many hours Krystal trains.

Find $8 \times 2\frac{3}{4}$.

$8 \times 2\frac{3}{4} = 8 \times \left(2 + \frac{3}{4}\right)$

$\qquad = (8 \times 2) + \left(8 \times \frac{3}{4}\right)$

$\qquad = 16 + \frac{24}{4}$

$\qquad = 16 + 6$

$\qquad = 22$

Krystal trains for 22 hours.

You can use the Distributive Property to help multiply.

C Find how many minutes Krystal spends on each activity during her training.

1 hour = 60 minutes
Find 60×22.

$\begin{array}{r} 22 \\ \times\ 60 \\ \hline 1,320 \end{array}$

In 8 days, Krystal spends 1,320 minutes sprinting, walking, and jogging.

Divide to find how many minutes Krystal spends on each activity. Find $1,320 \div 3$.

$\begin{array}{r} 440 \\ 3\overline{)1,320} \end{array}$

In 8 days, Krystal spends 440 minutes on each activity.

Convince Me! **Critique Reasoning** Ellie said, "You can regroup the 440 minutes Krystal spent on each activity as hours." What does Ellie mean? How many hours did Krystal spend on each activity?

Practice Buddy Tools Assessment

Another Example!

Adding Time

Find 2 hours 32 minutes + 3 hours 40 minutes.

$$
\begin{array}{r}
2 \text{ hours } 32 \text{ minutes} \\
+\ 3 \text{ hours } 40 \text{ minutes} \\
\hline
5 \text{ hours } 72 \text{ minutes} \\
=\ 6 \text{ hours } 12 \text{ minutes}
\end{array}
$$

Since 72 minutes > 1 hour, regroup 60 minutes as 1 hour.

Subtracting Time

Find 5 hours 8 minutes − 2 hours 32 minutes.

$$
\begin{array}{r}
\overset{4}{\cancel{5}} \text{ hours } \overset{68}{\cancel{8}} \text{ minutes} \\
-\ 2 \text{ hours } 32 \text{ minutes} \\
\hline
2 \text{ hours } 36 \text{ minutes}
\end{array}
$$

Since 8 minutes < 32 minutes, regroup 1 hour as 60 minutes.

Guided Practice*

Do You Understand?

1. **Construct Arguments** How is adding and subtracting measures of time like adding and subtracting whole numbers?

Do You Know How?

For **2–3**, multiply or divide. Remember there are 60 minutes in 1 hour and 7 days in 1 week.

2. How many minutes are in $6\frac{1}{4}$ hours?

3. How many weeks are in 7,077 days?

ndependent Practice

For **4–7**, add, subtract, multiply, or divide.

DATA	Units of Time	
	1 hour = 60 minutes	1 day = 24 hours
	1 year = 12 months	1 week = 7 days

4.
$$
\begin{array}{r}
8 \text{ hours } \quad 30 \text{ minutes} \\
+\ 7 \text{ hours } \quad 35 \text{ minutes} \\
\hline
\end{array}
$$
☐ hours ☐ minutes = ☐ hours ☐ minutes

5.   ☐   ☐
$$
\begin{array}{r}
2 \text{ years } 5 \text{ months} \\
-\ \qquad 9 \text{ months} \\
\hline
\end{array}
$$
☐ year ☐ months

6. $8 \times \frac{1}{4}$ hour $= \dfrac{\boxed{} \times 1}{\boxed{}} = \dfrac{\boxed{}}{4} = \boxed{}$ hours

7. How many weeks are in 588 days?
$588 \div 7 = \boxed{}$ weeks

Problem Solving

For **8–9**, use the table at the right.

8. If you attend all of the activities at the reunion, how long will you spend at all of the activities?

9. There are 55 minutes between the time dinner ends and the campfire begins. What is the elapsed time from the beginning of dinner to the beginning of the campfire?

DATA

Suarez Family Reunion Schedul

Trip to Scenic Lake Park	4 hours 15 minute
Slide show	55 minutes
Dinner	1 hour 30 minute
Campfire	1 hour 35 minute

---

10. **Make Sense and Persevere** The band boosters spent $4,520 on airline tickets and $1,280 on hotel costs for the 8 members of the color guard. How much was spent for each member of the color guard?

11. **Higher Order Thinking** There are 10 years in 1 decade. Dave's dog is 1 decade 2 years 10 months old. Dave is half as old as his dog. How old is Dave?

Assessment ⊙─ ISTEP+ Ready

12. Glen and Krys work at a shoe store. Glen worked 5 hours 8 minutes. Krys worked 3 hours 12 minutes. How much longer did Glen work than Krys? Write and solve an equation to find the difference.

13. Henry's first flight lasts 1 hour 12 minutes The second flight lasts 2 hours 41 minute How much time did Henry spend on the flights? Write and solve an equation to find the sum.

Name _____

Another Look!

You can add, subtract, multiply, or divide measures of time to solve problems.

Ann worked 5 years 7 months at her first job. She worked 3 years 3 months at her second job.

Add

How long did Ann work at her first and second job?

$$
\begin{array}{r}
5 \text{ years } \ 7 \text{ months} \\
+ \ 3 \text{ years } \ 3 \text{ months} \\
\hline
8 \text{ years } 10 \text{ months}
\end{array}
$$

Subtract

How much longer did Ann work at her first job than her second job?

$$
\begin{array}{r}
5 \text{ years } 7 \text{ months} \\
- \ 3 \text{ years } 3 \text{ months} \\
\hline
2 \text{ years } 4 \text{ months}
\end{array}
$$

Ann worked 6 times longer at her fourth job than her third job. Ann worked $1\frac{1}{2}$ years at her third job.

Multiply

How long did Ann work at her fourth job?

$$6 \times 1\frac{1}{2} = (6 \times 1) + \left(6 \times \frac{1}{2}\right)$$
$$= 6 + \frac{6}{2}$$
$$= 6 + 3$$
$$= 9 \text{ years}$$

Divide

Ann was employed for 546 days at her third job. How many weeks was Ann employed? There are 7 days in one week.

$546 \div 7 = 78$ weeks

For **1–9**, add, subtract, multiply, or divide.

	Units of Time		
DATA	1 hour = 60 minutes	1 day = 24 hours	1 decade = 10 years
	1 year = 12 months	1 week = 7 days	1 minute = 60 seconds

1. $\begin{array}{r} 8 \text{ hours } 12 \text{ minutes} \\ + \ 3 \text{ hours } 15 \text{ minutes} \\ \hline \end{array}$

2. $\begin{array}{r} 9 \text{ weeks } 5 \text{ days} \\ - \ 1 \text{ week } \ 6 \text{ days} \\ \hline \end{array}$

3. $\begin{array}{r} 3 \text{ hours } \ 6 \text{ minutes } 45 \text{ seconds} \\ + \ 8 \text{ hours } 55 \text{ minutes } 20 \text{ seconds} \\ \hline \end{array}$

4. $\begin{array}{r} 1 \text{ decade } 8 \text{ years} \\ - \ \ \ \ \ \ \ \ \ \ \ \ 9 \text{ years} \\ \hline \end{array}$

5. $\begin{array}{r} 12 \text{ days } \ 6 \text{ hours} \\ + \ \ 8 \text{ days } 18 \text{ hours} \\ \hline \end{array}$

6. $\begin{array}{r} 5 \text{ decades } 4 \text{ years } 3 \text{ months} \\ - \ 2 \text{ decades } 5 \text{ years } 6 \text{ months} \\ \hline \end{array}$

7. How many weeks are in 42 days?

8. What is $8 \times \frac{3}{4}$ hour?

9. How many minutes are in $9\frac{1}{4}$ hours?

10. Beth works $8\frac{2}{4}$ hours, drives $1\frac{1}{4}$ hours, cooks $\frac{3}{4}$ hour, and sleeps $7\frac{2}{4}$ hours each day. How many hours of free time does Beth have each day? Remember, there are 24 hours in a day.

11. Ryan spends $10\frac{1}{2}$ hours at work each day. He has a $\frac{3}{4}$-hour lunch and receives two $\frac{1}{4}$-hour breaks. How much time does Ryan spend working? Remember, you can write an equivalent fraction for $10\frac{1}{2}$.

12. The Baltimore Marathon features a relay race. The times for each leg run by a winning team are shown in the table at the right. What is the total time it took this team to run all four legs of the marathon?

Baltimore Marathon Winner Results

Leg of Race	Time Run
Leg 1	32 minutes 56 seconds
Leg 2	42 minutes 28 seconds
Leg 3	34 minutes 34 seconds
Leg 4	39 minutes 2 seconds

DATA

13. **Model with Math** What time does Mia have to leave for school if it takes 45 minutes to get to school? School starts at 7:30 A.M. Draw a number line to explain.

14. **Higher Order Thinking** Mr. Kent teaches 7 classes that are each 50 minutes long. He also has a 30-minute lunch break. How much time does Mr. Kent spend teaching class and at lunch?

Assessment ⟩⊙ ⟨ **ISTEP+ Ready** ⟩

15. If Tom brushes his teeth $\frac{1}{12}$ hour a day, how many minutes does Tom brush his teeth in 2 weeks? What units of time do you need to change to solve this problem? Write and solve equations.

16. A woman from England sneezed 978 days in a row. About how many weeks did she sneeze in a row? What units of time do you need to change to solve this problem? Write and solve an equation.

Name _____

Solve & Share

An ice cream company uses $4\frac{1}{4}$ gallons of vanilla extract and $2\frac{1}{4}$ gallons of almond extract in each vat of ice cream. How much extract is used to make 5 vats of ice cream? Use the bar diagrams to represent and solve this problem.

I can ...
use various representations to solve problems.

Process Standards PS.4 Also PS.1, PS.2, PS.6
Content Standard Extends 4.C.5

Thinking Habits

Be a good thinker! These questions can help you.

- How can I use math I know to help solve this problem?

- How can I use pictures, objects, or an equation to represent the problem?

- How can I use numbers, words, and symbols to solve the problem?

Look Back! **Model with Math** What number sentences can you write to model the problem?

How Can You Represent a Situation with a Math Model?

A

Finn gives the amount of snacks shown to the baseball team's coach every time the team wins a game. How many total pounds of snacks does Finn give the coach after the baseball team wins 3 games?

$\frac{5}{8}$ pound of red licorice

$\frac{7}{8}$ pound of peanuts

What hidden question do you need to find and solve first?

I need to find how many pounds of red licorice and peanuts Finn gives the coach when the baseball team wins a game.

Here's my thinking.

B **How can I model with math?**

I can

- use previously learned concepts and skills.

- find and answer any hidden questions.

- use bar diagrams and equations to represent and solve this problem.

C Find $\frac{5}{8} + \frac{7}{8}$ to show the total pounds of snacks.

p	
$\frac{5}{8}$	$\frac{7}{8}$

$\frac{5}{8} + \frac{7}{8} = \frac{12}{8}$ or $1\frac{4}{8}$ pounds

Find $3 \times 1\frac{4}{8}$ to show how many pounds Finn gives the coach after 3 wins.

t		
$1\frac{4}{8}$	$1\frac{4}{8}$	$1\frac{4}{8}$

$3 \times 1\frac{4}{8} = (3 \times 1) + \left(3 \times \frac{4}{8}\right)$

$= 3 + 1\frac{4}{8}$

$= 4\frac{4}{8}$ pounds

Finn gives the coach $4\frac{4}{8}$ pounds of snacks after the team wins 3 games.

Convince Me! **Reasoning** Would the answer change if $\frac{12}{8}$ pounds were used instead of $1\frac{4}{8}$ pounds to calculate the number of pounds of snacks Finn gives the coach after 3 wins? Explain.

⭐ Guided Practice *

Model with Math

Colton and his classmates are making maps of the streets where they live. How much green and black felt does his teacher need to buy so 25 students can each make a map?

Felt needed for each map

$\frac{1}{6}$ sheet of white
$\frac{2}{6}$ sheet of brown
$\frac{2}{6}$ sheet of blue
$\frac{4}{6}$ sheet of green
$\frac{5}{6}$ sheet of black

1. Draw bar diagrams and write equations to represent the problem.

2. How many green and black sheets of felt does the teacher need to buy in all? Explain.

When you model with math, you use math you know to solve a problem.

⭐ Independent Practice ⭐

Model with Math

Moira swims $\frac{3}{4}$ hour before school and $1\frac{3}{4}$ hours after school. For how long does she swim in 5 days? Use Exercises 3–5 to answer the question.

3. Draw bar diagrams and write equations to represent the problem.

4. What previously learned math can you use to solve the problem?

5. How long does Moira swim in 5 days? Explain.

Problem Solving

Seeing Orange

Perry mixed $4\frac{2}{3}$ ounces of red paint and $3\frac{1}{3}$ ounces of yellow paint to make the right shade of orange paint. He needs 40 ounces of orange paint to paint the top of a desk and 30 ounces of another color paint to paint the rest of the desk. How many ounces of red and yellow paint should Perry use to make enough orange paint to cover the top of the desk?

6. **Reasoning** What do you need to know to find how many ounces of each color Perry should use?

7. **Model with Math** Draw bar diagrams and write equations to represent finding how many ounces of paint are in a batch and how many batches Perry needs to make.

When you model with math, you use a picture to show how the quantities in the problem are related.

8. **Be Precise** How many batches does Perry need to make? Explain.

9. **Model with Math** Draw bar diagrams. Write and solve equations to show how to find how many ounces of each color Perry should use.

Name _____

Another Look!

How many more cups of bananas than cups of flour are in 3 loaves of banana bread?

Tell how you can model with math to solve problems.

- I can use previously learned concepts and skills.
- I can find and answer any hidden questions.
- I can use bar diagrams and equations to represent and solve this problem.

Draw bar diagrams and write equations to solve the hidden question and the original question.

Loaf of Banana Bread
$1\frac{3}{4}$ cups of mashed bananas
$1\frac{1}{4}$ cups flour
$\frac{1}{4}$ cup applesauce

$1\frac{3}{4}$

$1\frac{1}{4}$	m

d

$\frac{2}{4}$	$\frac{2}{4}$	$\frac{2}{4}$

$1\frac{3}{4} - 1\frac{1}{4} = \frac{2}{4}$

$3 \times \frac{2}{4} = \frac{6}{4}$ or $1\frac{2}{4}$

Each loaf uses $\frac{2}{4}$ cup more of mashed bananas than flour.

3 loaves of banana bread contain $1\frac{2}{4}$ or $1\frac{1}{2}$ cups more mashed bananas than flour.

When you model with math, you can write an equation to represent the relationships in the problem.

Model with Math

Aaron wraps presents in a store. In one hour, he wraps 8 games and one console. How much wrapping paper does Aaron use? Use Exercises 1–3 to answer the question.

Gaming console takes $4\frac{1}{3}$ feet of wrapping paper

Game takes $1\frac{2}{3}$ feet of wrapping paper

1. Draw bar diagrams and write equations to represent the problem.

2. What previously learned math can you use to solve the problem?

3. How much wrapping paper does Aaron use? Explain.

Cat Food

Tamara feeds her cat $\frac{1}{8}$ cup canned food each day and the rest dry. She also gives her cat one treat a day. How much dry food does Tamara feed her cat in a week?

4. **Reasoning** What quantities are given in the problem and what do the numbers describe?

$\frac{3}{8}$ cup of food per day

5. **Make Sense and Persevere** What do you need to find?

6. **Model with Math** Draw bar diagrams and write equations to represent the problem and show relationships.

When you model with math, you use math to represent a problem situation.

7. **Be Precise** How much dry food does Tamara feed her cat in a week? Explain. Write your answer as a mixed number.

8. **Reasoning** Explain how you know what units to use for your answer.

Name _____

Find a partner. Get paper and a pencil. Each partner chooses a different color: light blue or dark blue.

Partner 1 and Partner 2 each point to a black number at the same time. Each partner adds the two numbers.

If the answer is on your color, you get a tally mark. Work until one partner has twelve tally marks.

I can ...
add multi-digit whole numbers.

Partner 1					Partner 2
2,814	3,043	5,776	4,565	6,015	**369**
3,149	6,595	3,617	6,834	3,856	**194**
4,097	3,343	6,496	5,502	5,537	**229**
5,308	3,008	3,378	4,326	4,804	**468**
6,127	4,291	3,183	5,677	3,521	**707**
	3,518	6,356	3,282	4,466	

Tally Marks for Partner 1

Tally Marks for Partner 2

Vocabulary Review

Glossary

Word List

- benchmark fraction
- denominator
- equivalent fractions
- fraction
- mixed number
- numerator
- unit fraction

Understand Vocabulary

Write T for *true* and F for *false*.

1. _____ Benchmark fractions are commonly used fractions such as $\frac{1}{4}$ and $\frac{1}{2}$.

2. _____ Equivalent fractions are fractions where the numerator and the denominator have the same value.

3. _____ The denominator of a fraction tells the number of equal parts in the whole.

4. _____ A fraction names part of a whole, part of a set, or a location on a number line.

5. _____ The numerator is the number below the fraction bar in a fraction.

Write *always, sometimes,* or *never*.

6. A unit fraction _____ has a numerator of 1.

7. A numerator is _____ greater than its denominator.

8. A mixed number _____ has just a fraction part.

Use Vocabulary in Writing

9. Samatha wrote $\frac{1}{2}$. Use at least 3 terms from the Word List to describe Samantha's fraction.

> You can use all of the terms to describe Samantha's fraction.

Name _____

Set A | pages 543–548

Talia used $\frac{5}{8}$ yard of ribbon.

Write an equation for $\frac{5}{8}$ as a multiple of a unit fraction.

$$\frac{5}{8} = 5 \times \frac{1}{8}$$

Remember a unit fraction will always have a numerator of 1.

Reteaching

Write each fraction as a multiple of a unit fraction.

1. $\frac{5}{5}$ 2. $\frac{3}{8}$

3. $\frac{4}{3}$ 4. $\frac{6}{5}$

5. $\frac{15}{8}$ 6. $\frac{7}{4}$

Set B | pages 549–554

James runs $\frac{3}{5}$ mile each week. How far does James run after 2 weeks?

Use multiplication to find the product.

$2 \times \frac{3}{5} = \frac{2 \times 3}{5} = \frac{6}{5}$ or $1\frac{1}{5}$

James ran $\frac{6}{5}$ or $1\frac{1}{5}$ miles.

Remember you can record answers as fractions or mixed numbers.

Write and solve an equation.

1.

2.

Set C | pages 555–560

Alisa has 9 puppies. Each puppy eats $\frac{2}{3}$ cup of food each day. How many cups of food does Alisa need to feed the puppies for 7 days?

Use multiplication to find how much food the puppies eat in 7 days.

$9 \times \frac{2}{3} = \frac{9 \times 2}{3} = \frac{18}{3}$ or 6 cups

$6 \times 7 = 42$ cups

Alisa needs 42 cups of food to feed the puppies for 7 days.

Remember you multiply the whole number and the numerator and write the product above the denominator of the fraction.

1. Milo makes 5 batches of muffins. In each batch he uses $\frac{2}{3}$ bag of walnuts. How many bags of walnuts does Milo use?

2. A bird feeder can hold $\frac{7}{8}$ pound of seeds. How many pounds of seeds can 12 bird feeders hold?

Find $5 \times 3\frac{1}{3}$.

$5 \times 3 = 15$

$5 \times \frac{1}{3} = \frac{5}{3}$ or $1\frac{2}{3}$

$15 + 1\frac{2}{3} = 16\frac{2}{3}$

Remember you can use the distributive property to break apart multiplication problems.

1. It takes $2\frac{1}{4}$ yards of ribbon to make a bow for a gift. Serena made 7 bows. How much ribbon did she use?

2. There were 5 students that walked $3\frac{3}{8}$ miles as a group during a walk-a-thon. How many miles did the 5 students walk all together?

You can add, subtract, multiply, and divide measures of time.

Units of Time	
1 hour = 60 minutes	1 day = 24 hours
1 year = 12 months	1 week = 7 days

DATA

Remember you may need to regroup when solving problems with time.

1. 7 hours 12 minutes
   + 3 hours 53 minutes

2. $7 \times \frac{3}{4}$ hour

3. 5 weeks 4 days
   − 3 weeks 6 days

4. Write 560 days in weeks.

Think about these questions to help you **model with math**.

Thinking Habits

- How can I use math I know to help solve this problem?

- How can I use pictures, objects, or an equation to represent the problem?

- How can I use numbers, words, and symbols to solve the problem?

Remember you can draw a bar diagram to help write an equation.

Julie makes her famous chili recipe with $2\frac{3}{8}$ cups of red beans, $3\frac{4}{8}$ cups of chili beans, and $2\frac{6}{8}$ cups of onions.

1. How many more cups of chili beans are used than red beans?

2. How many cups of beans and onions does Julie use altogether?

Name _____

1. Margo practices her flute $\frac{1}{4}$ hour each day.

Units of Time
1 week = 7 days
1 hour = 60 minutes

Part A

Write and solve an equation to find how many hours Margo practices her flute in 1 week.

Part B

Use properties of operations to find how many minutes Margo practices her flute in 1 week.

$$60 \times \square\frac{\square}{\square} = 60 \times \left(\square + \frac{\square}{\square}\right)$$

$$= \left(60 \times \square\right) + \left(60 \times \frac{\square}{\square}\right)$$

$$= 60 + \frac{60 \times 3}{4}$$

$$= 60 + \frac{\square}{4}$$

$$= \square + 45$$

$$= \square \text{ minutes}$$

2. For questions 2a–2d, choose Yes or No to tell if $\frac{1}{2}$ will make each equation true.

2a. $6 \times \square = \frac{6}{2}$ ○ Yes ○ No

2b. $6 \times \square = 3$ ○ Yes ○ No

2c. $7 \times \square = \frac{7}{14}$ ○ Yes ○ No

2d. $7 \times \square = 3\frac{1}{2}$ ○ Yes ○ No

3. Ben played at a friend's house for 2 hours 35 minutes. Later he played at a park. He played for a total of 3 hours 52 minutes that day. How long did Ben play at the park?

Ⓐ 6 hours 27 minutes

Ⓑ 2 hours 17 minutes

Ⓒ 1 hour 17 minutes

Ⓓ 17 minutes

4. Choose numbers from the box to fill in the missing values in the multiplication equations. Use each number once.

$$\frac{7}{8} = \square \times \frac{\square}{8} \qquad \frac{1}{\square} \times 3 = \frac{\square}{4}$$

$$\frac{\square}{6} = 5 \times \frac{1}{\square} \qquad \frac{1}{2} \times 8 = \frac{\square}{\square}$$

| 1 | 2 | 3 | 4 | 5 | 6 | 7 | 8 |

5. Chris found the product of whole numbers and mixed numbers. Draw lines to match each expression with its product.

Expression	Product
$3 \times 2\frac{2}{3}$	$33\frac{6}{8}$
$5 \times 6\frac{6}{8}$	8
$4 \times 4\frac{3}{4}$	$22\frac{4}{8}$
$9 \times 2\frac{4}{8}$	19

6. Select all the expressions equal to the product of 4 and $1\frac{4}{8}$.

☐ $1\frac{4}{8} + 1\frac{4}{8} + 1\frac{4}{8} + 1\frac{4}{8}$

☐ $4 \times 1\frac{4}{8}$

☐ $4 - 1\frac{4}{8}$

☐ $4 + 1 + 4 + 8$

☐ $(4 \times 1) + \left(4 \times \frac{4}{8}\right)$

7. Complete the multiplication equation that describes what is shown by the model.

$$4 \times \frac{\square}{6} = 8 \times \frac{\square}{6}$$

8. Use a unit fraction and a whole number to write a multiplication equation equal to $\frac{7}{8}$.

9. Juan is making cookies. He makes 2 batches on Monday and 4 batches on Tuesday. He uses $\frac{3}{4}$ cup of flour in each batch. How much flour does Juan use? Explain.

10. Which multiplication expression describes the fraction shown on the number line?

Ⓐ $\frac{5}{6} + \frac{6}{6}$

Ⓑ $4 \times \frac{1}{6}$

Ⓒ $\frac{1}{6} + \frac{2}{6} + \frac{3}{6} + \frac{4}{6}$

Ⓓ $4 \times \frac{4}{6}$

11. Lucas is making one dozen snacks for his team. He uses $\frac{1}{4}$ cup of dried cherries and $\frac{2}{4}$ cup of dried apricots for each snack. How many cups of dried fruit does Lucas need for his one dozen snacks? Remember, there are 12 snacks in one dozen. Write and solve equations to show how you found the answer.

Name _____

School Mural

Paul has permission to paint a 20-panel mural for his school. Part of the mural is shown in the **Painting a Mural** figure. Paul decides he needs help. The **Helpers** table shows how much several of his friends can paint each day and how many days a week they can paint.

Painting a Mural

Paul paints $1\frac{2}{3}$ panels a day

Helpers		
Friend	**Panels a Day**	**Days a Week**
Leeza	$\frac{3}{4}$	3
Kelsey	$\frac{7}{8}$	4
Tony	$\frac{5}{6}$	3

1. The students want to find how long it will take to paint the mural if each works on a different part of the panels a different number of days a week.

Part A

How many panels can Leeza paint in a week?
Use fraction strips to explain.

Part B

How many panels can Kelsey paint in a week?
Use equations to explain.

Part C

Paul can work 5 days a week. How many panels can Paul paint in a week?
Use multiplication equations and properties of operations to explain.

Part D

How many panels can Tony paint in a week? Draw a bar diagram.
Write and solve an equation.

2. The **Time Spent Painting Each Day** table shows
how much time each of Paul's friends helped with
the mural each day that they worked on it.

How much more time did Kelsey spend each day
than Tony and Leeza combined? Explain.

Time Spent Painting Each Day	
Friend	**Time**
Leeza	30 minutes
Kelsey	2 hours 30 minutes
Tony	1 hour 45 minutes

TOPIC 11

Represent and Interpret Data on Line Plots

Essential Questions: How can you read data on a line plot? How can you make a line plot?

Digital Resources

Solve · Learn · Glossary · Practice Buddy · Tools · Assessment · Help · Games

Math and Science Project: Safety and Data

Do Research Use the Internet or other sources to find what causes an earthquake and how the power of an earthquake is measured. Tell how people can stay safe during earthquakes.

Journal: Write a Report Include what you found. Also in your report:

- The size, or *magnitude*, of an earthquake is measured with the Richter scale. Explain how the scale is used.

- Research the magnitudes of at least 6 earthquakes that have occurred in your lifetime. Make a table showing when they occurred and their magnitudes, and then show their magnitudes on a line plot.

Name _____

Review What You Know

Ⓐ-Ⓩ Vocabulary

Choose the best term from the box. Write it on the blank.

- compare
- data
- line plot
- scale

1. A _____ is a way to organize data on a number line.

2. Numbers that show the units used on a graph are called a _____.

3. _____ are pieces of information.

Comparing Fractions

Write $>$, $<$, or $=$ in the $\bigcirc$.

4. $\frac{7}{8} \bigcirc \frac{3}{4}$

5. $\frac{1}{2} \bigcirc \frac{5}{8}$

6. $\frac{1}{4} \bigcirc \frac{2}{8}$

Fraction Subtraction

Find the difference.

7. $10\frac{3}{8} - 4\frac{1}{8} =$ _____

8. $5\frac{1}{4} - 3\frac{3}{4} =$ _____

9. $7\frac{4}{8} - 2\frac{4}{8} =$ _____

Interpreting Data

Use the data in the chart to answer each exercise.

10. What is the greatest snake length? What is the least snake length?

DATA	Snake Lengths (Inches)			
	$12\frac{1}{2}$	$16\frac{1}{2}$	17	24
	16	16	13	$12\frac{1}{2}$
	$18\frac{1}{2}$	$17\frac{1}{2}$	17	16

11. Which of the snake lengths are recorded more than once? Which length was recorded the most?

12. What is the difference between the greatest length and the shortest length recorded?

In this topic, you will use data to create line plots.

My Word Cards

Use the examples for each word on the front of the card to help complete the definitions on the back.

A-Z
Glossary

line plot

outlier

Data Set: 2, 3, 3, 4, 5, 10

My Word Cards

Complete each definition. Extend learning by writing your own definitions.

Any number in a data set that is very different from the rest of the numbers is called an _____.

A_____ is a way to display data along a number line, where each dot represents one number in a set of data.

Homework & Practice 11-1
Read Line Plots

Another Look!

The data table shows the distances Freda ran over a period of 17 days.

A line plot shows data along a number line. Each dot represents 1 day. An outlier is a data point that is very different from the rest of the data. Which distance is the outlier?

Distance (miles)	Days
$\frac{1}{2}$	2
$1\frac{1}{2}$	4
2	5
$2\frac{1}{2}$	3
3	2
5	1

DATA

Freda's Daily Running Distance

0 $\frac{1}{2}$ 1 $1\frac{1}{2}$ 2 $2\frac{1}{2}$ 3 $3\frac{1}{2}$ 4 $4\frac{1}{2}$ 5

Miles

Five miles is an outlier because it is not close to the distances Freda ran on the other days.

For **1–5**, use the line plot at the right.

1. Identify any outliers in the data set.

2. Which weight is the most common?

Use a fraction to name points on a number line that are not whole numbers.

3. How many more puppies weighed 3 pounds than 7 pounds?

Weights of Puppies at a Pet Store

4. How many puppies weighed less than 7 pounds?

3 4 5 6 7 8 9 10 11 12 13

Pounds

5. What is the total weight of all the puppies weighing less than 6 pounds? Explain.

For **6–7**, use the line plot at the right.

6. Which height is the most common among the students in Ms. Jackson's class?

7. **Reasoning** Is there an outlier for the data in this line plot? Explain.

Heights of Students in Ms. Jackson's Class

Feet

For **8–9**, use the line plot at the right.

8. **Reasoning** Based on the line plot, how many more plants are less than $3\frac{2}{4}$ inches than are greater than $3\frac{2}{4}$ inches? Explain.

9. **Higher Order Thinking** Write a question that can be answered by using the line plot, and then give the answer.

Heights of Hal's Plants

Inches

For **10–11**, use the line plot at the right.

10. How many recipes use 2 cups of flour or more?

   Ⓐ 3 recipes

   Ⓑ 4 recipes

   Ⓒ 7 recipes

   Ⓓ 14 recipes

11. How many recipes are represented by the line plot?

   Ⓐ 7 recipes

   Ⓑ 9 recipes

   Ⓒ 12 recipes

   Ⓓ 14 recipes

The number of recipes is represented by the number of dots on the line plot.

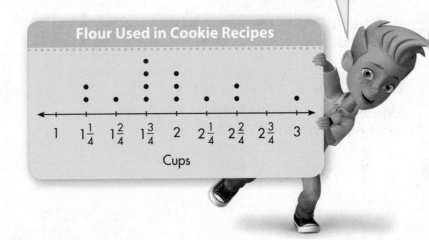

Flour Used in Cookie Recipes

Cups

Help · Practice Buddy · Tools · Games

Another Look!

Dorothy measured the lengths of the fingers on her left hand. She also measured the length of her thumb. Dorothy wants to make a line plot to show the measurements.

Follow these steps to make a line plot.

$2\frac{3}{4}$ in.
$2\frac{2}{4}$ in.
2 in.
2 in.

Step 1

Draw a number line and choose a scale based on the data collected. The scale should show data values from least to greatest.

2   $2\frac{1}{4}$ $2\frac{2}{4}$ $2\frac{3}{4}$

Step 2

Write a title for the line plot and a label for the numbers.

Lengths of Dorothy's Fingers

2   $2\frac{1}{4}$ $2\frac{2}{4}$ $2\frac{3}{4}$

Inches

Step 3

Draw a dot for each length.

Lengths of Dorothy's Fingers

2   $2\frac{1}{4}$ $2\frac{3}{4}$

Inches

For **1–4**, use the line plot at the right.

Lengths of Aiden's Cars

2   $2\frac{1}{8}$ $2\frac{2}{8}$ $2\frac{3}{8}$ $2\frac{4}{8}$ $2\frac{5}{8}$ $2\frac{6}{8}$ $2\frac{7}{8}$ 3
  $2\frac{1}{4}$ $2\frac{2}{4}$ $2\frac{3}{4}$
          $2\frac{1}{2}$

Inches

1. Aiden has two toy cars that measure $2\frac{1}{4}$ inches, three that measure $2\frac{3}{8}$ inches, one that measures $2\frac{7}{8}$ inches, one that measures $2\frac{1}{8}$ inches, and one that measures $2\frac{3}{4}$ inches. Use this data to complete the line plot at the right.

2. How long is Aiden's longest toy car?

3. Which length appears most often on the line plot?

4. Are more cars shorter or longer than $2\frac{1}{2}$ inches?

5. 🔤 **Vocabulary** Use a vocabulary word to complete the sentence.

An _____ fraction names the same region, part of a set, or part of a segment.

6. Math and Science Floodwalls are used to prevent damage from floods. A town built a floodwall $4\frac{4}{8}$ feet tall. Another town built a floodwall $7\frac{1}{8}$ feet tall. What is the difference between the heights of the floodwalls?

7. Reasoning Class members read the following number of pages over the weekend:

9, 11, 7, 10, 9, 8, 7, 13, 2, 12, 10, 9, 8, 10, 11, 12

Which number is an outlier? Explain your reasoning.

8. Higher Order Thinking Tony wants to make a line plot of the distances he rode his bike last week. He rode the following distances in miles:

$3, 4\frac{1}{2}, 6, 3, 5\frac{1}{2}, 3, 5\frac{1}{2}$

Make a line plot for the distances Tony rode.

You can draw a line plot to help you find outliers.

9. Caden collects insects. The table below lists the lengths in inches of insects in Caden's collection.

DATA	Insect	Length (in.)
	Ladybug	$\frac{2}{8}$
	Cross Spider	$\frac{6}{8}$
	Honey Bee	$\frac{2}{4}$
	Field Cricket	$\frac{3}{4}$
	Big Dipper Firefly	$\frac{4}{8}$
	Stag Beetle	1

Use the data set to complete the line plot. Draw the dots and write the scale values. Remember to use equivalent fractions to help write the scale values.

Lengths of Insects

Inches

ame _____

Another Look!

Belle made a bracelet using beads of different sizes. The line plot shows how many beads of each size Belle used. Which length of bead did Belle use most often? How many beads did Belle use to make her bracelet?

Lengths of Beads

Inches

The highest column of dots tells you which value occurs the most.

Belle used a $\frac{4}{8}$-inch bead most often.

Belle used 10 beads to make her bracelet.

For **1–2**, use the data set below.

DATA

Length of Time to Say the Alphabet (in seconds)

5, 4, $4\frac{1}{2}$, 6, 5, $6\frac{1}{2}$, $5\frac{1}{2}$, 7, $5\frac{1}{2}$, $7\frac{1}{2}$,

6, $4\frac{1}{2}$, $4\frac{1}{2}$, $4\frac{1}{2}$, 4, 6, $4\frac{1}{2}$, $5\frac{1}{2}$, 5, $6\frac{1}{2}$

1. The table lists the length of time in seconds it takes for each student in Ms. Sousa's class to say the alphabet. Make a line plot of the data.

2. Meghan says the difference between the least amount of time it takes a student to say the alphabet and the greatest amount of time is $4\frac{1}{2}$ seconds. Do you agree? Explain.

3. **Math and Science** To predict volcanic eruptions, scientists may use a seismograph to detect small earthquakes. Out of the 169 active volcanoes in the U.S., about 130 are in Alaska. About how many active U.S. volcanoes are **NOT** in Alaska?

4. **Make Sense and Persevere** Teddy has blue, red, and black shirts. He has six blue shirts and two red shirts. He has twice as many black shirts as red shirts. What fraction represents the number of blue shirts out of the total number of shirts?

For **5–7**, use the line plots at the right.

5. The line plots show the amount of rainfall in two cities during one month. How many total days of no rain did the two cities have?

6. Which city had fewer days of rain? How many fewer? Write and solve an equation to explain.

7. **Higher Order Thinking** Which city had the greatest amount of total rainfall? Explain.

8. How many pounds of oranges do the data in the line plot represent? Use equivalent fraction to select all that apply.

   ☐ $37\frac{4}{8}$ pounds

   ☐ $37\frac{7}{2}$ pounds

   ☐ $37\frac{28}{8}$ pounds

   ☐ $40\frac{1}{2}$ pounds

   ☐ $40\frac{4}{8}$ pounds

Name _____

Solve & Share

A class made a line plot showing the amount of snowfall for 10 days. Nathan analyzed the line plot and said, "The difference between the greatest amount of snowfall recorded and the least amount of snowfall recorded is 3 because the first measurement has one dot and the last measurement has 4 dots." How do you respond to Nathan's reasoning?

I can ...
use what I know about line plots to critique the reasoning of others.

Process Standards PS.3 Also PS.1, PS.2, PS.4
Content Standard 4.DA.2

Snowfall

$\frac{3}{4}$ 1 $1\frac{1}{4}$ $1\frac{2}{4}$ $1\frac{3}{4}$

Inches

Thinking Habits

Be a good thinker! These questions can help you.

• What questions can I ask to understand other people's thinking?

• Are there mistakes in other people's thinking?

• Can I improve other people's thinking?

Look Back! **Critique Reasoning** What question can you ask about the line plot above to find if Nathan's reasoning is correct?

A

The line plots show the amount of rainfall for two months.

Val said, "The total rainfall for February was greater than the total rainfall for January because $\frac{7}{8} + \frac{7}{8}$ equals $\frac{14}{8}$, and the highest rainfall in January was $\frac{5}{8}$."

Rainfall in January

Inches

What is Val's reasoning?

Val compared the two highest amounts of rainfall for each month.

Rainfall in February

Inches

Here's my thinking.

B **How can I critique the reasoning of others?**

I can

- ask questions for clarification.

- decide if the strategy used makes sense.

- look for flaws in estimates or calculations.

C Val's reasoning is not correct.

She compared the days with the greatest amount of rainfall for the two months. The days with the greatest amounts of rainfall are not the total for the months.

Val should have added the amounts for each month. Then she could compare the amounts.

January: $\frac{1}{8} + \frac{1}{8} + \frac{1}{8} + \frac{3}{8} + \frac{3}{8} + \frac{3}{8} + \frac{5}{8} = \frac{17}{8}$ inches

February: $\frac{1}{8} + \frac{1}{8} + \frac{5}{8} + \frac{7}{8} + \frac{7}{8} = \frac{21}{8}$ inches

During February, there was $\frac{21}{8} - \frac{17}{8} = \frac{4}{8}$ inch more rain than January.

Convince Me! **Critique Reasoning** Bev thought January had more rainfall because it rained on 7 days and February only had rain on 5 days. How do you respond to Bev's reasoning?

Guided Practice

Critique Reasoning

At a dog show, a judge wrote down the heights of 12 dogs. Cole made a line plot of the heights, shown to the right. He concluded, "The height with the most dots is $1\frac{1}{4}$ feet, so that is the greatest height of the dogs at the dog show."

Dog Heights

Feet

1. What is Cole's conclusion? How did he reach this conclusion?

When you critique reasoning, make sure you identify flaws in reasoning.

2. Is Cole's conclusion correct? Explain.

Independent Practice

Critique Reasoning

Natasha keeps a log of absences in her fourth-grade class. She creates the line plot shown. Each dot represents the number of absences in one week. Natasha says the total number of absences is 16 because there are 16 dots on the number line.

Fourth-Grade Attendance

Number of Absences in a Week

3. What is Natasha's argument? How does she support it?

4. Does Natasha's reasoning make sense? Explain.

5. Natasha also says there is an outlier in her data. Is she correct? Explain.

For another example, see Set D on page 618.

Taking Inventory

Mr. Pally is building a desk using screws of different lengths. The instructions show how many screws of each length he will need to use. Mr. Pally concludes he will use more of the shortest screws than the longest screws.

6. **Model with Math** Draw a line plot to show the screw lengths Mr. Pally will use to build the desk.

Screw Lengths (inches)			
$\frac{3}{8}$	1	$\frac{6}{8}$	$\frac{3}{8}$
$\frac{7}{8}$	$1\frac{4}{8}$	$\frac{7}{8}$	$\frac{3}{8}$
$1\frac{4}{8}$	$\frac{6}{8}$	$\frac{3}{8}$	1
$\frac{3}{8}$	$\frac{3}{8}$	$\frac{7}{8}$	$1\frac{4}{8}$

7. **Reasoning** How can you use the line plot to find which length of screw Mr. Pally will need the most?

When you critique reasoning, ask questions to help you understand someone's thinking.

8. **Critique Reasoning** Is Mr. Pally's conclusion reasonable? How did you decide? If not, what can you do to improve his reasoning?

Homework & Practice 11-4
Critique Reasoning

Another Look!

Ryan's dog just had a litter of 8 puppies. He measured the length of each of the puppies. The line plot below shows their lengths in inches. Ryan says the longest puppy in the litter is $7\frac{4}{8}$ inches because $7\frac{4}{8}$ has the most dots above it.

Lengths of Puppies

Inches: $7\frac{1}{4}$ $7\frac{4}{8}$ $7\frac{6}{8}$ 8 $8\frac{1}{4}$ $8\frac{4}{8}$ $8\frac{6}{8}$ 9

Tell how you can critique Ryan's reasoning.

Ryan's reasoning does not make sense. The most dots shows the most common length of puppy. To find the longest puppy, Ryan should find the dot farthest to the right on the line plot.

The longest puppy in the litter is 9 inches.

> When you critique reasoning, you explain why someone's reasoning is correct or incorrect.

Critique Reasoning

Sandy made this line plot to show how many hours she read on each of 10 days. She said the difference between the greatest time and the least time she read in one day was $1\frac{3}{4}$ hours.

Times Sandy Read

Hours: $\frac{1}{4}$ $\frac{2}{4}$ $\frac{3}{4}$ 1 $1\frac{1}{4}$ $1\frac{2}{4}$ $1\frac{3}{4}$ 2 $2\frac{1}{4}$ $2\frac{2}{4}$

1. Tell how you can critique Sandy's reasoning.

2. Critique Sandy's reasoning.

Critique Reasoning

Liana has a collection of book series in her library. The line plot below shows how many books are in each series Liana owns. She says she has a total of 24 books.

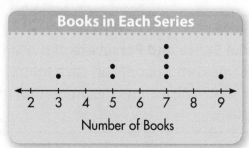

Books in Each Series

Number of Books: 2 3 4 5 6 7 8 9

3. Tell how you can critique Liana's reasoning.

4. Critique Liana's reasoning.

Trivia Contest

Wallace runs a monthly trivia contest. The table shows the number of people on each trivia team. Each contestant pays a $3 entry fee to enter the contest. Wallace finds the number of contestants in the contest and concludes he will earn $171.

Team	People on Each Team
A	3
B	3
C	3
D	4
E	4
F	4
G	4
H	5
I	6
J	6
K	7
L	8

5. **Reasoning** Draw a line plot to show the number of people on each team. Explain why a line plot can make it easier to find the most common number of people on a team.

6. **Make Sense and Persevere** If the largest team breaks into 4 teams with 2 people on each team, how will that affect the line plot? Will it affect the amount of money Wallace earns? Explain.

> When you critique reasoning, you consider all parts of an argument.

7. **Critique Reasoning** Explain if Wallace's conclusion is reasonable. How did you decide? If not, what can you do to improve his reasoning?

Find a Match

TOPIC
11

Fluency Practice Activity

Work with a partner. Point to a clue.

Read the clue.

Look below the clues to find a match. Write the clue letter in the box next to the match.

Find a match for every clue.

I can ...
add and subtract multi-digit whole numbers.

Clues

A The sum is between 3,510 and 3,520.

E The sum is exactly 3,584.

B The difference is exactly 3,515.

F The difference is between 3,590 and 3,600.

C The sum is between 3,560 and 3,570.

G The sum is exactly 3,987.

D The difference is between 3,530 and 3,540.

H The difference is between 1,000 and 2,000.

1,569 + 1,999	2,462 + 1,525	1,437 + 2,082	1,885 + 1,699
3,499 − 1,635	5,057 − 1,542	4,424 − 829	6,549 − 3,011

A-Z
Glossary

Word List

- bar diagram
- data set
- frequency table
- line plot
- number line
- outlier
- scale
- survey

Understand Vocabulary

Write T for *true* and F for *false*.

1. _____ A bar diagram is a tool used to help understand and solve word problems.

2. _____ A data set is a collection of pieces of information.

3. _____ A way to display data that shows how many times a response occurs in a set of data is called a frequency table.

4. _____ A line plot shows data along a line.

5. _____ Collecting information by asking each person a different question is called a survey.

Write *always*, *sometimes*, or *never*.

6. An outlier _____ sits outside of the rest of the data set on a line plot.

7. The scale on a line plot is _____ numbered using fractions.

8. A number line is _____ numbered out of order.

Use Vocabulary in Writing

9. Use at least 3 terms from the Word List to describe another way Patrick can display his data.

DATA	Patrick's Walking Log for 2 Weeks	
	Distance (miles)	**Days**
	1	3
	2	2
	3	4
	4	5

Set A pages 591–596

The line plot shows the average hang times of kickers in a football league.

Kickers' Average Hang Times

$3\frac{60}{100}$ $3\frac{70}{100}$ $3\frac{80}{100}$ $3\frac{90}{100}$

Seconds

Each dot above the line plot represents one value in the data set.

Remember an outlier is a number that is very different from the rest of the numbers in a data set.

1. How many hang times are shown on the line plot?

2. What hang time appears most often on the line plot?

3. Is there an outlier in the set?

Set B pages 597–602

Lilly measured the lengths of the ribbons in her craft kit.

Lengths of Lilly's Ribbons

Ribbon Colors	Length
Red	$5\frac{1}{2}$ in.
Blue	4 in.
White	$5\frac{1}{2}$ in.
Yellow	$4\frac{1}{4}$ in.
Pink	$4\frac{3}{4}$ in.

Lengths of Lilly's Ribbons

4   $4\frac{1}{4}$ $4\frac{2}{4}$ $4\frac{3}{4}$ 5 $5\frac{1}{4}$ $5\frac{2}{4}$

$4\frac{1}{2}$ $5\frac{1}{2}$

Inches

The number line shows the lengths from least to greatest. The labels show what the dots represent.

Remember to choose a reasonable scale for your number line.

A zoo in Australia studied platypuses. Their weights are recorded below.

Platypus Weights (kg)				
$1\frac{3}{4}$	2	$2\frac{1}{8}$	$2\frac{1}{2}$	$1\frac{3}{4}$
$2\frac{3}{4}$	2	2	2	$1\frac{3}{4}$
$1\frac{7}{8}$	$1\frac{5}{8}$	$2\frac{1}{4}$	$1\frac{7}{8}$	$2\frac{1}{2}$

1. Draw a line plot for the data set.

2. What scale did you use to create your line plot? Explain.

Carly and Freddie pick up trash. The line plots show how much they picked up each day for 14 days. What is the difference between the greatest and least amounts Carly picked up?

Trash Picked Up by Carly

Pounds

Trash Picked Up by Freddie

Pounds

The greatest amount of trash Carly picked up was 3 pounds. The least amount was $\frac{1}{2}$ pound.

Subtract. $3 - \frac{1}{2} = 2\frac{1}{2}$ pounds

Remember to use equivalent fractions when necessary to help solve problems on line plots.

For **1–3**, use the line plots at the left.

1. Explain how to find the total weight of the trash Freddie picked up.

2. Write and solve an equation to find the difference between the greatest amount Freddie collected and the least amount Carly collected.

3. What is the sum of Carly's most frequent weight and Freddie's most frequent weight? Explain.

Think about these questions to help you **critique the reasoning** of others.

Thinking Habits

- What questions can I ask to understand other people's thinking?

- Are there mistakes in other people's thinking?

- Can I improve other people's thinking?

Remember you can use math to identify mistakes in people's thinking.

Distance of Deliveries

Miles

1. Spencer says $2\frac{3}{8}$ miles is not an outlier because there are two dots above it. Do you agree? Explain.

Name _____

1. Which weights are least common?

Weights of Puppies in a Litter

Pounds

$2\frac{1}{2}$ $2\frac{3}{4}$ 3 $3\frac{1}{4}$ $3\frac{1}{2}$

2. How many dots would be placed above $1\frac{3}{4}$ in a line plot of this data?

Glasses of Water

DATA				
$1\frac{1}{2}$	$2\frac{1}{2}$	$1\frac{3}{4}$	2	$1\frac{3}{4}$
$2\frac{1}{4}$	3	$1\frac{1}{2}$	$2\frac{1}{2}$	$3\frac{1}{2}$
$1\frac{3}{4}$	2	$3\frac{1}{2}$	$1\frac{1}{4}$	$2\frac{1}{4}$

Ⓐ 3 dots   Ⓒ 1 dot

Ⓑ 2 dots   Ⓓ 0 dots

3. Which is the most common length of snail Fred has in his backyard?

Lengths of Snails

Inches

$2\frac{1}{4}$ $2\frac{2}{4}$ $2\frac{3}{4}$ 3 $3\frac{1}{4}$ $3\frac{2}{4}$ $3\frac{3}{4}$

4. During a sleep study, the number of hours 15 people slept was recorded in the table below.

Hours of Sleep in One Night

DATA				
9	6	7	$6\frac{1}{2}$	$5\frac{1}{2}$
8	$7\frac{1}{2}$	8	$7\frac{1}{2}$	7
6	$5\frac{1}{2}$	$7\frac{1}{2}$	$8\frac{1}{2}$	$6\frac{1}{2}$

Part A

Use the data in the table to draw a line plot.

Part B

How many more hours did the person who slept the greatest number of hours sleep than the person who slept the least number of hours? Explain.

5. Use the line plot below. Select all the true statements.

Heights of Bean Plants

Inches

☐ The greatest height is $2\frac{1}{2}$ inches.

☐ More plants have a height of 2 inches than $1\frac{1}{2}$ inches.

☐ There are 3 plants with a height of 1 inch.

☐ There are 3 plants with a height of 2 inches and 3 plants with a height of $2\frac{1}{2}$ inches.

☐ The tallest plant is $1\frac{1}{2}$ inches taller than the shortest plant.

6. Mr. Tricorn's class is tracking the number of books read each week. The class goal is to read 50 books. How many more books does the class need to read to meet their goal? Explain.

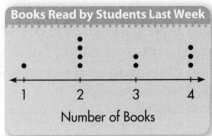

Books Read by Students Last Week

Number of Books

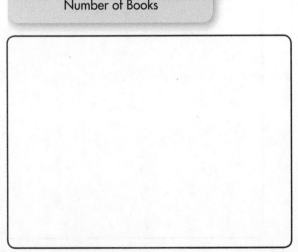

7. Use the line plot from Exercise 6. How many students read fewer than 4 books?

Ⓐ 9 students   Ⓒ 7 students

Ⓑ 8 students   Ⓓ 6 students

8. Ms. Garcia measured the heights of her students. Use the data in the table to draw a line plot.

DATA	Heights of Students in Ms. Garcia's Class (feet)				
	4	$3\frac{3}{4}$	$4\frac{1}{4}$	$4\frac{1}{2}$	4
	$3\frac{3}{4}$	$3\frac{1}{2}$	$4\frac{1}{2}$	4	$3\frac{3}{4}$
	4	$4\frac{1}{4}$	$4\frac{1}{4}$	4	$4\frac{1}{2}$

9. Use the data in Exercise 8. For 9a–9d, choose *Yes* or *No* to tell if each statement is true.

9a. There are no outliers.
○ Yes   ○ No

9b. The tallest student is $4\frac{1}{2}$ feet.
○ Yes   ○ No

9c. The shortest student is $3\frac{3}{4}$ feet.
○ Yes   ○ No

9d. The tallest student is 1 foot taller than the shortest student.
○ Yes   ○ No

Name _____

Measuring Pumpkins

Mr. Chan's class picked small pumpkins from the pumpkin patch and then weighed their pumpkins.

1. The class weighed their pumpkins and made the **Pumpkin Weights** line plot of the data.

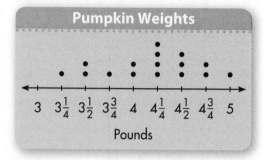

Part A

What is the most common weight of the pumpkins?

Part B

Write and solve an equation to find how much more the heaviest pumpkin weighs than the pumpkin that weighs the least.

Part C

Ayana said 3 pumpkins weigh $4\frac{1}{2}$ pounds.
Critique Ayana's reasoning. Is she correct?

2. The class also measures the length around their pumpkins to the nearest half-inch. They recorded their data in the **Pumpkin Size** list.

Pumpkin Size: $19\frac{1}{2}$, $20\frac{1}{2}$, $19\frac{1}{2}$, 20, $20\frac{1}{2}$, $21\frac{1}{2}$, 20, 21, 22, $19\frac{1}{2}$, $20\frac{1}{2}$, $21\frac{1}{2}$, 21, 21, $21\frac{1}{2}$, $20\frac{1}{2}$

Part A

Draw a line plot of **Pumpkin Size** data.

Part B

Drew says 1 more pumpkin was $20\frac{1}{2}$ inches around than was $19\frac{1}{2}$ inches around because $20\frac{1}{2} - 19\frac{1}{2} = 1$. Critique Drew's reasoning. Is Drew correct?

Part C

What is the difference between the longest length and the shortest length? Write and solve an equation.

Understand and Compare Decimals

Essential Questions: How can you write a fraction as a decimal? How can you locate points on a number line? How do you compare decimals?

Digital Resources

Solve   Learn   Glossary   Practice Buddy

Tools   Assessment   Help   Games

Curling is an Olympic sport that uses special stones and a target.

Players can make their stones move the other team's stones by transferring energy when they collide.

Curling must take a lot of energy! Here is a project about energy and decimals.

Math and Science Project: Energy and Decimals

Do Research Use the Internet or other sources to research other sports or games where players transfer energy to cause collisions in order to score points and win.

Journal: Write a Report Include what you found. Also in your report:

- Explain how the transfer of energy helps the player or team score.

- A game of curling is broken into ten rounds called *ends*. Suppose a team wins 6 of the 10 ends. Write a fraction with a denominator of 10 and an equivalent fraction with a denominator of 100. Then, write an equivalent decimal that represents the same value.

Name _____

Review What You Know

A-Z Vocabulary

Choose the best term from the box.
Write it on the blank.

| • hundredth | • tens |
| • place value | • tenth |

1. A _____ is one of 10 equal parts of a whole, written as $\frac{1}{10}$.

2. _____ is the position of a digit in a number that is used to determine the value of the digit.

3. A _____ is one of 100 equal parts of a whole, written as $\frac{1}{100}$.

Comparing Fractions

Write >, <, or = in the ◯.

4. $\frac{5}{100}$ ◯ $\frac{5}{10}$

5. $\frac{1}{10}$ ◯ $\frac{1}{100}$

6. $\frac{2}{10}$ ◯ $\frac{20}{100}$

Parts of a Whole

Complete each fraction to represent the shaded part of the whole.

7. $\frac{\square}{10}$

8. $\frac{\square}{10}$

9. $\frac{\square}{10}$

Shade the part of the whole that represents the fraction.

10. $\frac{22}{100}$

11. $\frac{79}{100}$

12. $\frac{37}{100}$

Problem Solving

13. **Reasoning** Rob walked $\frac{2}{10}$ block. Drew walked $\frac{5}{10}$ block. Write a comparison for the distance Rob and Drew each walked.

My Word Cards

Use the examples for each word on the front of the card to help complete the definitions on the back.

tenth

hundredth

decimal

0.07
0.25
1.45

decimal point

0.07   0.25   1.45

My Word Cards

One part of 100 equal parts of a whole is called a _____.

One part of 10 equal parts of a whole is called a _____.

A dot used to separate dollars from cents in money or separate ones from tenths in a number is called a _____.

A number with one or more digits to the right of the decimal point is called a _____.

ame _____

Help Practice Tools Games
Buddy

Homework
& Practice 12-1
Fractions and
Decimals

Another Look!

How can you represent
a number as a fraction or
a decimal?

 30 parts out
of 100 is 0.30.

$\frac{30}{100} = 0.30$

 3 parts out of
10 is 0.3.

$\frac{3}{10} = 0.3$

You can use grids
to help write fractions
and decimals.

So, $\frac{30}{100} = \frac{3}{10}$ and $0.30 = 0.3$.
These decimals and fractions
are equivalent.

For **1–3**, write a decimal and fraction for each grid.

1.

2.

3.

For **4–7**, shade the grid for each fraction and write the decimal.

4. $\frac{1}{10}$

5. $\frac{8}{10}$

6. $\frac{29}{100}$

7. $\frac{4}{100}$

8. On Tuesday, Pierce ran $\frac{3}{4}$ mile and walked $\frac{3}{4}$ mile. On Wednesday, he ran $\frac{2}{4}$ mile and walked $1\frac{1}{4}$ miles. How much farther did Pierce run and walk on Wednesday than on Tuesday? Explain.

9. **Critique Reasoning** Monique said, "0.7 is greater than 0.7 because 70 is greater than 7." Do you agree with Monique? Wh or why not?

10. Jaclynn had 84 cents. Her brother gave her another 61 cents. Write the amount of money Jaclynn now has as a decimal. Explain.

11. **Higher Order Thinking** Hugh uses 0.6 of a piece of canvas to paint a picture. Draw a model to represent this decimal. How much of the canvas is left?

12. Look at the floor plan below. Which fraction and decimal describe the part of the grocery store that is used for food?

☐ Food ■ Kitchenware
☐ Toiletries ■ Pharmacy

Ⓐ $\frac{7}{100}$; 0.07

Ⓑ $\frac{1}{10}$; 0.1

Ⓒ $\frac{73}{100}$; 0.73

Ⓓ $\frac{73}{10}$; 7.3

Use the key for the floor plan to find the part of the store that is used for food.

13. Which grid represents 0.85?

Ⓐ

Ⓑ

Ⓒ

Ⓓ

Help　Practice Buddy　Tools　Games

Another Look!

You can use a number line to locate decimals and fractions.

There are 10 sections between each whole number. That means each section is one tenth, or 0.1. You can count the sections to determine the decimal for the point on the number line.

7 sections means the point is at 0.7.

There are ten sections between each tenth. That means each section is one hundredth, or $\frac{1}{100}$. You can count the sections to determine the fraction for the point on the number line.

6 sections means the point is at $5\frac{76}{100}$.

For **1–5**, name the point on the number line for each decimal.

1. 10.1　　**2.** 10.28　　**3.** 10.25　　**4.** 9.6　　**5.** 10.0

For **6–10**, name the fraction for each point on the number line.

6. Q　　**7.** R　　**8.** S　　**9.** T　　**10.** V

11. Which two points on the number line represent the same point?

12. Model with Math Ben says $7\frac{9}{100}$ must be less than $7\frac{2}{10}$ because 9 hundredths is less than 2 tenths. Do you agree? Draw a number line to show how you know.

13. Higher Order Thinking According to the Greek mathematician Zeno, if each bounce of a ball is half the height of the bounce before it, the ball will never stop bouncing. Write the fractions in hundredths that should be written at points *B* and *C*.

14. The girls have to each write a 10-page paper.

Joanna has written 7 pages.
Amber has written 3 pages.
Esme has written 6 pages.
Lisa has written 9 pages.

Choose names to match the girl with the decimal that represents how much of the paper she written.

The scale on a bar graph is a vertical number line.

Name _____

Solve & Share

A penny made in 1982 weighs about 0.11 ounce. A penny made in 2013 weighs about 0.09 ounce. Which penny weighs more? **Solve this problem any way you choose.**

I can ...
compare decimals by reasoning about their size.

Content Standard 4.NS.7
Process Standards PS.2, PS.3, PS.5

You can construct arguments. Thinking about what you know about place value can help justify your reasoning.

Look Back! **Construct Arguments** Simon and Danielle are eating oranges. Danielle says, "Because we each have 0.75 of an orange left, we have the same amount left to eat." Do you agree with Danielle? Explain.

Essential Question **How Do You Compare Decimals?**

A

Donovan ran the 100-meter race in 10.11 seconds. Sal ran the same race in 10.09 seconds. Who had the faster time?

Donovan 10.11s

Sal 10.09 s

There is more than one way to compare decimals when they refer to the same whole.

B ## One Way

Use hundredths grids.

The digits in the tens and ones places are the same. Compare the digits in the tenths place.

10.11   10.09

10.11 > 10.09

~~faster time~~

C ## Another Way

Use place value.

The whole number parts are the same.

The decimal parts are both to the hundredths.

11 hundredths is greater than 9 hundredths.

10.11 > 10.09

Sal had the faster time.

D ## Another Way

Start at the left.

Compare each place value. Look for the first place where the digits are different.

10.11   10.09

1 tenth > 0 tenths

10.11 > 10.09

Sal had the faster time.

Convince Me! **Reasoning** Write four different digits in the blank spaces to make each comparison true. Explain your reasoning.

0. ___ 8 < 0. ___ 7   0. 5 ___ > 0. ___ 9

Another Example!

Compare 0.23 and 0.32.

0.23 < 0.32

 = 1 = 0.1 = 0.01

> You can use place-value blocks to compare.

Guided Practice

Do You Understand?

1. **Critique Reasoning** Cy says, "0.20 is greater than 0.2 because 20 is greater than 2." Do you agree? Explain.

Do You Know How?

For **2–5**, write >, <, or = in each ◯. Use place-value blocks or grids as needed to compare.

2. 0.70 ◯ 0.57   3. 0.41 ◯ 0.14

4. 6.28 ◯ 7.31   5. 1.1 ◯ 1.10

Independent Practice

Leveled Practice For **6–14**, write >, <, or = in each ◯. Use place-value blocks, grids, or number lines to help as needed.

6.

0.01 ◯ 0.1

7.

0.31 ◯ 0.29

8.

0.44 ◯ 0.22

9. 0.1 ◯ 0.10

10. $2.98 ◯ $2.56

11. 7.01 ◯ 7.1

12. 0.08 ◯ 0.7

13. 3.40 ◯ 3.4

14. $21.50 ◯ $20.99

For **15–20**, write a decimal to make the comparison true.

15. _____ < 0.23

16. 8.60 = _____

17. _____ > 4.42

18. 13.2 > _____

19. 5.2 < _____

20. 6.21 = _____

Problem Solving

21. Use Appropriate Tools Maria timed how long it took her Venus Fly Trap to close. The first time it took 0.43 seconds to close. The second time took 0.6 seconds to close. Which was the faster time? Draw place-value blocks to show your comparison.

22. Fishing lures have different weights. Which lure weighs more?

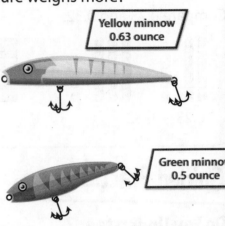

Yellow minnow
0.63 ounce

Green minnow
0.5 ounce

23. Number Sense Ellen wants to give about 125 toys to each of 7 charities. In one week, she collects 387 toys. The next week, she collects 515 toys. Has Ellen reached her goal? Explain.

24. Higher Order Thinking Tori has two different-sized water bottles. In the large bottle, she has 0.81 liter of water. In the smaller bottle, she has 1.1 liters of water. Can you tell whether one bottle has more water? Explain.

25. Stanley found the weights of two minerals, quartz and garnet. The quartz weighed 3.76 ounces and the garnet weighed 3.68 ounces.

Explain how Stanley can use a model to find which mineral weighed more.

Explain how Stanley can use place value to find which mineral weighed less.

Name _____

Another Look!

Patrick collected change for charity. On Friday, he collected $7.28. On Saturday, he collected $7.15. On which day did Patrick collect more money? Use a number line to compare the amounts.

```
        $7.15       $7.28
←++++++|++++++•++++|+++++•++++|++++++|++++++→
 $7.00   $7.10   $7.20   $7.30   $7.40   $7.50
```

Because $7.28 is farther to the right on the number line, it is the greater number.

So, $7.28 > $7.15.

Patrick collected more money on Friday.

There are different ways to compare decimals.

For **1–11**, write $>$, $<$, or $=$ in each ◯. Use place-value blocks, grids, or number lines to help as needed.

1.

0.37 ◯ 0.77

2.

2.40 ◯ 2.5

3. 0.6 ◯ 0.55

4. 0.2 ◯ 0.20

5. 0.68 ◯ 0.59

6. $10.45 ◯ $10.54

7. 0.99 ◯ 1.0

8. 0.05 ◯ 0.04

9. 4.1 ◯ 4.10

10. 6.44 ◯ 6.4

11. $0.93 ◯ $0.39

For **12–20**, write a decimal to make the comparison true.

12. _____ > 1.45

13. $7.8 =$ _____

14. _____ > 4.42

15. $29.20 >$ _____

16. $8.99 <$ _____

17. $13.41 =$ _____

18. $22.18 <$ _____

19. _____ > 3.48

20. $9.4 >$ _____

21. Maria told Patrick that her quarter weighs less than what a nickel weighs because 0.2 has fewer digits than 0.18. How can Patrick show Maria that 0.2 is greater than 0.18?

Quarter 0.2 oz

Nickel 0.18 oz

22. Construct Arguments Kimmy drew the number line below and wrote the comparison shown. Is her comparison correct? Explain?

10   11   12

10.9 days   11.5 hours

10.9 days < 11.5 hours

23. 🔤 **Vocabulary** Use a vocabulary term to make the sentence true.

In 37.2, the ones place and the tenths place are separated by a _____.

24. Higher Order Thinking Tamar is thinking of a number in the hundredths. Her number is greater than 0.8 and less than 0.9. The greatest digit in the number is in the hundredths place. What number is Tamar thinking of? Explain.

Assessment ISTEP+ Ready

25. Andy mailed two packages. The first package weighed 2.48 pounds, and the second weighed 2.6 pounds. Andy said, "The first package will cost more to send because it weighs more."

Part A

What mistake could Andy have made? What can he do to correct it?

Part B

Andy mailed a third package weighing 2.5 pounds. Did the third package weigh more or less than the first package? Describe how you would use place-value blocks to compare the weights.

Name _____

☆ ☆
Solve & Share

     The mural is divided into 100 equal parts. Marilyn's class painted $\frac{3}{10}$ of the mural, and Cal's class painted $\frac{27}{100}$ of the mural. How much of the mural have the two classes painted? *Solve this problem any way you choose.*

Lesson 12-4
Add Fractions with Denominators of 10 and 100

I can ...
use equivalence to add fractions with denominators of 10 and 100.

Content Standard 4.C.5
Process Standards PS.1, PS.2, PS.3, PS.4, PS.5

You can use appropriate tools. Think about how you can use the grid to find how much of the mural the two classes painted. *Show your work in the space above!*

Look Back! **Reasoning** How much of the mural remains to be painted? Write the amount as a decimal.

How Can You Add Fractions with Denominators of 10 and 100?

A

Jana and Steve collected money for an animal shelter. Jana collected $\frac{5}{100}$ of their goal while Steve collected $\frac{4}{10}$. How much of their goal did Jana and Steve collect?

Use like denominators to add fractions.

Paws and Tails Animal Shelter

0                 $\frac{10}{10}$

B

The red shows $\frac{4}{10}$ of the goal and the blue shows $\frac{5}{100}$ of the goal.

The amount they collected can be written as $\frac{4}{10} + \frac{5}{100}$.

You can use equivalent fractions to write tenths as hundredths.

C

Rewrite $\frac{4}{10}$ as an equivalent fraction with a denominator of 100.

Multiply the numerator and denominator by 10.

$$\frac{4}{10} \times \frac{10}{10} = \frac{40}{100}$$

D

Add the numerators and write the sum over the like denominator.

$$\frac{40}{100} + \frac{5}{100} = \frac{45}{100}$$

Jana and Steve collected $\frac{45}{100}$ of their goal.

Convince Me! **Construct Arguments** In the problem above, why is the denominator 100 and not 200?

---

646   **Topic 12** | Lesson 12-4

Guided Practice

Practice Buddy Tools Assessment

Do You Understand?

1. Suppose Jana collected another $\frac{25}{100}$ of their goal. What fraction of the goal have they now collected?

2. **Model with Math** Write a problem that represents the addition shown below, then solve.

Do You Know How?

For **3–8**, add the fractions.

3. $\frac{3}{10} + \frac{4}{100}$

4. $\frac{71}{100} + \frac{5}{10}$

5. $\frac{3}{100} + \frac{38}{10}$

6. $\frac{90}{100} + \frac{1}{10}$

7. $\frac{8}{10} + \frac{1}{10} + \frac{7}{100}$

8. $\frac{38}{100} + \frac{4}{10} + \frac{2}{10}$

Independent Practice

Leveled Practice For **9–23**, add the fractions.

9. $\frac{21}{100} + \frac{2}{10} = \frac{21}{100} + \frac{\square}{100}$

10. $\frac{\square}{10} + \frac{68}{100} = \frac{30}{100} + \frac{68}{100}$

11. $\frac{4}{10} + \frac{60}{100} = \frac{\square}{10} + \frac{\square}{10}$

12. $\frac{32}{100} + \frac{28}{100} + \frac{6}{10}$

13. $\frac{11}{10} + \frac{41}{100}$

14. $\frac{72}{100} + \frac{6}{10}$

15. $\frac{5}{10} + \frac{3}{10} + \frac{18}{100}$

16. $\frac{7}{100} + \frac{6}{10}$

17. $\frac{9}{10} + \frac{4}{100}$

18. $\frac{30}{100} + \frac{5}{10}$

19. $\frac{39}{100} + \frac{2}{10}$

20. $\frac{8}{10} + \frac{9}{100}$

21. $\frac{44}{100} + \frac{34}{100} + \frac{9}{10}$

22. $\frac{70}{10} + \frac{33}{100}$

23. $\frac{28}{10} + \frac{72}{10} + \frac{84}{100}$

Problem Solving

24. Algebra A mail carrier made a total of 100 deliveries in a day. $\frac{76}{100}$ of the deliveries were letters, $\frac{2}{10}$ were packages, and the rest were postcards. Write and solve an equation to find the fraction that represents how many of the deliveries were postcards.

25. Make Sense and Persevere Balloons are sold in bags of 30. There are 5 giant balloons in each bag. How many giant balloons will you get if you buy 120 balloons? Explain.

There is a hidden question in this problem.

26. Higher Order Thinking Of the first 100 elements on the periodic table, $\frac{13}{100}$ were discovered in ancient times, and $\frac{21}{100}$ were discovered in the Middle Ages. Another $\frac{5}{10}$ were discovered in the 1800s. What fraction of the first 100 elements was discovered *after* the 1800s? Explain.

27. Delia knocked over 7 out of 10 pins in the first frame of bowling. The next 9 frames, she knocked over a total of 67 more pins of the 100 possible pins in the game. Delia wanted to find the fraction that represented the number of pins she knocked over in the game. Her work is shown below.

$$\frac{7}{10} + \frac{67}{100}$$

$$\frac{70}{100} + \frac{67}{100} = \frac{137}{100} \text{ pins}$$

Is Delia's work correct? If not, explain her mistake.

Another Look!

In the morning, Duncan sold
$\frac{27}{100}$ of the items in his yard sale.
In the afternoon, he sold another
$\frac{6}{10}$ of the items.

What fraction of the items did
Duncan sell?

Find $\frac{27}{100} + \frac{6}{10}$.

Use equivalent fractions
to find how many of the
items Duncan sold.

Rename one of the fractions using
a common denominator.

$\frac{6}{10} \times \frac{10}{10} = \frac{60}{100}$

Add

$\frac{27}{100} + \frac{60}{100} = \frac{87}{100}$

Duncan sold $\frac{87}{100}$ of the items.

For **1–15**, add the fractions.

1. $\frac{31}{100} + \frac{4}{10} = \frac{31}{100} + \frac{\square}{100} = \frac{\square}{100}$

2. $\frac{17}{100} + \frac{9}{10} = \frac{17}{100} + \frac{\square}{\square} = 1\frac{7}{100}$

3. $\frac{\square}{\square} + \frac{3}{\square} = \frac{2}{\square} + \frac{\square}{10} = \frac{5}{10}$

4. $\frac{6}{10} + \frac{39}{100}$

5. $\frac{7}{10} + \frac{22}{100}$

6. $\frac{9}{100} + \frac{3}{10} + \frac{5}{10}$

7. $2\frac{4}{10} + \frac{33}{100}$

8. $\frac{19}{100} + \frac{21}{100} + \frac{3}{10}$

9. $\frac{9}{10} + \frac{30}{100}$

0. $\frac{1}{100} + \frac{25}{10}$

11. $1\frac{3}{10} + 2\frac{8}{100}$

12. $\frac{27}{100} + \frac{2}{10}$

3. $\frac{3}{10} + \frac{4}{10} + \frac{53}{100}$

14. $\frac{64}{100} + \frac{33}{100}$

15. $3\frac{3}{10} + \frac{42}{100} + \frac{33}{100}$

16. Model with Math Cecily purchases a box of 100 paper clips. She puts $\frac{37}{100}$ of the paper clips in a jar on her desk and puts another $\frac{6}{10}$ in her drawer at home. Shade a grid that shows how many of the paper clips are in Cecily's jar and drawer, then write the fraction the grid represents.

17. Robyn sells 100 tickets to the fourth-grade play. The table shows how many c each ticket she sold. What fraction of the tickets were adult and student tickets?

DATA	Ticket	Number
	Adult	$\frac{38}{100}$
	Child	$\frac{22}{100}$
	Student	$\frac{4}{10}$

18. Math and Science Balls colliding on a pool table are an example of how energy changes when objects collide. When two balls collide, the first ball loses speed and the second ball moves. What is the combined distance the two balls traveled?

19. Higher Order Thinking Alecia walked $\frac{3}{10}$ of a mile from school, stopped at the grocery store on the way, then walked another $\frac{4}{10}$ of a mile home. Georgia walked $\frac{67}{100}$ of a mile from school to her home. Which of the girls lives farther from school? Explain.

20. Regina kept a reading log of how much of her 100-page book she read each day. She read $\frac{33}{100}$ of the book on Monday, $\frac{4}{10}$ of the book on Tuesday, and another 35 pages on Wednesday. Did Regina fill out her reading log correctly? Explain.

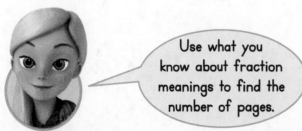

Use what you know about fraction meanings to find the number of pages.

Name _____

☆ ☆
Solve & Share

A flash drive costs $24, including tax. A customer purchases 3 flash drives and pays the cashier $80. How much change should the cashier give back to the customer? *Solve this problem any way you choose.*

I can ...
use fractions or decimals to solve word problems involving money.

Content Standard 4.M.3
Process Standards PS.1, PS.2, PS.4, PS.7, PS.8

You can make sense and persevere. What do you need to find first to answer the question?

$24.00

Look Back! **Generalize** How can you estimate and check if your solution is reasonable?

How Can You Solve Word Problems Involving Money?

A

Marcus buys a toy airplane and a toy car. How much does Marcus spend? How much more does the toy airplane cost than the toy car?

$1.12

$3.32

You can draw or use bills and coins to solve problems involving money.

B

Find $3.32 + $1.12.

Cost of Airplane   **Cost of Car**

Add the bills, then count on to add each type of coin.

$4.00 + $0.40 + $0.04 = $4.44

Marcus spent $4.44.

C

Find $3.32 − $1.12.

Start with the cost of the airplane, then subtract the cost of the car.

Count the remaining bills and coins.

$2.00 + $0.20 = $2.20

The toy airplane costs $2.20 more than the toy car.

Convince Me! **Use Structure** In the examples above, how can you use place value to help add or subtract?

Help   Practice Buddy   Tools   Games

Another Look!

Add

$1.25 + $2.01

$1.25 + $2.01 = $3.26

You can use coins and bills to add, subtract, multiply, and divide with money.

Subtract

$2.28 − $1.25

$2.28 − $1.25 = $1.03

Multiply

$2.01 × 2

$2.01 × 2 = $4.02

Divide

$3.03 ÷ 3

$3.03 ÷ 3 = $1.01

For **1–2**, draw or use coins and bills to solve.

1. Mrs. Hargrove owes the doctor $34.56. She gives the clerk $50.00.

   a. List Mrs. Hargrove's change using the least number of coins and bills.

   b. What is the total amount of change Mrs. Hargrove should receive?

2. Emma buys a game for $26.84. She gives the clerk $30.00.

   a. List Emma's change using the least number of coins and bills.

   b. What is the total amount of change Emma should receive?

3. **Model With Math** Three friends combine their money to buy tickets for a hockey game. If they share the change evenly, how much will each friend receive? Write equations to represent the problem, then solve.

Money given for tickets

4. **Reasoning** Niall has a half dollar, Krista has a quarter dollar, Mary has a tenth of a dollar, and Jack has a hundredth of a dollar. If they combine their money, do the 4 students have more or less than a dollar? Explain.

5. Jessie has 14 half-dollar coins, but she needs quarters to do her laundry. If she trades her half-dollar coins for quarters, how many quarters will Jessie have? Explain.

6. **Higher Order Thinking** Julia and Carl buy 2 sandwiches, 1 salad, 1 piece of fruit, and 2 drinks for lunch. They give the cashier $20.03. What coins and bills could they receive in change? Draw or use coins and bills to solve.

Menu	
Sandwich	$3.96
Chips	$0.79
Fruit	$1.24
Salad	$2.17
Drink	$1.55

Assessment ISTEP+ Ready

7. Claire has a $60 gift card. She uses the whole value of the card to buy 4 copies of the same book to give as gifts. How much does each book cost?

Ⓐ $15

Ⓑ $20

Ⓒ $40

Ⓓ $60

8. Larisa buys 3 purses. Each purse costs $126.32. How much did Larisa spend? Draw or use bills and coins to solve.

Ⓐ $126.32

Ⓑ $256.64

Ⓒ $378.96

Ⓓ $505.28

Name _____

☆ Solve & Share ☆

Three people hiked the same 1-mile trail. The distance for each hiker is represented in the drawings. Show about where the 1-mile mark should be on each drawing. Explain.

Start   0.5 mi ⟶

Start   0.25 mi ⟶

Start   0.75 mi ⟶

Problem Solving

Lesson 12-6
Look For and Use Structure

I can ...
use the structure of the place-value system to solve problems.

ⓙ **Process Standards** PS.7 Also PS.1, PS.2, PS.3, PS.4, PS.6
Content Standard 4.M.3

Thinking Habits

Be a good thinker! These questions can help you.

- What patterns can I see and describe?

- How can I use the patterns to solve the problem?

- Can I see expressions and objects in different ways?

Look Back! **Look For Relationships** The three drawings represent 0.5, 0.25, and 0.75 mile with equivalent lengths. How does this affect where 1-mile is located on each drawing?

How Can You Look for and Make Use of Structure to Solve Problems?

A

Maps from two different ski resorts show a 1-mile cross-country ski trail for beginners. Show about where to mark 0.25, 0.5, and 0.75 mile on each trail.

How can you determine where to mark the points on each drawing?

I need to analyze each drawing and decide about where the given decimals should be located on each.

Start   1 mile

Start   1 mile

B How can I make use of structure to solve this problem?

I can

- break the problem into simpler parts.

- use what I know about decimal meanings to locate the points.

- use equivalent forms of numbers.

C Here's my thinking.

The size of a decimal depends on the size of the whole. The size of the whole is not the same for each drawing. Divide each whole in half to show **0.5** on each whole.

Divide each half into two equal parts to show **0.25** and **0.75** on each whole.

Convince Me! **Use Structure** Use the drawing of the trail shown. Where is the 1.5-mile mark on the trail? How did you decide?

Guided Practice *

Use Structure

Margie painted 0.4 of her banner blue.
Helena painted 0.5 of her banner blue.

Margie's banner

0   0.4

Helena's banner

0   0.5

1. Complete the drawings to show the whole, or 1, for each banner.

2. Explain how you determined where to draw 1 whole for each banner.

> You can use the structure of the place value system to locate decimals on a number line.

3. Do the drawings show 0.4 < 0.5? Explain.

ndependent Practice *

e Structure

itlin is making a map for a 1-mile scavenger hunt. She wants
e stops to be 0.5 mile, 0.3 mile, and 0.85 mile from the start.

Start   End

. Label 0.25, 0.5, 0.75 on the number line as a scale reference. Explain how you decided where to mark the number line.

. Estimate where 0.3 and 0.85 are located compared to the other points. Mark the points 0.3 and 0.85. Explain how you estimated.

r another example, see Set F on page 666.
Topic 12 | Lesson 12-6

Problem Solving

Watching Savings Grow

Tomas deposits money in his savings account every month. If he continues to save $3.50 each month, how much money will he have at the end of 6 months? 12 months? Use the table and Exercises 6–11 to help solve.

Month	Money in Savings Account
0	$10.00
1	$13.50
2	$17.00
3	$20.50

6. **Reasoning** What quantities are given in the problem and what do the numbers mean?

7. **Make Sense and Persevere** What do you need to find?

8. **Use Structure** What is the relationship between the amount of money Tomas will have in his savings account in the fourth month and the amount in the third month?

> When you look for and make use of structure, you break a problem into simpler parts.

9. **Model with Math** Write an expression that can be used to find the amount saved at the end of 6 months.

10. **Model with Math** Complete the table to find how much Tomas will have saved in 6 months.

11. **Be Precise** Use the answers from the table to find how much money Tomas will have at the end of 12 months. Show your work.

Another Look!

Do the number lines show 0.2 = 0.5?

Tell how you can use the structure of a number line to analyze the relationships between decimals.

- I can break the problem into simpler parts.

- I can use what I know about decimal meanings.

Use the number line to help you find if the decimals represent parts of the same whole.

On the third number line, you can use the distance between 0 and 0.2 as a guide to mark **0.4**, **0.6**, **0.8**, and **1**.

On the fourth number line, you can use the distance between 0 and 0.5 as a guide to mark **1**.

To find **1**, you can make a mark that is the same distance to the right of 0.5 as 0.5 is from 0.

When the size of the whole is not the same on the two number lines, the number lines cannot be used to show equivalent decimals.

se Structure

nton knows it is $\frac{1}{2}$ mile from his home to the store along Main reet. He wants to find how far it is from his home to school.

Home   Store   School

. Label 1, 1.5, and 2 on the drawing. Explain how you determined where to label each number.

> When you look for relationships, you use equivalent forms of numbers.

. How far does Anton live from school? Explain.

Training

Liz trains for rock climbing 4 days a week. Her first 4 days of training are shown in the table. She plans to increase the distance each time she climbs. Did Liz climb farther on the first two days than the last two days?

Day	Distance Liz Climbed
1	0.09 km
2	0.1 km
3	0.11 km
4	0.07 km

3. **Reasoning** What quantities are given in the problem and what do the numbers mean?

4. **Make Sense and Persevere** What do you need to find?

5. **Reasoning** What hidden questions need to be answered before answering the main question?

When you look for relationships, you break problems into simpler parts to solve.

6. **Model with Math** Use equivalent fractions to write equations to find the distances Liz climbed the first two days and the last two days.

7. **Construct Arguments** Did Liz climb farther the first two days or the last two days? Use a number line to justify your answer.

Follow the Path

Shade a path from **Start** to **Finish**. Follow the sums or differences that round to 2,000 when rounded to the nearest thousand. You can only move up, down, right, or left.

I can ...

add and subtract multi-digit whole numbers.

Start				
954 + 871	2,000 − 1,876	3,887 + 369	2,195 − 737	2,698 + 400
8,998 − 7,399	1,810 + 789	8,917 − 5,252	6,295 − 3,290	8,506 − 3,282
1,789 + 210	1,340 − 771	2,615 + 347	9,000 − 6,233	5,896 + 5,601
6,726 − 4,309	1,199 + 468	3,300 − 298	9,444 + 9,444	3,922 − 923
3,856 + 1,144	4,239 − 2,239	5,999 − 4,370	5,607 − 3,605	2,203 + 122

Finish

TOPIC 12 **Vocabulary Review**

Glossary

Word List

- decimal
- decimal point
- equivalent
- fraction
- greater than symbol (>)
- hundredth
- less than symbol (<)
- tenth

Understand Vocabulary

Choose the best term from the box. Write it on the blank.

1. A dot used to separate dollars from cents or ones from tenths in a number is called a _____.

2. One part of 100 equal parts of a whole is called a _____.

3. Numbers that name the same amount are _____.

4. A symbol, such as $\frac{2}{3}$, $\frac{5}{1}$, or $\frac{8}{5}$, used to name part of a whole, part of a set, or a location on a number line is called a _____.

5. One out of ten equal parts of a whole is called a _____.

For each of these terms, give an example and a non-example.

	Example	**Non-example**
6. greater than symbol (>)	_____	_____
7. less than symbol (<)	_____	_____
8. decimal	_____	_____

Use Vocabulary in Writing

9. Krista wrote $\frac{75}{100}$ and 0.75. Use at least 3 terms from the Word List to describe Krista's work.

Set A | pages 627–632

Reteaching

e essay question on a 100-point test was
orth 40 points. Write this amount as a
action and a decimal.

ere are 100 points, so each point is $\frac{1}{100}$.
is 0.40.

$\frac{}{0} = \frac{4}{10}$ and 0.40 = 0.4

Remember that the name
of a fraction can help you
write it as a decimal.

> Write a decimal and a fraction
> for each model.

1.   **2.**

3. Donnie has 4 dollars, 6 pennies, and
9 dimes. Write a decimal for the amount
of money Donnie has.

Set B | pages 633–638

cate 0.8 and 0.62 on a number line.

e distance from 0 to 0.8 is eight-tenths the
stance from 0 to 1.

$\frac{8}{10}$ or 0.8

0.8

1

0.6 0.62   0.7

aw a number line showing hundredths.
2 is between 0.6 and 0.7.

J   K L   M   N   O
5.40 5.45 5.50 5.55 5.60 5.65 5.70

> Name the decimal at each point.

1. K   **2.** M   **3.** O

> Name the point for each decimal.

4. 5.6   **5.** 5.5   **6.** 5.42

Set C | pages 639–644

mpare 1.74 and 1.08.

e digits in the ones place are the same,
look at the digits after the decimal point
compare.

1.74   1.08
7 tenths > 0 tenths
1.74 > 1.08

Remember you can use place-value blocks or
grids to visualize decimal amounts.

> Write >, <, or = in each ◯.

1. $4.13 ◯ $4.32   **2.** 0.6 ◯ 0.60

3. 5.29 ◯ 52.9   **4.** 12.91 ◯ 12.19

Find $\frac{9}{10} + \frac{49}{100}$.

Rewrite $\frac{9}{10}$ as an equivalent fraction with a denominator of 100.

$$\frac{9}{10} \times \frac{10}{10} = \frac{90}{100}$$

$$\frac{90}{100} + \frac{49}{100} = \frac{139}{100} \text{ or } 1\frac{39}{100}$$

Remember to find equivalent fractions with like denominators to help add.

Add. Use grids or place-value blocks as needed to help solve.

1. $\frac{8}{10} + \frac{40}{100}$

2. $\frac{24}{100} + \frac{6}{100}$

Find $5.21 + $1.52.

Add the bills, then count on to add each type of coin.

$6.00 + $0.50 + $0.20 + $0.03 = $6.73

Remember to take away each type of bill and coin when subtracting money.

1. Chelsea had $71.18. She bought a new pair of glasses for $59.95. Can she buy a case that costs $12.95? Explain.

2. Eddie bought 3 train tickets for $17.00 each. If he paid with three $20 bills, how much change did Eddie receive?

Think about these questions to help you **look for and make use of structure.**

Thinking Habits

- What patterns can I see and describe?

- How can I use the patterns to solve the problem?

- Can I see expressions and objects in different ways?

Remember you can use structure to break problem into simpler parts.

Raven joined a walk-a-thon. The red dot shows how far Raven walked in one hour.

1. Complete the number line below.

```
0                    1.25
        Miles
```

2. Estimate how far Raven walked in the fir hour. Explain.

ame _____

ature Club

he nature club at the school devoted a month to learning about
fferent local birds. The **Bird Traits** photos show information about
veral birds they observed.

Bird Traits

Red-tailed Hawk
Mass: 0.78 kg
Wingspan: 1.2 m

Great Horned Owl
Mass: 1.8 kg
Wingspan: 1.3 m

Blue Jay
Mass: 0.08 kg
Wingspan: 0.28 m

Sandpiper
Mass: 0.06 kg
Wingspan: 0.2 m

**. The club leader asked students to analyze and compare the measures
from the Bird Traits photos.**

Part A

Randall was asked to write the mass of a red-tailed hawk as a fraction.
Label the mass on the number line and write the equivalent fraction.

Part B

Melanie was assigned to compare the wingspans of the blue jay and the
sandpiper. Which bird had longer wings? Show the comparison on the
grids, and write the comparison using symbols.

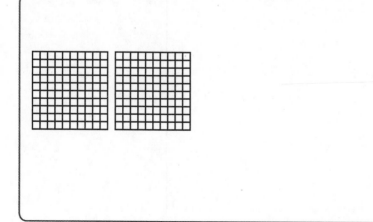

Part C

Mila compared the wingspans of the red-tailed hawk and the great horned owl. Explain how to use place value to find the longer wingspan. Show the comparison using symbols.

2. Gerald found the mass of a great horned owl and a sandpiper combined. Show how to write each mass as a fraction and then write and solve an addition equation.

3. The **Blue Jay** photo shows the wingspan of a blue jay Susannah observed.

   Susannah said the wingspan of the blue jay was greater than the wingspan of the great horned owl since 1.4 > 1.3. Do you agree? Explain.

Blue Jay

Wingspan: 1.4 ft

Measurement: Find Equivalence in Units of Measure

Essential Questions: How can you convert from one unit to another? How can you be precise when solving math problems?

Digital Resources

Solve · Learn · Glossary · Practice Buddy

Tools · Assessment · Help · Games

> The Grand Canyon in Arizona was formed by erosion.

> The Colorado River cut through the layers of rock. In some places, the canyon is more than a mile deep!

> Imagine how it will look in the future! Here is a project on erosion and measurement.

Math and Science Project: Erosion and Measurement

Do Research The Colorado River has played a large part in shaping North America. Use the Internet and other resources to research the states through which the river travels.

Journal: Write a Report Include what you found. Also in your report:

- Look up *geology* and *geometry* in the dictionary. Write the definitions and explain how these words are related. What does the prefix "geo" mean in both words?

- A.J. takes a 4-mile tour of the Grand Canyon. Explain how to convert the length of A.J.'s tour from miles to feet.

Name _____

Review What You Know

A-Z Vocabulary

Choose the best term from the box. Write it on the blank.

• capacity
• gram
• liter
• mass

1. The amount of liquid a container can hold is called its _____.

2. _____ is the amount of matter that something contains.

3. One metric unit of capacity is a _____.

Perimeter

Find the perimeter of each shape.

4.
42 centimeters

25 centimeters

5. 7 feet

6.
3 yards

7.
17 inches

12 inches   12 inches

21 inches

8. $15\frac{1}{4}$ centimeters

9.
$19\frac{11}{12}$ feet

$7\frac{5}{12}$ feet

Area

Find the area of each shape.

10.
5 yards

$2\frac{1}{2}$ yards

11.
$\frac{1}{4}$ inch 2 inches

12.
$7\frac{1}{10}$ centimeters

3 centimeters

Problem Solving

13. **Make Sense and Persevere** A league is a nautical measurement equal to about 3 miles. If a ship travels 2,000 leagues, about how many miles did the ship travel?

My Word Cards

Use the examples for each word on the front of the card to help complete the definitions on the back.

A-Z Glossary

capacity

quart (qt)

1 quart = 2 pints

gallon (gal)

1 gallon = 4 quarts

cup (c)

pint (pt)

1 pint = 2 cups

fluid ounce (fl oz)

weight

ounce (oz)

A small piece of cheese weighs about 1 ounce.

A _____ is a customary unit of capacity. One quart equals 2 pints.

_____ is the amount a container can hold, measured in liquid units.

A _____ is a customary unit of capacity.

A _____ is a customary unit of capacity. One gallon equals 4 quarts.

A _____ is a customary unit of capacity equal to 2 tablespoons.

A _____ is a customary unit of capacity. One pint equals 2 cups.

An _____ is a customary unit of weight.

_____ is how heavy an object is.

My Word Cards

Use the examples for each word on the front of the card to help complete the definitions on the back.

pound (lb)

1 pound = 16 ounces

ton (T)

A small car weighs about a ton.

1 ton = 2,000 pounds

millimeter (mm)

1 mm

CENTIMETERS

10 mm = 1 cm

1 cm

centimeter (cm)

CENTIMETERS

1 cm = 10 mm

meter (m)

METER

100 cm = 1 m

kilometer (km)

1 kilometer is about the length of 4 city blocks.

mass

milliliter (mL)

My Word Cards

Complete each definition. Extend learning by writing your own definitions.

A _____ is a customary unit of weight. One ton equals 2,000 pounds.

A _____ is a customary unit of weight. One pound equals 16 ounces.

A_____ is a metric unit of length. One hundred centimeters equals 1 meter.

A_____ is a metric unit of length. Ten millimeters equals 1 centimeter. One thousand millimeters equals 1 meter.

A _____ is a metric unit of length. One kilometer equals 1,000 meters.

A _____ is a metric unit of length equal to 100 centimeters.

A _____ is a metric unit of capacity. One thousand milliliters equals 1 liter.

_____ is the amount of matter that something contains.

My Word Cards

Use the examples for each word on the front of the card to help complete the definitions on the back.

A-Z
Glossary

liter (L)

1 L

gram (g)

1 gram

milligram (mg)

Three typical grains of salt have a combined mass of about 1 mg.

kilogram (kg)

1 kilogram

perimeter

$5 + 10 + 5 + 10 = 30$ units

area

= 9 square unit

formula

$$P = (2 \times \ell) + (2 \times w)$$
$$A = \ell \times w$$

☆
Inde

For 4

4. A
co
m

*For anoth

My Word Cards

Complete each definition. Extend learning by writing your own definitions.

A _____ is a metric unit of mass. One thousand grams equals 1 kilogram.

A_____ is a metric unit of capacity equal to 1,000 milliliters.

A_____ is a metric unit of mass equal to 1,000 grams.

A_____ is a metric unit of mass. One thousand milligrams equals 1 gram.

The number of square units needed to cover a region is its _____.

The distance around a figure is its _____.

A_____ is an equation that uses symbols to relate two or more quantities.

Name _____

☆ ☆
Solve & Share

Casey has $2\frac{1}{2}$ gallons of juice. How many 1-pint containers can he fill? *Solve this problem any way you choose.*

I can ...
convert customary units of capacity from one unit to another and recognize the relative size of different units.

You can use reasoning. Use what you know about converting a larger unit to a smaller unit. *Show your work in the space below!*

Customary Units of Capacity

DATA

1 cup (c) = 8 fluid ounces (fl oz)

1 pint (pt) = 2 c = 16 fl oz

1 quart (qt) = 2 pt = 4 c

1 gallon (gal) = 4 qt = 8 pt

Content Standards 4.M.2, 4.M.3
Process Standards PS.1, PS.2, PS.8

Look Back! **Generalize** How did you change from a larger unit of capacity to a smaller unit of capacity? Did you use the same process you used to change from a larger unit of length to a smaller unit of length? Explain.

Essential Question

How Can You Convert from One Unit of Capacity to Another?

A

Ms. Nealy's class needs 5 gallons of punch for family math night. How much of each ingredient is needed to make enough punch with the recipe shown?

Units of capacity include gallons, quarts, pints, cups, and fluid ounces.

RECIPE #116

Punch Recipe

5 pints of apple juice
4 pints lemon/lime soda
1 pint frozen orange juice

1 gal							
1 qt		1 qt		1 qt		1 qt	
1 pt	1 pt	1 pt	1 pt	1 pt	1 pt	1 pt	1 pt
1 c	1 c	1 c	1 c	1 c	1 c	1 c	1 c	1 c	1 c	1 c	1 c	1 c	1 c	1 c	1 c

B

Step 1

Convert 5 gallons to pints.

DATA

Gallons	Quarts	Pints
1	4	8
2	8	16
3	12	24
4	16	32
5	20	40

5 gallons = 40 pints

C

Step 2

Add the number of pints in the recipe to find how many batches the class needs to make.

$5 + 4 + 1 = 10$

$10 \times n = 40$

$n = 4$

The class needs to make 4 batches of the recipe.

D

Step 3

Find how much of each ingredient is in 4 batches.

$4 \times 5 = 20$ pints
$4 \times 4 = 16$ pints
$4 \times 1 = 4$ pints

20 pints of apple juice, 16 pints of lemon/lime soda, and 4 pints of frozen orange juice are needed.

Convince Me! **Reasoning** Complete the sentence below.

One gallon equals _____ quarts, _____ pints, or _____ cups.

Guided Practice

Do You Understand?

1. **Make Sense and Persevere** How many cups of punch does one batch of the recipe on the previous page make? Explain.

Do You Know How?

For **2–4**, convert each unit.

2. 2 cups = _____ fluid ounces

3. $3\frac{1}{2}$ quarts = _____ pints

4. 1 pint = _____ fluid ounces

Independent Practice

For **5–12**, convert each unit.

5. 7 quarts = _____ cups

6. 12 gallons = _____ quarts

7. 3 gallons = _____ cups

8. $1\frac{1}{2}$ quarts = _____ cups

9. $3\frac{3}{4}$ gallons = _____ pints

10. $2\frac{3}{4}$ pints = _____ fluid ounces

11. 9 cups = _____ fluid ounces

12. $3\frac{1}{2}$ pints = _____ fluid ounces

For **13–14**, complete each table.

13.

Pints	Fluid Ounces
$1\frac{1}{2}$	
$2\frac{1}{2}$	
$3\frac{1}{2}$	
$4\frac{1}{2}$	
$5\frac{1}{2}$	
$6\frac{1}{2}$	

14.

Quarts	Cups
$1\frac{1}{2}$	
$2\frac{1}{2}$	
$3\frac{1}{2}$	
$4\frac{1}{2}$	
$5\frac{1}{2}$	
$6\frac{1}{2}$	

r another example, see Set A on page 723.

Problem Solving

15. Math and Science Scientists measure how much water and debris flow past a river station at different times of the year. The water and debris are called discharge. The table shows the average discharge at the Camp Verde station on the Verde River in two months. How many more quarts of discharge per second are there in December than November?

Verde River Discharge at Camp Verde, Arizona	
Month	**Average Gallons per Second**
November	1,619
December	2,285

16. **Vocabulary** Use *capacity, length,* and *meters* to complete the definitions.

_____ is the amount of liquid a container can hold.

_____ are one unit that can be used to measure _____.

17. Higher Order Thinking A caterer combines 3 quarts of orange juice, 5 pin of milk, and 5 cups of pineapple juice to make smoothies. How many cups can be filled with smoothies? Explain.

Assessment ISTEP+ Ready

18. Annabelle had the following containers of paint leftover: $\frac{1}{2}$ gallon, $\frac{3}{4}$ quart, and $\frac{1}{4}$ gallon.

Part A
How many quarts of paint does Annabelle have left over? Explain.

Part B
Annabelle put the leftover paint in pint containers. How many pint containers d Annabelle fill? Explain.

ame _____

Homework & Practice 13-2

Equivalence with Customary Units of Capacity

Another Look!

Lance has an 8-gallon aquarium. How many 2-quart containers will it take to fill the aquarium?

Customary Units of Capacity
DATA
1 cup (c) = 8 fluid ounces (fl oz)
1 pint (pt) = 2 c = 16 fl oz
1 quart (qt) = 2 pt = 4 c
1 gallon (gal) = 4 qt = 8 pt

Step 1

Convert 8 gallons to quarts.

Gallons	Quarts
2	8
4	16
6	24
8	32

8 gallons = 32 quarts

Use the correct units as you solve measurement problems.

Step 2

Divide 32 quarts by 2.

$$
\begin{array}{r}
16 \\
2\overline{)32} \\
-2 \\
\hline
12 \\
-12 \\
\hline
0
\end{array}
$$

It takes 16 of the 2-quart containers to fill the tank.

For **1–6**, convert each unit.

. 9 pints = _____ fluid ounces

. 2 gallons = _____ pints

. $1\frac{1}{4}$ gallons = _____ pints

2. 16 quarts = _____ cups

4. $1\frac{1}{2}$ quarts = _____ cups

6. $5\frac{1}{2}$ pints = _____ fluid ounces

For **7–8**, complete each table.

.

Quarts	Fluid Ounces
$1\frac{1}{2}$	
$2\frac{1}{2}$	
$3\frac{1}{2}$	
$4\frac{1}{2}$	
$5\frac{1}{2}$	
$6\frac{1}{2}$	

8.

Gallons	Pints
$1\frac{1}{2}$	
$2\frac{1}{2}$	
$3\frac{1}{2}$	
$4\frac{1}{2}$	
$5\frac{1}{2}$	
$6\frac{1}{2}$	

9. **Number Sense** Lauren hiked 16,900 feet in the morning and 14,850 feet in the afternoon. Estimate the total number of miles Lauren hiked that day. Explain.

10. How many minutes are in 3 hours? There are 60 minutes in one hour. Complete the table.

Hours	Minutes
1	
2	
3	

11. **Math and Science** How many pounds of eroded material does the Verde River carry past a given point each hour?

12. How many pounds of eroded material does the Verde River carry past a given point in $\frac{1}{4}$ of a day?

The Verde River in Arizona carries an average of $14\frac{1}{3}$ pounds of eroded material past a given point each minute.

13. A car with a 20-gallon gas tank can go 25 miles on 1 gallon of gas. If the tank is full at the beginning of a 725-mile trip, how many times does the driver have to refill the gas tank?

14. **Higher Order Thinking** Janice needs 3 gallons of lemonade for a party. She h 4 quarts, 6 pints, and 4 cups of lemonad already made. How many cups of lemonade does Janice need? How many more cups does she need?

 Assessment ⓖ◎ (**ISTEP+ Ready**)

15. Edgar has a birdbath that holds 2 gallons of water. He only wants to fill it $\frac{3}{4}$ full.

Part A

How much water, in gallons, should Edgar put in the birdbath? Explain.

Part B

How many 1-pint containers does it tak to fill the birdbath? Explain.

ame _____

Another Look!

The world's largest horse weighed almost $1\frac{1}{2}$ tons. An average mature male horse weighs about 1,200 pounds. How much more did the largest horse weigh than an average horse?

Step 1

Convert the weight of the world's largest horse to pounds.

Tons	Pounds
$\frac{1}{2}$	1,000
1	2,000
$1\frac{1}{2}$	3,000

$1\frac{1}{2}$ tons = 3,000 pounds

Step 2

Find the difference.

3,000 lb

1,200 lb	d

$3,000 - 1,200 = d$
$d = 1,800$

The world's largest horse weighed 1,800 pounds more than an average male horse.

There are 2,000 pounds in a ton.

For **1–6**, convert each unit.

1. 21 pounds = _____ ounces

2. 8 tons = _____ pounds

3. $8\frac{3}{4}$ pounds = _____ ounces

4. $4\frac{3}{8}$ pounds = _____ ounces

5. 6 tons = _____ pounds

6. $6\frac{1}{2}$ pounds = _____ ounces

For **7–8**, complete each table.

7.

Tons	Pounds
1	
2	
3	
4	
5	

8.

Pounds	Ounces
1	
2	
3	
4	
5	

For **9–11**, use the table and art shown at the right.

9. **Be Precise** What is the total weight in ounces of Heidi's 2 guinea pigs?

10. **Be Precise** What is the total weight in ounces of the food for Heidi's guinea pigs?

Heidi's 2 guinea pigs each weigh $2\frac{1}{2}$ pounds.

11. **Higher Order Thinking** A pound of guinea pig pellets is about 3 cups of food. Each guinea pig eats $\frac{1}{4}$ cup of pellets a day. How many days will the pellets last? Explain.

DATA

Food for Heidi's Guinea Pigs	
Food	**Weight**
Grass or hay	$2\frac{1}{2}$ pounds
Vegetables	15 ounces
Pellets	5 pounds

12. **Reasoning** Which product is greater, 9×15 or 9×17? Explain how you can tell without finding the products.

13. **Make Sense and Persevere** What two 1-digit factors could you multiply to get a product between and including 40 and 50?

Assessment ISTEP+ Ready

14. Which is most likely to weigh 4 tons?

Ⓐ A watermelon

Ⓑ A man

Ⓒ A clothes dryer

Ⓓ A helicopter

15. Each stone in Ally's collection weighs about 4 ounces. Her collection weighs about 24 pounds in all. About how many stones are in Ally's collection?

Ⓐ 3 stones

Ⓑ 4 stones

Ⓒ 36 stones

Ⓓ 96 stones

Another Look!

Jasmine finished 9 centimeters of the scarf she is knitting. Manuella finished 108 millimeters of her scarf. How much longer is Manuella's scarf than Jasmine's?

> To change from a larger unit like centimeters to a smaller unit like millimeters, multiply.

Step 1

Convert 9 centimeters to millimeters.

1 centimeter = 10 millimeters

$9 \times 10 = 90$ millimeters
↑ ↑
Number of   Millimeters
centimeters per centimeter

9 centimeters = 90 millimeters

Step 2

Find the difference.

```
|---------------- 108 mm ----------------|
| 90 mm                          |   d   |
```

$108 - 90 = d$

$d = 18$

Manuella's scarf is 18 millimeters longer than Jasmine's scarf.

For **1–6**, convert each unit.

1. 7 meters = _____ centimeters

2. 8 kilometers = _____ meters

3. 65 centimeters = _____ millimeters

4. 2 meters = _____ centimeters

5. 7 kilometers = _____ meters

6. 8 meters = _____ centimeters

For **7–8**, complete each table.

7.

Kilometers	Meters
1	
2	
3	
4	
5	

8.

Meters	Centimeters
1	
2	
3	
4	
5	

For **9–11**, use the pictures at the right.

9. **Make Sense and Persevere** José bought the items shown and paid $0.53 tax. He gave the cashier a $10 bill. How much change should José get? Use coins and bills to solve.

$2.88

10. Brittney bought two bottles of shampoo like the one shown and paid $0.52 tax. How much did she spend? Use coins and bills to solve.

11. **Number Sense** How can you tell, without adding, that two bottles of shampoo cost less than a bottle of shampoo and a 2-pack of toothpaste?

$2.9

---

12. Martha had 2.35 centimeters of her hair cut off. Neil had 2.53 centimeters cut. Who had more hair cut off? Explain.

13. A spider traveled 3 meters in one minut How many centimeters did it travel?

---

14. **Be Precise** The ceiling of Mr. Vega's classroom is 3 meters high. The ceiling in the hall is 315 centimeters high. How much taller is the ceiling in the hall than in the classroom?

15. **Higher Order Thinking** A yellow ribbo is 56 centimeters long. It is twice as long as a green ribbon. A brown ribbon is 4 times as long as the green ribbon. Wh is the length of the brown ribbon?

Assessment 🕐⊙ ISTEP+ Ready

16. Select all the true statements.

- ☐ 1,000 kilometers = 100 meters
- ☐ 11 meters = 110 centimeters
- ☐ 17 centimeters = 170 millimeters
- ☐ 5 meters = 500 millimeters
- ☐ 5 kilometers = 5,000 meters

17. Select all the true statements.

- ☐ 5 meters = 5,000 millimeters
- ☐ 18 kilometers = 1,800 meters
- ☐ 20 centimeters = 200 millimete
- ☐ 7 meters = 70 centimeters
- ☐ 6 meters = 60,000 millimeters

Name _____

Another Look!

Convert each unit.

To convert from kilograms to grams, multiply by 1,000.

To convert from liters to milliliters, multiply by 1,000.

Convert 8 liters to milliliters.

1 liter = 1,000 milliliters

$8 \times 1,000 = 8,000$

8 liters = 8,000 milliliters

Convert 9 grams to milligrams.

1 gram = 1,000 milligrams

$9 \times 1,000 = 9,000$

9 grams = 9,000 milligrams

For **1–6**, convert each unit.

1. 2 liters = _____ milliliters

2. 8 grams = _____ milligrams

3. 3 kilograms = _____ grams

4. 7 liters = _____ milliliters

5. 4 grams = _____ milligrams

6. 8 kilograms = _____ grams

For **7–8**, complete each table.

7.

Liters	Milliliters
5	
6	
7	
8	
9	

8.

Kilograms	Grams
4	
5	
6	
7	
8	

9. **Vocabulary** Fill in the blank:
_____ is the amount of matter something contains.
_____ is a measure of how heavy an object is.

10. Jake walks dogs and delivers papers to earn money. This month, he earned $52 delivering papers and $44 walking dogs. Each month, he puts half of his money into his savings account. How much money did Jake save this month?

11. **Math and Science** A glacier moved a boulder with a mass of 9 kilograms. What was the mass of the boulder in grams?

12. Another glacier moved a boulder that weighed 2 tons. How many pounds did the boulder weigh?

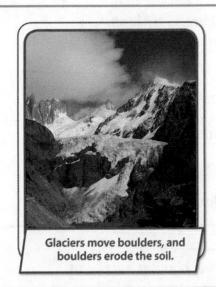

Glaciers move boulders, and boulders erode the soil.

13. **Reasoning** Hannah has 3 boxes of rice. One box contains 3 kilograms, the second box contains 150 grams, and the third box contains 500 grams. She wants to divide the rice equally into 5 bags. How much rice should she put into each bag? Explain.

14. **Higher Order Thinking** Rob has a 2-liter bottle of iced tea. He poured an equal amount of the iced tea into 8 containers. How many milliliters did Rob pour into each container?

Assessment ISTEP+ Ready

15. Which shows a correct comparison?

   Ⓐ 1,000 liters < 1,000 milliliters

   Ⓑ 40 liters = 400 milliliters

   Ⓒ 5,000 milliliters = 5 liters

   Ⓓ 900 milliliters > 900 liters

16. Which shows a correct comparison?

   Ⓐ 5 grams = 500 milligrams

   Ⓑ 1 gram < 10 milligrams

   Ⓒ 910 kilograms < 910 grams

   Ⓓ 2 kilograms > 2 grams

Name _____

Solve

Solve & Share

A can of paint is used to cover all 168 square feet of a wall. The wall is 8 feet high. Tape is placed along the top, bottom, and sides of the wall. What is the width of the wall? How much tape is needed? *Solve this problem any way you choose.*

I can ...
find the unknown length or width of a rectangle using a known area or perimeter.

Content Standard 4.M.4
Process Standards PS.1, PS.2, PS.3

$A = \boxed{}$ square feet $\boxed{}$ feet

$\boxed{}$ feet

You can use reasoning to find the width and the perimeter of the wall. *Show your work in the space above!*

Look Back! **Make Sense and Persevere** Describe the steps you would use to solve the problem.

Essential Question **How Can You Use Perimeter and Area to Solve Problems?**

A

The state park shown has a perimeter of 37 miles. What is the area of the state park?

Use formulas or equations, that use symbols to relate two or more quantities to solve this problem.

The formula for perimeter is:
$P = (2 \times \ell) + (2 \times w)$

The formula for area is:
$A = \ell \times w$

length (ℓ)

width (w) = $7\frac{1}{2}$ miles

B **Step 1**

Find the length of the state park.

Use the perimeter, 37 miles, and the width, $7\frac{1}{2}$ miles, to find the length.

Opposite sides of a rectangle are the same length, so multiply the width by 2.

$7\frac{1}{2} \times 2 = 15$

Subtract 15 from the perimeter.

$37 - 15 = 22$

22 miles is the length of two sides of the park. Divide 22 by 2 to find the length of one side.

$22 \div 2 = 11$

The length of the park is 11 miles.

C **Step 2**

Find the area of the state park.

$w = 7\frac{1}{2}$ miles

$\ell = 11$ miles

$A = \ell \times w$
$= 11 \times 7\frac{1}{2}$
$= 82\frac{1}{2}$

11 miles

$7\frac{1}{2}$ miles

The area of the state park is $82\frac{1}{2}$ square miles.

Convince Me! **Make Sense and Persevere** If the area of another state park is 216 square miles, and the park has a width of 8 miles, what is the park's length? What is the perimeter of this state park?

Guided Practice*

Do You Understand?

1. Construct Arguments A sandbox is shaped like a rectangle. The area is 16 square feet. The side lengths are whole numbers. What are the possible dimensions of the sandbox? Do all possible dimensions make sense?

2. Write and solve an equation to find the width of a room if the length of the floor is 8 feet and the area of the room is 96 square feet.

Do You Know How?

For **3–5**, complete each calculation.

3. Find n. Perimeter = 46 in.

8 in.

n

4. Find n. Perimeter = 26 cm

9 cm

$A =$ _____ sq cm

n

5. Find the perimeter.

$5\frac{1}{2}$ yd

ndependent Practice

For **6–9**, find the missing dimension.

6. Find n.

Area = 60 sq ft   6 ft

n

7. Find n. Perimeter = 65 in.

n

$11\frac{2}{4}$ in.

8. Find n. Perimeter = 84 yd

22 yd

n

9. A rectangle has a length of 9 millimeters and an area of 270 square millimeters. What is the width? What is the perimeter?

9 mm

w

Problem Solving

10. Greg built the picture frame shown to the right. It has a perimeter of $50\frac{2}{4}$ inches. How wide is the picture frame?

11. Greg covered the back of the picture with a piece of felt. The felt covers both the picture and the frame. What is the area of the felt?

$\ell = 15\frac{1}{4}$ in.

---

12. Number Sense Al has a goal to read 2,000 pages over summer break. He has read 1,248 pages. How many more pages does Al need to read to reach his goal?

13. The area of a tabletop is 18 square feet. The perimeter of the same table is 18 feet. What are the dimensions of the tabletop?

---

14. Amy and Zach each have 24 feet of fencing for their rectangular gardens. Amy makes her fence 6 feet long. Zach makes his fence 8 feet long. Whose garden has the greater area? How much greater?

15. Higher Order Thinking Nancy made a table runner that has an area of 80 squa inches. The length and width of the tab runner are whole numbers. The length i 5 times greater than the width. What are the dimensions of the table runner?

---

16. Which has the greater area: a square with a side that measures 7 meters or a $6\frac{1}{2}$-meter by 8-meter rectangle? How much more a.... ...oes that figure have?

You can draw pictures to model the math you use to solve the problem.

Homework & Practice 13-6

Solve Perimeter and Area Problems

Another Look!

Find the perimeter of the rectangle.

Area = 20 sq cm | 5 cm

w

The length and width of a rectangle are used to find both the perimeter and the area of the figure.

Use the formula for the area of a rectangle to find the width.

$A = \ell \times w$

$20 = 5 \times w$

$w = 4$

The width of the rectangle is 4 centimeters.

Use the formula for perimeter to find the perimeter of the rectangle.

$P = (2 \times \ell) + (2 \times w)$

$P = (2 \times 5) + (2 \times 4)$

$P = 10 + 8 = 18$

The perimeter of the rectangle is 18 centimeters.

For **1–4**, use the formulas for perimeter and area to solve each problem.

1. Find n.

$\vdash$—n—$\dashv$

2 ft | Area = 28 sq ft

2. Find n. Perimeter = 86 in.

25 in.

n

3. Find n. Then find the perimeter.

3 ft | Area = 33 sq ft

$\vdash$—n—$\dashv$

4. Find n. Then find the area.
Perimeter = $60\frac{2}{4}$ in.

$\vdash$—n—$\dashv$

$12\frac{1}{4}$ in.

5. On Friday, 39,212 fans attended the baseball game at a major league baseball park. On Saturday, 41,681 attended and on Sunday 42,905 attended. How many more fans attended on Saturday and Sunday than on Friday?

6. Write 352,619 in expanded form and using number names.

7. One side of the flower garden is 3 times as great as the other. What are the dimensions of the flower garden?

Area = 48 sq m

8. The sides of each square in the potholder measure 1 inch. What is the perimeter and area of the potholder?

9. How many seconds are in 3 minutes? There are 60 seconds in one minute. Complete the table.

Minutes	Seconds
1	
2	
3	

10. Higher Order Thinking An art class is planning to paint a rectangular mural with an area of 60 square feet. It has to be at least 4 feet high but no more than 6 feet high. The length and width have to be whole numbers. List all possible widths for the mural.

Assessment ISTEP+ Ready

11. The area of a square-shaped rug is 81 square feet. If the rug is 9 ft long, what is its perimeter? Explain.

Use what you know about squares to help solve the problem.

Name _____

★ ☆ ★
Solve & Share

Mr. Beasley's science class wants to decorate one wall in the classroom like an underwater scene. They use sheets of blue poster board that are 2 feet long and 2 feet wide. How many sheets of blue poster board are used to cover the entire area of the wall? Use math words and symbols to explain how you solve.

I can ...
be precise when solving math problems.

⬛ **Process Standards** PS.6 Also PS.1, PS.2, PS.4
Content Standards 4.M.3, 4.M.4

8 feet high

14 feet wide

Thinking Habits

Be a good thinker!
These questions can help you.

• Am I using numbers, units, and symbols appropriately?

• Am I using the correct definitions?

• Am I calculating accurately?

• Is my answer clear?

Look Back! **Be Precise** How can calculating the area of the whole wall and the area of one sheet of poster board help you determine the total number of sheets of poster board needed to cover the entire area of the wall?

How Can You Be Precise When Solving Math Problems?

length = 12 inches

A

Piper has a fish tank and wants to cover all four sides $\frac{6}{10}$ of the way to the top with clear plastic for insulation. She measures and finds the dimensions shown. How much plastic does Piper need? Use math words and symbols to explain how to solve.

height = 15 inches

width = 24 inches

What do you need to know so you can solve the problem?

I need to find how much plastic is needed for the fish tank. I need to be precise in my calculations and explanation.

Here's my thinking

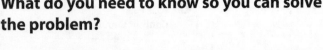

B

How can I be precise in solving this problem?

I can

- correctly use the information given.

- calculate accurately.

- decide if my answer is clear and appropriate.

- use the correct units.

C

The height of the plastic is $\frac{6}{10}$ times 15 inches.

$\frac{6}{10} \times 15 = \frac{90}{10}$ or 9   The plastic is 9 inches high.

Front and back: $A = 9 \times 24$
$A = 216$ square inches

Each side: $A = 9 \times 12$
$A = 108$ square inches

Add: $216 + 216 + 108 + 108 = 648$ square inches

Piper needs 648 square inches of plastic.

Convince Me! **Be Precise** How did you use math words and numbers to make your explanation clear?

Guided Practice *

Be Precise

Jeremy uses $1\frac{1}{2}$ feet of tape for each box he packs for shipping. How many inches of tape does Jeremy need to pack 3 boxes?

1. How can you use the information given to solve the problem?

2. How many inches of tape does Jeremy need to pack 3 boxes? Explain.

3. Explain why you used the units you did in your answer.

When you are precise, you calculate accurately.

ndependent Practice *

e Precise

rs. Reed collects shells. Each shell in her collection weighs
out 4 ounces. Her collection weighs about 12 pounds in all.
out how many shells are in Mrs. Reed's collection? Use
ercises 4–6 to solve.

4. How can you use the information given to solve the problem?

5. What is the total weight of Mrs. Reed's shell collection, in ounces?

6. How many shells are in Mrs. Reed's shell collection?

Problem Solving

Making Thank You Cards
Tanesha is making cards by gluing 1 ounce of glitter on the front of the card and then making a border out of ribbon. She makes each card the dimensions shown. How much ribbon does Tanesha need?

9 cm

85 mm

7. **Reasoning** What quantities are given in the problem and what do the numbers mean?

8. **Make Sense and Persevere** What do you need to find?

9. **Model with Math** What are the hidden questions which must be answered to solve the problem? Write equations to show how to solve the hidden questions.

> When you are precise, you specify and use units of measure appropriately.

10. **Be Precise** How much ribbon does Tanesha need? Use math language and symbols to explain how you solved the problem and computed accurately.

11. **Reasoning** What information was not needed in the problem?

Another Look!

Mia has a length of string that is 2 meters long. She cuts it into 4 equal pieces. Is one of the pieces of string long enough to tie around the perimeter of a square box with a side length of 16 centimeters? Explain.

Tell how you can solve the problem with accuracy.

When you are precise, you use math symbols and language appropriately.

- I can correctly use the information given.

- I can calculate accurately.

- I can decide if my answer is clear and appropriate.

- I can use the correct units.

Attend to precision as you solve.

First, convert 2 meters to centimeters.

$2 \times 100 = 200$ centimeters

Next, find the length of each piece Mia has after she cuts the string into 4 equal pieces.

$200 \div 4 = 50$ centimeters

Then, find the perimeter of the square box.

$P = 4 \times 16 = 64$ centimeters

The 50-centimeter piece is not long enough to go around the 64-centimeter perimeter of the box.

Precise

san bought a 1 kilogram bag of grapes. On the way home, she ate 5 grams of the grapes. How many grams of grapes does Susan have t? Use Exercises 1–3 to solve.

. How can you use the information given to solve the problem?

. How many grams of grapes does Susan have left? Show that you compute accurately.

. Use math language and symbols to explain how you solved the problem.

Cell Phone Pouches

Lex wants to make phone bags like the one shown. The pattern shows the material he needs for each side of the bag. He needs to know how much material he will need to make each bag.

Pattern   6 i

7 ½ inches of string

$2\frac{3}{4}$ in.

4. **Make Sense and Persevere** What do you know and what do you need to find?

5. **Model with Math** What is the hidden question? Write an equation to show how to solve it.

6. **Make Sense and Persevere** How much material does Lex need to make each bag?

When you are precise, you give carefully formulated explanations that are clear and appropriate.

7. **Be Precise** Explain how you know what units to use for your answer.

8. **Reasoning** What information was not needed to solve the problem?

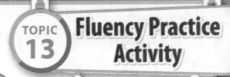

TOPIC 13 **Fluency Practice Activity**

nd a Match

Work with a partner. Point to a clue.

Read the clue.

Look below the clues to find a match. Write the clue letter in the box next to the match.

Find a match for every clue.

I can ...
add and subtract multi-digit whole numbers.

Clues

A The sum is between 2,000 and 2,500.

B The difference is exactly 10,000.

C The sum is exactly 6,000.

D The difference is exactly 4,500.

E The sum is exactly 16,477.

F The sum is between 5,500 and 5,600.

G The difference is between 1,000 and 2,000.

H The difference is between 8,000 and 9,000.

10,005 + 6,472	7,513 − 5,676	35,000 − 25,000	1,234 + 4,321
1,050 + 1,200	3,778 + 2,222	10,650 − 2,150	9,000 − 4,500

Vocabulary Review

 A-Z Glossary

Word List

- area
- capacity
- centimeter (cm)
- cup (c)
- fluid ounce (fl oz)
- formula
- gallon (gal)
- gram (g)
- kilogram (kg)
- kilometer (km)
- liter (L)
- mass
- meter (m)
- milligram (mg)
- milliliter (mL)
- millimeter (mm)
- ounce (oz)
- perimeter
- pint (pt)
- pound (lb)
- quart (qt)
- ton (T)
- weight

Understand Vocabulary

1. Cross out the units that are **NOT** used to measure length.

centimeter (cm)   pint (pt)

pound (lb)   kilogram (kg)

2. Cross out the units that are **NOT** used to measure capacity.

millimeter (mm)   ounce (oz)

gallon (gal)   milliliter (mL)

3. Cross out the units that are **NOT** used to measure weight.

cup (c)   liter (L)

meter (m)   ton (T)

4. Cross out the units that are **NOT** used to measure mass.

fluid ounce (fl oz)   kilometer (km)

milligram (mg)   quart (qt)

Label each example with a term from the Word List.

5. $2 \times 4 = 8$ square units   _____

6. $3 + 7 + 3 + 7 = 20$ units   _____

7. Area $= \ell \times w$ _____

Use Vocabulary in Writing

8. Mike uses 24 meters of fence to enclose a rectangular garden. The length of the garden is 10 meters, what is the width? Use at least 3 terms from the Word List to explain.

et A | pages 679–696 _____

stomary units can be used when
asuring length, capacity, and weight.

Length	1 foot (ft) = 12 inches (in.)
	1 yard (yd) = 3 ft = 36 in.
	1 mile (mi) = 1,760 yd = 5,280 ft

Capacity	1 cup (c) = 8 fluid ounces (fl oz)
	1 pint (pt) = 2 c = 16 fl oz
	1 quart (qt) = 2 pt = 4 c
	1 gallon (gal) = 4 qt = 8 pt

| Weight | 1 pound (lb) = 16 ounces (oz) |
| | 1 ton (T) = 2,000 lb |

nvert 26 quarts to cups.

Larger Unit		Smaller Unit		Converted to Smaller Unit
26	×	4 cups	=	104 cups

Remember when converting from a larger unit to a smaller unit, you multiply. Use the conversion charts to help solve.

Reteaching

1. 9 yards = _____ inches

2. 5 miles = _____ yards

3. 215 yards = _____ feet

4. 9 pints = _____ fluid ounces

5. 372 quarts = _____ cups

6. 1,620 gallons = _____ pints

7. 9 pounds = _____ ounces

8. 5 tons = _____ pounds

9. 12 feet = _____ inches

et B | pages 697–708 _____

tric units are commonly used by
entists to measure length, capacity,
d mass.

Length	1 centimeter (cm) = 10 millimeters (mm)
	1 meter (m) = 100 cm = 1,000 mm
	1 kilometer (km) = 1,000 m

Capacity and Mass	1 liter (L) = 1,000 milliliters (mL)
	1 gram (g) = 1,000 milligrams (mg)
	1 kilogram (kg) = 1,000 g

nvert 30 centimeters to millimeters.

Larger Unit		Smaller Unit		Converted to Smaller Unit
30	×	10 mm	=	300 mm

Remember metric units can be converted using multiples of 10. Use the conversion charts to help.

1. 9 kilometers = _____ meters

2. 55 centimeters = _____ millimeters

3. 2 meters = _____ centimeters

4. 9 liters = _____ milliliters

5. 4 grams = _____ milligrams

6. 5 kilograms = _____ grams

7. 8 kilograms = _____ grams

8. 5 grams = _____ milligrams

The perimeter of Ted's pool is 16 yards. The pool is 3 yards wide. He has a 150-square foot plastic cover. Is Ted's plastic cover large enough to cover his pool?

Use the formula for perimeter to find the length. Substitute the numbers you know.

$$\text{Perimeter} = (2 \times \ell) + (2 \times w)$$
$$16 = (2 \times \ell) + (2 \times 3)$$
$$\ell = 5$$

The length of the pool is 5 yards.

Convert yards to feet.

3 yards wide × 3 feet = 9 feet wide

5 yards long × 3 feet = 15 feet long

$$A = 15 \times 9$$
$$A = 135$$

The area of the pool is 135 square feet. $135 < 150$, so Ted's plastic cover is large enough to cover his pool.

Remember to label your answer with the appropriate unit.

1. Find n.
   $P = 108$ inches

   18 inches

2. Find the area.

   $A = $ ____ sq m   4 m
   9 m

3. Find the perimeter of the square.

   $2\frac{1}{2}$ yards

Think about these questions to help you **be precise.**

Thinking Habits

- Am I using numbers, units, and symbols appropriately?

- Am I using the correct definitions?

- Am I calculating accurately?

- Is my answer clear?

Remember to give an explanation that is cle and appropriate.

A puppy pen is 4 feet wide and 5 feet long.

1. Is 21 square feet of fabric large enough to make a mat for the pen? Explain.

2. Puppy fencing comes in sizes that are 12 feet, 24 feet, and 30 feet in length. Which length would be the best for the pen? How much, if any, will have to be cut off to fit the pen?

atermelons

sia grows watermelons.

. Kasia plants her watermelons in rows. Kasia's watermelon field has a perimeter of $71\frac{1}{3}$ yards and is 44 feet wide. The rows will be planted $2\frac{2}{3}$ yards apart.

Part A

How many rows of watermelons can Kasia plant? Explain.

Watermelon Field

width = 44 feet

First and last row are 6 feet from the edge.

Part B

What is the area of Kasia's field? Complete the table to convert the perimeter to feet. Explain.

Yards	Feet
$1\frac{1}{3}$	4
$11\frac{1}{3}$	
$21\frac{1}{3}$	
$31\frac{1}{3}$	
$41\frac{1}{3}$	
$51\frac{1}{3}$	
$61\frac{1}{3}$	
$71\frac{1}{3}$	

Part C

Explain why you used the units you did in your answer to Part B.

2. Use the information in the 20-Pound **Watermelon** table.

Part A

If there are twenty-eight 8-ounce servings in a 20-pound watermelon, how many pounds does the rind weigh? Explain.

DATA	
	20-pound watermelon
	28 8-ounce servings
	1 pound = $1\frac{1}{2}$ pints of fruit

The part of the watermelon that you do not eat is the rind.

Part B

How many cups of fruit does Kasia get from a 20-pound watermelon? Explain. Show your computations.
Do not include the weight of the rind.

3. Use the information from the **Watermelon and Nutrition** picture to answer the question.

Watermelon and Nutrit

How many more milligrams of fiber than potassium are in a serving of watermelon? Explain.

Each serving has 1 gram of fiber and 270 mg of potassium.

TOPIC 14

Algebra: Generate and Analyze Patterns

Essential Questions: How can you use a rule to continue a pattern? How can you use a table to extend a pattern? How can you use a repeating pattern to predict a shape?

Digital Resources

Solve Learn Glossary Practice Buddy

Tools Assessment Help Games

Scientists can use an instrument called an oscilloscope to see sounds as waves.

Higher sounds have shorter wavelengths.

I can see what you are saying on the oscilloscope. Here is a project about patterns and waves.

Math and Science Project: Patterns and Waves

Do Research Use the internet or other sources to learn about 2 industries where oscilloscopes can be used. Name the industry and what can be observed using the oscilloscope.

Journal: Write a Report Include what you found. Also in your report:

• Oscilloscopes are also used to observe patterns in waves. Suppose a scientist created a pattern with three levels of sounds: *quiet, loud, medium*. If the scientist repeats the pattern of sounds, what would be the 41st sound in the pattern? Explain.

Name _____

Review What You Know

Review What You Know

A-Z Vocabulary

Choose the best term from the box.
Write it on the blank.

• even number	• odd number
• inverse operations	• variable

1. A(n) _____ can be divided into groups of 2 without a remainder.

2. A symbol or letter that stands for a number is called a(n) _____.

3. Operations that undo each other are called _____.

Addition and Subtraction Patterns

Add or subtract to find the missing number in each pattern.

4. 3, 6, 9, 12, _____, 18

5. 4, 8, 12, _____, 20, 24

6. 8, 7, 6, _____, 4, 3

7. 30, 25, 20, 15, _____, 5

8. 1, 5, 9, _____, 17, 21

9. 12, 10, 8, 6, _____, 2

Multiplication and Division Patterns

Multiply or divide to find the missing number in each pattern.

10. 1, 3, 9, 27, _____, 243

11. 64, 32, 16, _____, 4, 2

12. 1, 5, 25, _____, 625

13. 1, 2, 4, 8, _____, 32

14. 1, 4, 16, _____, 256

15. 729, 243, 81, 27, 9, _____

Problem Solving

16. **Look for Relationships** James places 1 counter in the first box. He places 2 counters in the second box, 4 counters in the third box, 8 counters in the fourth box, and continues the pattern until he gets to the tenth box. How many counters did James place in the tenth box?

My Word Cards

Use the examples for each word on the front of the card to help complete the definitions on the back.

rule

Rule: Multiply by 3

Input	1	2	3	4
Output	3	6	9	12

repeating pattern

Rule: Triangle, Square

Complete each definition. Extend learning by writing your own definitions.

A _____ is made up of shapes or numbers that form a part that repeats.

A mathematical phrase that tells how numbers or shapes in a pattern are

related is called a _____.

Another Look!

Melanie has to create a pattern using the rule "Add 11." Her starting number is 11. What are the next 5 numbers in Melanie's pattern? Describe a feature of the pattern.

You can use a rule to describe a number pattern.

Use the rule to continue the pattern.

+11 +11 +11 +11 +11

11   22   33   44   55   66

The next 5 numbers in Melanie's pattern are 22, 33, 44, 55, and 66.

Describe features of the pattern.

- The numbers in the pattern are multiples of 11.

- The digits in the ones place increase by one as the pattern continues.

For **1–6**, continue each pattern. Describe a feature of each pattern.

1. Subtract 2: 30, 28, 26, _____, _____

2. Add 8: 14, 22, 30, _____, _____

3. Add 9: 9, 18, 27, _____, _____

4. Subtract 7: 49, 42, 35, _____, _____

5. Add 10: 213; 223; 233; _____; _____

6. Subtract 8: 92, 84, 76, _____, _____

For **7–12**, use the rule to fill in the missing number in each pattern.

7. Add 3

41, 44, _____, 50

8. Subtract 10

429, 419, 409, _____

9. Add 6

11, _____, 23, 29

10. Add 7

1, _____, 15, 22

11. Subtract 2, Add 3

6, 4, 7, _____, _____

12. Add 2, Subtract 4

10, 12, 8, _____, _____

13. **Use Appropriate Tools** Emily buys a sandwich, a salad, and a drink. If she gives the cashier $20, how much change will she receive? Use bills and coins to solve.

Item	Price
Sandwich	$5.75
Salad	$3.25
Drink	$1.45

14. Mimi started a pattern with 5 and used the rule "Add 10." What are the first five numbers in Mimi's pattern? Describe the numbers in the sequence.

15. **Reasoning** Jack arranged the pencils in groups of 6 to make a pattern. His rule is "Add 6." His starting number is 6. What are the next 4 numbers in Jack's pattern?

16. Presidential elections are held every 4 years. There were Presidential elections in 1840, 1844, 1848, and 1852. When were the next three Presidential elections? Describe a feature of the pattern.

17. **Higher Order Thinking** Sarah created a pattern. Her rule was "Add 4." All the numbers in Sarah's pattern were odd. Three of the numbers in Sarah's pattern were less than 10. What was the starting number for Sarah's pattern?

Assessment ISTEP+ Ready

18. The house numbers on Carr Memorial Avenue follow a pattern. The first four houses on the left side of the street are numbered 8, 14, 20, and 26. The rule is "Add 6." How many more houses are on the left side of the street with numbers less than 50?

ⓐ 1 house

ⓑ 2 houses

ⓒ 3 houses

ⓓ 4 houses

19. Noreen is training for a race. The first week she runs the route in 54 minutes. The second week, she runs the route in 52 minutes. The third week, she runs the route in 50 minutes. Noreen runs 2 minutes faster each week. If the pattern continues, how many minutes will it take Noreen to run the route the fifth week?

ⓐ 44 minutes

ⓑ 46 minutes

ⓒ 48 minutes

ⓓ 50 minutes

Another Look!

Stephanie wants to know how many players are participating in a competition. There are 6 teams. Each team has 11 players. The rule is "Multiply by 11."

Use the rule to complete the table.

Number of Teams	Number of Players
1	11
2	22
3	33
4	44
5	55
6	66

Describe features of the pattern.

- The number of players are multiples of 11.

- The digits in the ones place increase by 1 for each team added.

- The number of teams is a factor of the number of players for each number pair.

There are 66 players participating.

For **1–4**, use the rule to complete each table. Describe a feature of each pattern.

1. Rule: Multiply by 12

Number of Dozens	4	5	6	7
Number of Eggs	48		72	

2. Rule: Divide by 9

Number of Baseball Players	54	63	72	81
Number of Teams	6	7		

3. Rule: Divide by 6

Number of Legs	162	168	174	180
Number of Insects		28	29	

4. Rule: Multiply by 10

Number of Phone Numbers	33	34	35	36
Number of Digits in Phone Numbers	330	340		

5. **Look for Relationships** The table shows the amounts of money Emma earns for different numbers of chores. How much money does Emma earn when she does 6 chores?

Rule: Multiply by 9

Number of Chores	Amount Earned
3	$27
4	$36
5	$45
6	

6. **Math and Science** A *wavelength* is the distance between 1 peak of a wave of light, heat, or other energy to the next peak. Greta measured the distance for 3 wavelengths. What is distance for 1 wavelength?

├────── 168 feet ──────┤

7. Write 894,217 in expanded form and using number names.

8. There are 21,611 more students enrolle in elementary school than in middle school in a city district. If there are 16,2 students enrolled in middle school, how many are enrolled in elementary school

For **9–10**, the rule is "Divide by 7."

9. Using the rule from the table, how many T-shirts would sell for $168?

Do you need to find the price of 30 T-shirts and 9 T-shirts to solve Exercise 10?

10. **Higher Order Thinking** How much more do 30 T-shirts cost than 9 T-shirts? Explain.

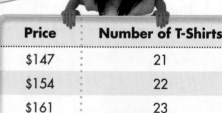

	Price	Number of T-Shirts
DATA	$147	21
	$154	22
	$161	23

11. There are 24 hours in a day. Use the rule "Multiply by 24" to show the relationship between the number of days and the number of hours. Use each digit from the box once to complete the table.

Number of Days	13	14	15	16	17
Number of Hours	□□□	336	360	384	□□□

0	1
2	3
4	8

Help Practice Tools Games
Buddy

Another Look!

Alan is using the rule below to make a repeating pattern. What is the 31st shape in Alan's pattern?

Rule: Rectangle, Circle, Square, Triangle

 ...

Divide: $31 ÷ 4 = 7$ R3

The pattern repeats 7 times. Then 3 more shapes appear.

The third shape in the repeating pattern is the square.
The square is the 31st shape in the repeating pattern.

> Every fourth shape is the same because there are four repeating items in the pattern.

For **1–4**, draw or write the next three items to continue each repeating pattern.

1. The rule is "Oval, Triangle."

 ...

2. The rule is "Short, Tall, Medium."

 ...

3. The rule is "2, 8, 9."

2, 8, 9, 2, 8, 9, 2, 8, 9, …

4. The rule is "1, 2, 3, 4, 5."

1, 2, 3, 4, 5, 1, 2, 3, 4, …

For **5–8**, determine the given shape or number in each repeating pattern.

5. The rule is "Star, Circle, Heart." What is the 17th shape?

 ...

6. The rule is "Add, Subtract, Multiply, Divide." What is the 100th shape?

 ...

7. ... "What is the 87th number?

1, 1, 1, 2, ...

*For another ...

8. The rule is "8, 9." What is the 100th number?

8, 9, 8, 9, 8, 9, …

---

9. Stonehenge is an ancient monument in England thought to have been originally made up of a repeating pattern of rocks that looks like this:

The rule is "Vertical, Horizontal, Vertical." Draw the 26th shape in the pattern.

10. Reasoning Marcia is using the rule "Heart, Star, Star" to make a repeating pattern. She wants the pattern to repeat 6 times. How many stars will be in Marcia's pattern?

♥ ☆ ☆ ♥ ☆ ☆ ...

11. Vocabulary Describe the difference between *perimeter* and *area*.

12. Higher Order Thinking Tanji creates a "Square, Circle" repeating pattern. Kenji creates a "Square, Circle, Triangle, Circle" repeating pattern. If both Tanji and Kenji have 100 shapes in their patterns, which pattern contains more circles? Explain.

Tanji's Pattern

Kenji's Pattern

Assessment ISTEP+ Ready

13. Which rules give a repeating pattern that has a 9 as the 20th number? Select all that apply.

- ☐ 1, 9, 4
- ☐ 1, 2, 3, 9
- ☐ 9, 9, 9
- ☐ 1, 2, 9
- ☐ 9, 1, 4

14. Which rules give a repeating pattern that has a circle as the 20th shape? Select all that apply.

- ☐ Square, Circle
- ☐ Circle, Square, Triangle
- ☐ Trapezoid, Circle, Square
- ☐ Circle, Circle, Circle
- ☐ Circle, Triangle, Circle

Name _____

Solve

★ ☆ ★
Solve & Share

Evan's baby brother is stacking blocks. Using the rule "Add 1 block to the number of blocks in the previous stack," how many blocks will be in the 6th stack? Explain. Justify your answer.

1st   2nd   3rd

I can ...
use patterns to help solve problems.

Process Standards PS.7 Also PS.1, PS.2
Content Standards 4.AT.6, 4.M.4

Thinking Habits

• What patterns can I see and describe?

• How can I use the patterns to solve the problem?

• Can I see expressions and objects in different ways?

Look Back! **Look For Relationships** ~~~v~~ many blocks are in the 10th stack? Explain.

Essential Question **How Can I Look for and Make Use of Structure?**

A

Alisa made three walls with cubes. She recorded her pattern. If she continues the pattern, how many cubes will be in a 10-layer wall? a 100-layer wall?

Rule: Each layer has 4 cubes.

1 layer
4 cubes

2 layers
8 cubes

3 layers
12 cubes

What do you need to do to find the number of cubes in a 10-layer and 100-layer wall?

I need to continue the pattern using the rule and analyze the pattern to find features not stated in the rule itself.

Here's my thinking.

B **How can I make use of structure to solve this problem?**

I can

- look for and describe patterns in three-dimensional shapes.

- use the rule that describes how objects or values in a pattern are related.

- use features of the pattern not stated in the rule to generate or extend the pattern.

C Make a table and look for patterns.

Number of Layers	1	2	3	4	5
Number of Cubes	4	8	12	16	20

1 layer
4 cubes

2 layers
8 cubes

3 layers
12 cubes

4 layers
16 cubes

5 layers
20 cubes

There are 4 cubes in each layer. Multiply the number of layers by 4 to calculate the number of cubes.

A 10-layer wall contains 10 × 4 = 40 cubes.

A 100-layer wall contains 100 × 4 = 400 cubes.

Convince Me! **Look For Relationships** How could you use multiples to describe Alisa's pattern?

Guided Practice *

Use Structure

Leah arranged triangular tiles in a pattern like the one shown. She used the rule "Multiply the number of rows by itself to get the number of small triangles." How many small triangles would be in the pattern if there were 10 rows?

1 row	2 rows	3 rows
$1 \times 1 = 1$	$2 \times 2 = 4$	$3 \times 3 = 9$

1. Complete the table to help describe the pattern.

Number of Rows	1	2	3	4	5
Number of Small Triangles	1	4	9		

> When you look for relationships, you use features of the pattern not stated in the rule to extend the pattern.

2. Describe the pattern another way.

3. How many triangles would be in 10 rows?

Independent Practice *

Look for Relationships

[Le]an built the towers shown using the rule "Each story has [b]locks." How many blocks will a 10-story tower have? [Us]e Exercises 4–6 to answer the question.

[4]. Complete the table to help describe the pattern.

Number of Stories	1	2	3	4	5
Number of Blocks	2	4	6		

[5]. What is another way to describe the pattern that is not described by the rule?

[6]. How many blocks are in a 10-story tower? Explain.

another example, see Set D on page 760.   **Topic 14** | Lesson 14-4

Glass Stairs

An art gallery staircase is built using glass cubes. The diagram below shows 4 steps are 4 cubes high and 4 cubes across. Five steps are 5 cubes high and 5 cubes across. How many glass cubes are used to make 7 steps? Use Exercises 7–10 to answer the question.

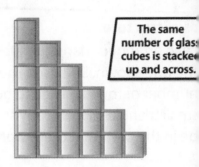

The same number of glass cubes is stacked up and across.

4 cubes high

4 cubes across

5 cubes high

5 cubes across

7. **Make Sense and Persevere** What do you know, and what do you need to find?

When you look for relationships, you use the rule that describes how objects or values in a pattern are related.

8. **Reasoning** Complete the table.

Cubes Up or Across	2	3	4	5	6
Total Cubes Needed	3	6			

9. **Look For Relationships** What pattern can you determine from the table?

10. **Reasoning** How many cubes are needed for 7 steps? Write and solve an equation.

Another Look!

Dwayne built the towers shown. He used the rule that each tower has 1 more block than the tower before it. How many blocks are needed for the 10th tower?

Tell how you can solve the problem.

- I can use the rule that describes how objects or values in a pattern are related.

- I can use features of the pattern not stated in the rule to extend the pattern.

Tower 1 Tower 2 Tower 3 Tower 4

Extend the pattern and find features not stated in the rule.

When you look for relationships, you recognize, describe, and use patterns.

Tower Number	1	2	3	4	5
Number of Blocks	2	3	4	5	6

The number of blocks in a tower is 1 more than the tower number. The 10th tower contains $10 + 1 = 11$ blocks.

e Structure

ah is making diamond shapes with yarn like the es shown. She adds the length of the sides to termine how much yarn she needs. What is the eatest side length Sarah could make with 48 inches yarn? Use Exercises 1–3 to answer the question.

. Complete the table to help describe the pattern.

Inches on One Side	2	3	4	5	6
Inches of Yarn Needed	8	12	16		

. What is another feature of the pattern that is not described in the rule?

. What is the side length of the diamond Sarah can make with 48 inches of yarn? Explain.

Swimming Pools

Pete's Pools installs rectangular pools that are all 10 feet wide. The length can vary from 10 feet to 30 feet. The company installed a pool with a perimeter of 76 feet. What was the length of the pool?

10 feet · 10 feet · 12 feet · 10 feet · 14 feet · 10 feet

4. **Reasoning** What quantities are given in the problem and what do the numbers mean?

5. **Make Sense and Persevere** What do you need to find?

When you use structure, you break the problem into simpler parts.

6. **Reasoning** Complete the table.

Feet in Length	10	12	14	16	18	20	22	24
Perimeter	40	44	48					

7. **Use Structure** What is the length of a pool with a perimeter of 76 feet? Explain how you found the answer. Then describe how you can use a feature of the pattern to find the length.

me _____

Find a partner. Get paper and a pencil. Each partner chooses a different color: light blue or dark blue.

Partner 1 and Partner 2 each point to a black number at the same time. Each partner adds the two numbers.

If the answer is on your color, you get a tally mark. Work until one partner has twelve tally marks.

I can ...
add multi-digit whole numbers.

Partner 1

5,150	
10,101	
11,000	
23,231	
40,400	

49,495	14,245	47,250	30,081
32,326	17,850	40,900	12,000
8,650	11,500	16,951	42,399
26,731	12,100	23,731	7,149
13,601	10,601	19,196	43,900
14,500	20,095	5,650	12,999

Partner 2

500	
1,999	
3,500	
6,850	
9,095	

Tally Marks for Partner 1

Tally Marks for Partner 2

A-Z
Glossary

Understand Vocabulary

1. Circle the term that best describes 28.

even   odd   equation   unknown

2. Circle the term that best completes this sentence:
4 is a _____ of 16.

even   odd   factor   multiple

3. Circle the term that best describes 17.

even   odd   equation   unknown

4. Circle the term that best completes this sentence:
9 is a _____ of 3.

even   odd   factor   multiple

Draw a line from each term to its example.

equation	Multiply by 3
repeating pattern	$14 \div 2 = n$
rule	▲ ■ ▲ ■
[unk]nown	$4 + 7 = 11$

Use Vocabulary in Writing

6. Use at least [two] terms from the Word List to describe the pattern.

50, 48, 46, ...

Set A pages 733–738

You can use the rule "Subtract 3" to continue the pattern.

21 18 15 12 9 6 3
−3 −3 −3 −3 −3 −3 −3

The next three numbers in the pattern are 9, 6, and 3.

A feature of the pattern is all the numbers are multiples of 3.

Another feature is all the numbers in the pattern alternate even, odd.

Remember to check that the numbers in your pattern follow the rule.

Use the rule to continue each pattern. Describe a feature of the pattern.

1. Rule: Add 2

   1, 3, 5, _____, _____, _____

2. Rule: Subtract 4

   22, 18, 14, _____, _____, _____

Set B pages 739–744

The regular price is twice the sale price. You can use the rule "Divide by 2" to continue the pattern.

Regular Price	Sale Price
$44	$22
$42	$21
$40	$20
$38	$19
$36	$18
$34	$17

The regular price is a multiple of the sale price, and the sale price is a factor of the regular price.

Remember to look for features of the pattern not described by the rule.

Use the rule to continue each pattern. Describe a feature of the pattern.

1. Rule: Multiply by 18

Trucks	3	5	7	9
Wheels	54	90	126	

2. Rule: Divide by 3

Earned	$12	$18	$24	$30
Saved	$4	$6	$8	

3. Rule: Multiply by 4

Chairs	5	10	15	20
Legs	20	40	60	

You can use the rule "Circle, Triangle, Square" to continue the repeating pattern.

You can use the rule to find the 25th shape in the pattern.

$25 \div 3 = 8 \text{ R}1$.

The pattern will repeat 8 times, then the 1st shape will appear.

The circle is the 25th shape in the pattern.

Remember to use the rule to continue the pattern.

1. **a.** Draw the next three shapes in the repeating pattern. The rule is "Right, Up, Up."

   b. Draw the 50th shape in the pattern.

2. **a.** Write the next three numbers in the repeating pattern. The rule is "3, 5, 7, 9

   3, 5, 7, 9, 3, 5, 7, _____, _____, _____

   b. What will be the 100th number in the pattern?

Think about these questions to help you **look for relationships**.

Thinking Habits

- What patterns can I see and describe?

- How can I use the patterns to solve the problem?

- Can I see expressions and objects in different ways?

Remember to use the rule that describes ho objects or values in a pattern are related.

Sam creates a pattern using the rule "Each layer has 3 cubes."

1. Draw the next shape in Sam's pattern.

2. Use the rule to continue Sam's pattern.

Stories	1	2	3	4
Blocks	3	6	9	

3. How many blocks are in the 10th shape Sam's pattern?

ll Hangings

hael uses knots to make wall hangings to sell.

The **Michael's Basic Wall Hanging** figure shows a simple wall hanging Michael makes by repeating the shapes shown. What is the 16ᵗʰ shape in the repeating pattern? The rule is "Circle, Triangle, Square." Explain.

Michael's Basic Wall Hanging

The **Snowflake Design** figure shows a knot Michael likes to use.

Snowflake Design

Uses 11 knots

Part A

List the number of knots that Michael uses to form 1 to 6 snowflake designs. The rule is "Add 11."

Part B

Describe a feature of the pattern you listed in Part A that is not part of the rule. Explain why it works.

3. The **Michael's Wall Hanging** figure shows the design of a wall hanging Michael makes using the **Snowflake Design**. Answer the following to find how many knots Michael ties to make a wall hanging with 28 snowflakes.

Part A

Each up-and-down row of 4 snowflakes has 4 connectors. There are also 4 connectors between rows. Complete the **Connectors** table using the rule "Add 8 connectors for each row." Describe a feature of the pattern.

Each connector uses 3 knots.

Connectors

Rows	1	2	3	4	5
Connectors	4	12			

Part B

Complete the **Total Knots** table using the following rules.

Snowflake Knots rule: Multiply the number of snowflakes by 11.

Connector Knots rule: Multiply the number of connectors from the **Connectors** table by 3.

Total Knots rule: Add the number of snowflake knots and the number of connector knots.

Total Knots

Columns	Snowflakes	Snowflake Knots	Connector Knots	Total Knots
1	4	44	12	56
2	8			
3	12			
4	16			
5	20			

Geometric Measurement: Understand Concepts of Angles and Angle Measurement

Essential Questions: What are some common geometric terms? How can you measure angles?

Digital Resources

Solve   Learn   Glossary   Practice Buddy

Tools   Assessment   Help   Games

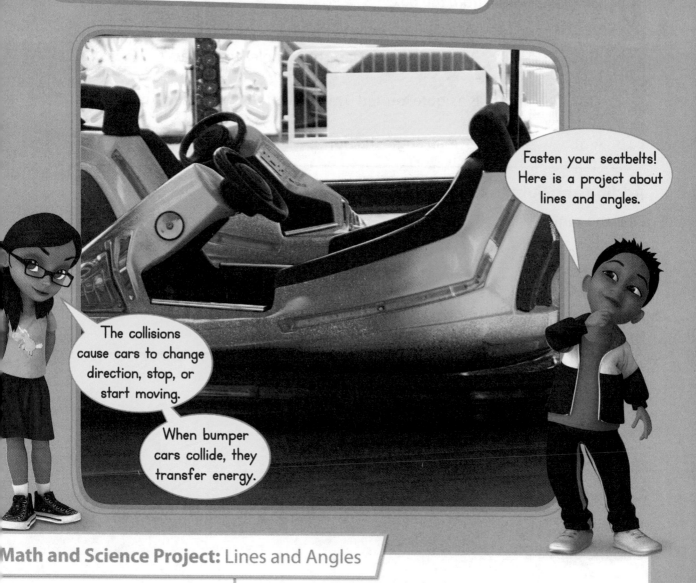

The collisions cause cars to change direction, stop, or start moving.

When bumper cars collide, they transfer energy.

Fasten your seatbelts! Here is a project about lines and angles.

Math and Science Project: Lines and Angles

Do Research Use the internet or other sources to research the area of the world's largest bumper car floor. Find where it is located and when it was built.

Journal: Write a Report Include what you found. Also in your report:

- Draw a diagram of a bumper car collision. Use an angle to show how a car might change direction after it collides with something. Measure and label the angle you drew.

- Describe your angle using some of the vocabulary terms on the My Word Cards.

Name _____

Review What You Know

A-Z Vocabulary

Choose the best term from the box.
Write it on the blank.

| • angle | • right angle |
| • line | • sixth |

1. A(n) _____ is one of 6 equal parts of a whole, written as $\frac{1}{6}$.

2. A(n) _____ is a figure formed by two rays that share the same endpoint.

3. A(n) _____ is an angle that forms a square corner.

Adding and Subtracting

Find the sum or difference.

4. $45 + 90$

5. $120 - 45$

6. $30 + 150$

7. $180 - 135$

8. $60 + 120$

9. $90 - 45$

Parts of a Whole

Tell the fraction that represents the shaded part of the whole.

10. $\frac{\square}{\square}$

11. $\frac{\square}{\square}$

12. $\frac{\square}{\square}$

Dividing

Find the quotient.

13. $360 \div 6$

14. $180 \div 9$

15. $360 \div 4$

Problem Solving

16. **Make Sense and Persevere** Gary has $4. Mary has twice as many dollars as Gary. Larry has 4 fewer dollars than Mary. How much money do Gary, Mary, and Larry have in all?

My Word Cards

Use the examples for each word on the front of the card to help complete the definitions on the back.

point

A

line

A B

$\overleftrightarrow{AB}$

line segment

Q R

$\overline{QR}$

ray

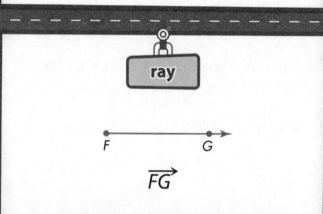

F G

$\overrightarrow{FG}$

right angle

A

B C

$\angle ABC = 90°$

acute angle

D

E F

$\angle DEF < 90°$

obtuse angle

G

H J

$\angle GHJ > 90°$ and $\angle GHJ < 180°$

straight angle

J K L

$\angle JKL = 180°$

My Word Cards

Complete each definition. Extend learning by writing your own definitions.

A straight path of points that goes on and on in opposite directions is called a
_____.

A _____ is an exact location in space.

A part of a line that has one endpoint and continues on forever in one direction is called a _____.

A part of a line with two endpoints is called a _____.

An _____ is an angle that is open less than a right angle and has a measure less than 90°.

A _____ is an angle that forms a square corner and has a measure of 90°.

A _____ is an angle that forms a straight line and has a measure of 180°.

An _____ is an angle that is open more than a right angle but less than a straight angle. This angle measures between 90° and 180°.

My Word Cards

Use the examples for each word on the front of the card to help complete the definitions on the back.

A-Z
Glossary

degree (°)

The angle measure is 45°.

unit angle

The angle measure is 1°.

angle measure

60°

protractor

vertex

Topic 15 | My Word Cards   769

My Word Cards

Complete each definition. Extend learning by writing your own definitions.

An angle that turns through $\frac{1}{360}$ of a circle and measures 1° is called a

_____,

or a one-degree angle.

Angles can be measured using a unit called a _____.

A _____ is a tool used to measure and draw angles.

The number of degrees an angle turns through is its

_____.

The point where two rays meet to form an angle is called a _____.

Help · Practice Buddy · Tools · Games

Another Look!

Here are some important geometric terms.

• C			
Point	**Line**	**Line segment**	**Ray**
A point is an exact location in space. This is point C.	A line is a straight path of points that goes on and on in opposite directions. This is $\overleftrightarrow{AB}$.	A line segment is part of a line. It has two endpoints. This is $\overline{XY}$.	A ray is part of a line. It has one endpoint and goes on and on in one direction. This is $\overrightarrow{AB}$.

Right angle	**Obtuse angle**	**Acute angle**	**Straight angle**
A right angle forms a square corner. This is ∠QRS.	An obtuse angle is greater than a right angle. This is ∠LMN.	An acute angle is less than a right angle. This is ∠HIJ.	A straight angle forms a straight line. This is ∠STU.

For **1–3**, use geometric terms to describe what is shown. Be as specific as possible.

1.

2.

3.

For **4–6**, use the diagram at the right.

4. Name three different rays.

5. Name two different line segments.

6. Name two different acute angles.

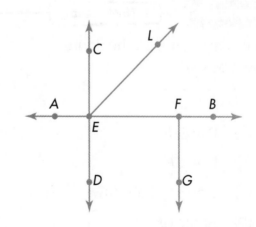

For **7–9**, use the diagram at the right.

There may be more than one name for the same geometric figure.

7. Name two lines.

8. Name two obtuse angles.

9. Name one point that lies on two lines.

---

10. Model with Math Randy used 92 sticks to build a model. Bryan used 3 times as many sticks. Complete the bar diagram to represent how many sticks Bryan used. Then find how many more sticks Bryan used than Randy. Write and solve equations.

n sticks

Bryan ____ ____ ____ times as many

Randy ____

---

11. **A-Z Vocabulary** What is the difference between a *line* and a *line segment*? Draw an example of each.

12. Higher Order Thinking Name two ray with the same endpoint in the figure below. Do they form an angle? Explain.

A   B   C

---

13. What is the name for the figure shown below?

G   H

Ⓐ Ray *GH*

Ⓑ Line *GH*

Ⓒ Line Segment *HG*

Ⓓ Angle *GH*

14. Mary drew $\overleftrightarrow{XY}$. Which of the following Mary's drawing?

Ⓐ • *X*

Ⓑ *X* *Y*

Ⓒ *X* *Y*

Ⓓ *X*   *Y*

Help Practice Tools Games
       Buddy

Another Look!

You can find the measure of an angle using fractions of a circle.

The angle shown is $\frac{2}{5}$ of a circle.

What is the measure of this angle?

Remember that $\frac{2}{5} = \frac{1}{5} + \frac{1}{5}$.
Divide to find the angle measure of $\frac{1}{5}$ of a circle.

$360° \div 5 = 72°$

An angle that turns through $\frac{1}{5}$ of a circle measures 72°.

$72° + 72° = 144°$

The measure of this angle is 144°.

Fractions of a circle can help with the understanding of angle measures.

For **1–4**, find the measure of each angle.

1. The angle turns through $\frac{1}{9}$ of the circle.

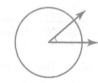

2. A circle is divided into 6 equal parts. What is the total angle measure of 1 part?

$\frac{1}{6} \times$ _____ = _____

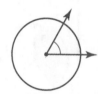

3. A circle is divided into 5 equal parts. What is the total angle measure of 4 parts?

4. A circle is divided into 8 equal parts. What is the total angle measure of 4 parts?

5. **Reasoning** Noah used a bar diagram to find the measure of an angle that turns through $\frac{1}{5}$ of a circle. Write an equation to find the measure of the angle.

angle measure

6. **Number Sense** Miguel cut $\frac{1}{4}$ from a round pie. Mariah cut a piece from the same pie with an angle measure of 60°. Who cut the larger piece? Explain.

7. **Construct Arguments** Janie served 4 same-size pizzas at the class party. Explain how to find how many slices of pizza Janie served if the angle for each slice turns through a right angle.

8. Wendy's older brother is buying a car. He can make 24 payments of $95 or 30 payments of $80 each. Which costs less? How much less?

9. **Higher Order Thinking** A circle is divided into 18 equal parts. How many degrees is the angle measure for each part? How many degrees is the angle measure for 5 of those parts? Break apart 18 to solve. Explain.

10. Draw a line to match the angle in the circle with its angle measure.

90°   120°   144°   60°

Name _____

☆ ☆
Solve & Share

The smaller angles on the tan pattern block shown each measure 30°. How can you use the angles on the pattern block to determine the measure of the angle below? *Solve this problem any way you choose.*

I can ...
use angles I know to measure angles I do not know.

Content Standard 4.M.6
Process Standards PS.1, PS.3, PS.4, PS.5, PS.8

You can make sense and persevere in solving the problem. *Show your work in the space below!*

?

Look Back! **Make Sense and Persevere** Two right angles make a straight angle. How many 45° angles form a straight angle? Explain.

Essential Question **How Can You Measure Angles?**

A

Holly traced around a trapezoid pattern block. She wants to find the measure of the angle formed shown to the right. What can Holly use to measure the angle?

The measure of a unit angle is 1 degree.

B Use an angle you know to find the measure of another angle.

30°

The smaller angle of the tan pattern block measures 30°.

A 30-degree angle turns through 30 one-degree angles.

C The angle of the trapezoid pattern block is equal to 2 of the smaller angles of the tan pattern block. Each smaller angle is 30°.

$2 \times 30° = 60°$

The measure of the trapezoid angle is 60°.

A 60-degree angle turns through 60 one-degree angles.

Convince Me! **Generalize** What do you notice about the number of one-degree angles in an angle measure?

Guided Practice

Do You Understand?

1. How many 30° degree angles are in a 180° angle? Explain.

2. **Make Sense and Persevere** How many 15° angles are in a 180° angle? Use your answer to Exercise 1 to explain.

Do You Know How?

For **3–4**, use angles you know to find the measure of each angle. Explain how the angles in the square can help.

3.

4.

dependent Practice

or **5–13**, find the measure of each angle. se pattern blocks to help.

6.

7.

9.

10.

12.

13.

14. Use Appropriate Tools What is the measure of the angle of the yellow hexagon pattern block?

15. What is the measure of the smaller angle formed by the clock hands when it is 5:0

16. Model with Math How many 30° angles are in a circle? Write and solve a multiplication equation to explain.

17. Make Sense and Persevere How mar unit angles make up the smaller angle formed by the hands of a clock when it 3:00? Explain.

18. Veronica purchases a rug with a length of 16 feet and a width of 4 feet. One fourth of the rug is purple and the rest is blue. What is the area of the blue part of the rug?

19. Higher Order Thinking The hands of a clock form a 120° angle. Name two different times it could be.

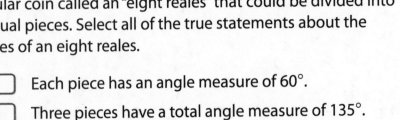

Assessment 🔾 ⊙ ISTEP+ Ready

20. Before creating their own dollar, American colonists used a circular coin called an "eight reales" that could be divided into 8 equal pieces. Select all of the true statements about the pieces of an eight reales.

☐ Each piece has an angle measure of 60°.

☐ Three pieces have a total angle measure of 135°.

☐ Five pieces turn through 225 one-degree angles.

☐ Three 30° angles can fit into 2 pieces of an eight reales.

☐ Half of an eight reales has an angle measure of 90°.

Another Look!

The smaller angle of the tan pattern block measures 30°.

Use the tan pattern block to find the measure of the angle below.

30°

> You can use an angle you know to find the measure of an angle you do not know.

Four of the 30° angles will fit into the angle.

$30° + 30° + 30° + 30° = 120°$

The measure of this angle is 120°.
It turns through 120 one-degree angles.

For **1–6**, find the measure of each angle.
Use pattern blocks to help.

120°   150°   30°

60°

2.

3.

5.

6.

7. Construct Arguments A round classroom table is made from 5 identical wedges. What is the measure of each angle formed at the center of the classroom table? Explain.

8. Generalize How many unit angles does the smaller angle of a tan pattern block turn through? Explain.

9. Mario cut a circular pizza into 9 equal slices. He put a slice of pizza on each of 5 plates. What is the measure for the angle of the slices that are left?

10. Number Sense How many 30° angles are there in a 150° angle? Use repeated subtraction to solve. Draw a picture to justify your solution.

11. Matt's parents pay him $5.50 for each half hour he babysits his sister, plus a two dollar tip. If Matt made $18.50, for how long did he babysit?

12. Higher Order Thinking If a clock face reads 1:00, how many hours must pass for the hands to form a straight angle?

13. Shirley uses pattern blocks to measure the straight angle. Select all the combinations of pattern block angles that Shirley could use to measure the angle.

150°   30°

120°

60°

- ☐ 6 small angles on the tan pattern block

- ☐ 1 large angle and one small angle on the red pattern block

- ☐ 1 large angle on the red pattern block and 3 small angles on the tan pattern block

- ☐ 4 small angles on the tan pattern block and one small angle on the red pattern block

- ☐ 2 large angles on the red pattern block

Help Practice Tools Games
       Buddy

Another Look!

To measure an angle:

Place the protractor's center on the vertex of the angle and the 0° mark on one of the angle's rays. Read the number in degrees where the other ray of the angle crosses the protractor. If the angle is acute, use the lesser number. If the angle is obtuse, use the greater number.

You can use a protractor to measure or draw angles.

To draw an angle:

Draw a dot to show the vertex of the angle. Place the center of the protractor on the vertex point. Draw another point at the 0° mark and another point at the angle degree mark. Draw rays from the vertex through the other points.

For **1–4**, measure each angle. Tell if each angle is acute, right, or obtuse.

2.

3.

4.

For **5–12**, use a protractor to draw an angle for each measure.

5. 75°

6. 80°

7. 155°

8. 45°

9. 135°

10. 180°

11. 5°

12. 90°

13. Reasoning The angle turns through $\frac{1}{5}$ of the circle. What is the measure of the angle?

There are multiple ways to determine an angle's measure.

---

14. Use Appropriate Tools Joanie is making a map of the trails in the community park. Two of the trails start at the same point and form a 40° angle. Use a protractor to draw the angle that Joanie will use on her map.

15. Math and Science Watts, volts, and amps are used to measure electricity. There is a formula that shows the relationship between watts, volts, and amps. Volts × Amps = Watts. If the vo are 120 and the amps are 5, how many watts are there?

For **16–18**, use the figure at the right.

16. Reasoning Does the measure of ∠COA equal the measure of ∠EOD? What are their measures?

17. Name an acute, an obtuse, and a right angle.

18. Higher Order Thinking The measure of ∠EOF is 35°. The measure of ∠FOB is 120°. What is the measure of ∠BOC?

---

19. Stuart drew 4 angles. Which of Stuart's angles measures 25°?

Ⓐ   Ⓑ   Ⓒ   Ⓓ

---

me _____

Homework & Practice 15-5

Add and Subtract Angle Measures

Another Look!

Addition

∠ADC is decomposed into 2 non-overlapping angles, ∠BDC and ∠ADB.

If the measure of ∠ADB is 90° and the measure of ∠BDC is 75°, what is the measure of ∠ADC?

$90° + 75° = 165°$
$∠ADC = 165°$

Subtraction

∠ADC is decomposed into 2 non-overlapping angles, ∠ADB and ∠BDC.

If the measure of ∠ADC is 165° and the measure of ∠ADB is 90°, what is the measure of ∠BDC?

$165° - 90° = 75°$
$∠BDC = 75°$

You can write and solve addition and subtraction equations to find unknown angle measures.

or **1–5**, add or subtract to find the missing angle measures.

TUW and ∠WUV share a ray.
gether, they form ∠TUV.

A table can help you see the relationships between angles.

	Angle Measure		
	∠TUW	∠WUV	∠TUV
1.	120°	45°	
2.	105°		155°
3.	100°		170°
4.		25°	150°
5.	112°	36°	

or **6–8**, write and solve an addition or subtraction equation to find the missing angle measure.

45°
n
45°

7.

50°
n

8.

60° n 60°

9. Ms. Willer wanted to donate 27 cans of food to each of 8 food banks. Each of the 23 students in Ms. Willer's class donated 9 cans. How many more cans does Ms. Willer need? Explain.

10. Construct Arguments Two nonoverlapping acute angles that share a ray form an obtuse angle. If one of the acute angles has a measure of 50°, what could be the measure of the other acute angle?

For **11–13**, use the diagram at the right.

11. Algebra Write and solve an equation to find the measure of ∠NPO.

12. Algebra What is the measure of ∠SPR if the measure of ∠RPQ is 40°? Write and solve an equation.

13. Higher Order Thinking ∠NPO and ∠RPQ both share rays with ∠QPO. Do ∠NPO and ∠RPQ have the same measure? How do you know?

14. ∠CMW and ∠WML together form ∠CML. ∠CMW is a right angle.

Part A

Describe ∠CML.

Part B

Write an equation showing one possible su▮ for ∠CMW and ∠WML.

ame _____

Solve & Share

Caleb is standing next to the tallest building in a city. Determine the measure of the 3 angles with the vertex at the tallest building and rays on the music hall, the live theater, and the art museum. Tell what tool you used and explain why the measures make sense relative to each other.

Problem Solving

Lesson 15-6
Use Appropriate Tools

I can ...
use appropriate tools strategically to solve problems.

Process Standards PS.5 Also PS.1, PS.2, PS.4
Content Standard 4.M.6

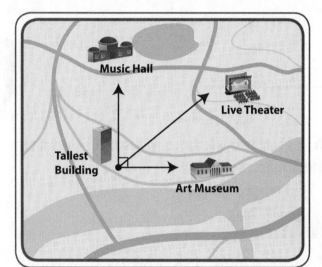

Music Hall

Live Theater

Tallest
Building

Art Museum

Thinking Habits

Be a good thinker!
These questions can help you.

- Which tools can I use?

- Why should I use this tool to help me solve the problem?

- Is there a different tool I could use?

- Am I using the tool appropriately?

Look Back! **Use Appropriate Tools** Could you use a ruler to find the angle measures? Explain.

Essential Question # How Can You Select and Use Appropriate Tools to Solve Problems?

A

Trevor and Holly are tracing large trapezoids to make a wall mural. They need to find the measures of the angles formed by the sides of the trapezoid and the length of each side of the trapezoid. What tools are needed to find the measures of the angles and the lengths of the sides?

What do you need to do to copy the trapezoid?

I need to measure the angles, then measure the sides.

Here's my thinking.

B **Which tool can I use to help me solve this problem?**

I can

- decide which tool is appropriate.

- explain why it is the best tool to use.

- use the tool correctly.

C

First, use a protractor to measure the angles. The angles measure 120° and 60°.

Then, use a meterstick to measure the length of each side. The lengths are 1 meter, 1 meter, 1 meter, and 2 meters.

Convince Me! **Use Appropriate Tools** What other tools could be used to solve this problem? Why are a protractor and a meterstick more appropriate than other tools?

Practice Buddy   Tools   Assessment

Guided Practice*

Use Appropriate Tools

Lee brought $1\frac{3}{5}$ pounds of apples to the picnic. Hannah brought $\frac{4}{5}$ pounds of oranges. Lee said they brought $2\frac{2}{5}$ pounds of fruit in all. Lee needs to justify that $1\frac{3}{5} + \frac{4}{5} = 2\frac{2}{5}$.

1. What tool could Lee use to justify the sum?

2. How can Lee use a tool to justify the sum? Draw pictures of the tool you used to explain.

> When you use appropriate tools, you select the best tool to use.

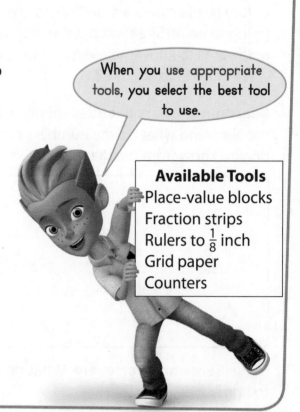

Available Tools
Place-value blocks
Fraction strips
Rulers to $\frac{1}{8}$ inch
Grid paper
Counters

Independent Practice

Use Appropriate Tools

What are the measures of the sides and angles of the parallelogram shown? Use Exercises 3–5 to help solve.

3. What tools can you use to solve this problem?

4. Explain how to use the tool you chose to find the measures of the angles. Label the figure with the measures you find.

5. Explain how to use the tool you chose to find the lengths of the sides. Label the figure with the measures you find.

For another example, see Set F on page 810.

Topic 15 | Lesson 15-6   **803**

Problem Solving

Mural

Before Nadia paints a mural, she plans what she is going to paint. She sketches the diagram shown and wants to know the measures of ∠WVX, ∠WVY, ∠XVY, and ∠YVZ.

6. **Reasoning** What quantities are given in the problem and what do the numbers mean? What do you know from the diagram?

7. **Make Sense and Persevere** What do you need to find?

8. **Use Appropriate Tools** Measure ∠WVX, ∠WVY, and ∠YVZ. What is the best tool to use?

When you use appropriate tools, you decide if the results you get with the tool make sense.

9. **Model with Math** Write and solve an equation which could be used to find the measure of ∠XVY. What is the measure of the angle?

me _____

Another Look!

When light hits a mirror, it reflects at the same angle as it hits. In the diagram shown, $\angle ABC$ has the same measure as $\angle CBD$, where $\overline{BC}$ makes a right angle with the mirror.

Measure $\angle ABC$. Then, write and solve an equation to find the measure of $\angle DBE$.

Tell how you can strategically choose a tool to solve the problem.

- I can decide which tool is appropriate.

- I can explain why it is the best tool to use.

- I can use the tool correctly.

The measure of $\angle ABC$ is 25°. The measure of $\angle CBD$ is also 25° and the sum of $\angle CBD$ and $\angle DBE$ is 90°. So, $25° + d = 90°$, $d = 90° - 25° = 65°$. The measure of $\angle DBE$ is 65°.

Mirror

Appropriate Tools

Jason wants to set up blocks for a game. He wants to set up the blocks in an array, so there are the same number of rows as columns. He wants to use between 20 and 90 blocks. How can Jason set up the blocks? Use Exercises 1–2 to help solve.

1. What tool could Jason use? Explain how Jason could use the tool to find at least one way to set up the blocks.

When you use appropriate tools, you consider options before selecting a tool.

Available Tools
Place-value blocks
Fraction strips
Rulers
Grid paper
Counters

2. What are all the ways Jason can set up the blocks?

Tiling

Marcus created the tile pattern shown. All the angles of each hexagon have the same measure and all the angles of each equilateral triangle have the same measure. Find the measure of each angle.

3. **Make Sense and Persevere** What do you know and what do you need to find?

4. **Use Appropriate Tools** What tool could you use to measure the angle of a hexagon? Explain how to use the tool you chose. What is the measure?

When you use appropriate tools, you use the tool you chose correctly.

5. **Model with Math** Write and solve an equation which could be used to find the measure of one angle of a triangle. What is the measure of the angle? Explain.

TOPIC 15 **Fluency Practice Activity**

Shade a path from **START** to **FINISH**. Follow sums and differences that are between 20,000 and 25,000. You can only move up, down, right, or left.

I can …

add and subtract multi-digit whole numbers.

Start				
66,149 − 44,297	13,000 + 13,000	11,407 + 13,493	35,900 − 12,605	30,000 − 9,825
40,350 − 20,149	18,890 + 190	13,050 + 11,150	60,000 − 33,900	41,776 − 18,950
89,000 − 68,900	12,175 + 18,125	12,910 + 12,089	67,010 − 42,009	42,082 − 19,582
56,111 − 32,523	22,009 + 991	11,725 + 11,450	75,000 − 45,350	65,508 − 42,158
99,000 − 81,750	9,125 + 9,725	18,517 + 8,588	38,000 − 19,001	37,520 − 16,215

Finish

Word List

- acute angle
- angle measure
- degree (°)
- line
- line segment
- obtuse angle
- point
- protractor
- ray
- right angle
- straight angle
- unit angle
- vertex

Understand Vocabulary

1. Cross out the terms that do **NOT** describe an angle with a square corner.

   acute angle   right angle

   obtuse angle   straight angle

2. Cross out the terms that do **NOT** describe an angle open less than a right angle.

   acute angle   right angle

   obtuse angle   straight angle

3. Cross out the terms that do **NOT** describe an angle that forms a straight line.

   acute angle   right angle   obtuse angle   straight angle

4. Cross out the terms that do **NOT** describe an angle open more than a right angle, but less than a straight angle.

   acute angle   right angle   obtuse angle   straight angle

Label each example with a term from the Word List.

5. ←——→ _____

6. •——• _____

7. •——→ _____

8. _____

Use Vocabulary in Writing

9. Describe how to measure an angle. Use at least 3 terms from the Word List in your explanation.

ncient Roads

e ancient Romans built roads throughout their empire.
any roads were paved with stones that fit together.
e spaces between the stones were filled with sand
d gravel. Many of these roads still exist today,
er 2,000 years after they were built.

. As seen in the **Roman Road** figure, the stones formed
angles and other geometric figures.

Roman Road

Part A

What geometric figure has one endpoint at *F* and goes on
forever through point *G*?

Part B

Is ∠*EDA* right, acute, or obtuse? Explain.

Part C

∠*EDG* turns through $\frac{1}{8}$ of a circle. What is its angle
measure? Explain.

2. Answer the following to find the measure of $\angle HJK$ and $\angle HJL$ in the **Measuring a Roman Road** figure.

Part A

Name two tools you could use to measure the angles.

Part B

The smaller angle of the tan pattern block measures $30°$, as shown in the **Tan Pattern Block** figure. A 30-degree angle is 30 one-degree angles. What is the measure of $\angle HJK$ in the **Measuring a Roman Road** figure? Explain.

Tan Pattern Block

30°

You can write and solve equation to find unknown angle measures.

Part C

What is the measure of $\angle HJL$ in the **Measuring a Roman Road** figure? Write and solve an equation to find the measure of the angle.

Lines, Angles, and Shapes

Essential Questions: How can you classify triangles and quadrilaterals? What is line symmetry?

Digital Resources

Solve   Learn   Glossary   Practice Buddy

Tools   Assessment   Help   Games

They can see the math that is all around them! Here is a project about senses and symmetry!

Chameleons can move their eyes one at a time!

When they do, they are able to see in two directions at once, helping them find food and stay safe.

Math and Science Project: Senses and Symmetry

Do Research The location of an animal's eyes helps it to survive in the wild. Use the Internet or other sources to find why some animals have eyes on the sides of their head and others have eyes on the front.

Journal: Write a Report Include what you found. Also in your report:

• Most animals are the same on both sides of their body. Use a line of symmetry to help make a simple drawing of your favorite animal's face. Draw both sides of the animal's face the same. Explain how you know that both sides of your drawing are the same.

Name _____

Review What You Know

A-Z Vocabulary

Choose the best term from the box.
Write it on the blank.

• angle • quadrilateral
• polygon • triangle

1. A polygon with four sides is a(n) _____.

2. A polygon with three sides is a(n) _____.

3. A(n) _____ is formed by two rays with the same endpoint.

Shapes

Choose the best term to describe each shape. Use each term once.

      Rectangle   Rhombus   Trapezoid

4.   **5.**   **6.**

Lines

Use geometric terms to describe what is shown.

7.   **8.**   **9.**

Problem Solving

10. Generalize Which generalization about these figures is **NOT** true?

  Ⓐ   Each figure is a quadrilateral.

  Ⓑ   Each figure has two pairs of parallel sides.

  Ⓒ   Each figure has at least two sides of equal length.

  Ⓓ   Each figure has 4 angles.

My Word Cards

Use the examples for each word on the front of the card to help complete the definitions on the back.

parallel lines

perpendicular lines

intersecting lines

right triangle

obtuse triangle

acute triangle

equilateral triangle

isosceles triangle

5.

6. Us to is

_____
are lines that intersect to form right angles.

_____
are lines that never intersect.

A _____
is a triangle that has one right angle.

_____
are lines that pass through the same point.

An _____
is a triangle that has three acute angles.

An _____
is a triangle that has one obtuse angle.

An _____

_____
is a triangle with at least two sides that are the same length.

An _____

_____
is a triangle with three sides that are the same length.

My Word Cards

Use the examples for each word on the front of the card to help complete the definitions on the back.

A-Z Glossary

scalene triangle

parallelogram

rectangle

square

rhombus

trapezoid

line symmetric

line of symmetry

Complete each definition. Extend learning by writing your own definitions.

A _____
is a quadrilateral that has two pairs of parallel sides.

A _____
is a triangle with no sides that are the same length.

A _____
is a quadrilateral that has four right angles and all sides are the same length.

A _____
is a quadrilateral that has four right angles.

A _____
is a quadrilateral with only one pair of parallel sides.

A _____
is a quadrilateral that has opposite sides that are parallel and all of its sides are the same length.

The line on which a figure can be folded so both halves are the same is called a

_____

A figure is _____
if it can be folded on a line to form two halves that fit exactly on top of each other.

Solve

Lesson 16-1
Lines

☆ ☆
Solve & Share

The number line below is an example of a line. A line goes on forever in a straight path in two directions. Draw the following pairs of lines: two lines that will never cross, two lines that cross at one point, two lines that cross at two points. If you cannot draw the lines, tell why.

I can ...
draw and identify perpendicular, parallel, and intersecting lines.

Content Standard 4.G.4
Process Standards PS.2, PS.3, PS.5, PS.6, PS.7

0 1 2 3 4 5 6 7 8 9

Be precise. Think of and use math language you already know. *Show your work in the space below!*

Look Back! **Be Precise** Terry said, "The lines shown intersect at three points." Is Terry correct? Explain.

A

A line is a straight path of points that goes on and on in opposite directions. A pair of lines can be described as parallel, perpendicular, or intersecting.

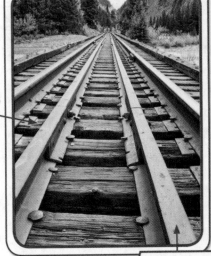

Railroad tie

The railroad tracks in the picture are parallel because they never meet. The railroad ties are perpendicular to the railroad tracks because they intersect at right angles.

Railroad track

B Pairs of lines are given special names depending on their relationship.

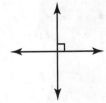

Parallel lines never intersect.

Intersecting lines pass through the same point.

Perpendicular lines are lines that intersect to form right angles.

Convince Me! **Be Precise** Find examples in your classroom where you can identify parallel lines, intersecting lines, and perpendicular lines. Explain.

Guided Practice*

Do You Understand?

1. **Be Precise** What geometric term could you use to describe the top and bottom edges of a book? Why?

2. What pair of lines looks like the blades of an open pair of scissors? Why?

Do You Know How?

> For **3–6**, use the diagram.

3. Name four points.

4. Name four lines.

5. Name two pairs of parallel lines.

6. Name two pairs of perpendicular lines.

Independent Practice

> For **7–12**, use geometric terms to describe what is shown. Be as specific as possible.

8.

9. •
   A

11.

12.

> For **13–15**, draw what is described by the geometic terms.

13. Perpendicular lines

14. Intersecting lines

15. Parallel lines

another example, see Set A on page 859.

Topic 16 | Lesson 16-1   **823**

Problem Solving

16. Construct Arguments Bella names this line $\overleftrightarrow{LM}$. Miguel names the line $\overleftrightarrow{LN}$. Who is correct? Explain.

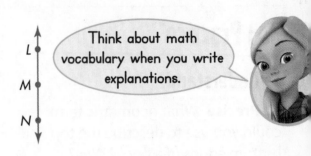

Think about math vocabulary when you write explanations.

17. Construct Arguments If all perpendicular lines are also intersecting lines, are all intersecting lines also perpendicular lines? Explain.

18. Model with Math Draw three lines so two of the lines are perpendicular and the third line intersects the perpendicu[lar] lines at exactly one point. Label the line[s] with points.

19. Higher Order Thinking $\overleftrightarrow{AB}$ is parallel to $\overleftrightarrow{CD}$, and $\overleftrightarrow{CD}$ is perpendicular to $\overleftrightarrow{EF}$. Describe the relationship between $\overleftrightarrow{AB}$ and $\overleftrightarrow{EF}$.

 Assessment ISTEP+ Ready

20. Which geometric term would you use to describe the power cables shown at the right?

Ⓐ Perpendicular lines

Ⓑ Parallel lines

Ⓒ Intersecting lines

Ⓓ Points

What relationship do the power cables have to each other?

Another Look!

You can use geometric terms to describe what you draw.

Parallel lines

Parallel lines never intersect.

Intersecting lines

Intersecting lines pass through the same point.

Perpendicular lines

Perpendicular lines form right angles.

r **1–3**, use geometric terms to describe what is shown. Be as specific as possible.

2.

3.

r **4–7**, use the figure at the right.

Name three different lines.

Name a pair of parallel lines.

Name two lines that are perpendicular.

Name two intersecting lines.

8. Name two lines.

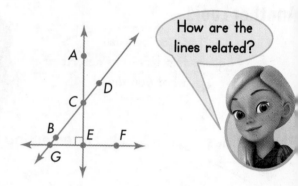

How are the lines related?

9. Name two lines that are perpendicular.

10. Draw a $\overleftrightarrow{HF}$ on the diagram that is parallel to $\overleftrightarrow{AE}$ and perpendicular to $\overleftrightarrow{GF}$.

---

11. A-Z **Vocabulary** Describe a point. What could you use as a model of a point?

12. **Critique Reasoning** Ali says if two lines share a point, they cannot be parallel. Do you agree? Explain.

---

13. Draw and label parallel lines $\overleftrightarrow{XY}$ and $\overleftrightarrow{RS}$. Then draw and label $\overleftrightarrow{TS}$ so it is perpendicular to both $\overleftrightarrow{XY}$ and $\overleftrightarrow{RS}$. Draw point Z on $\overleftrightarrow{TS}$.

14. **Higher Order Thinking** $\overleftrightarrow{RS}$ is perpendicular to $\overleftrightarrow{TU}$. $\overleftrightarrow{RS}$ is parallel to $\overrightarrow{VW}$. What is the relationship between and $\overrightarrow{VW}$? Draw lines if needed.

🅹 **Assessment** 🔘 ISTEP+ Ready

15. Which geometric term would you use to describe the lines to the right?

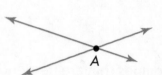

Ⓐ Perpendicular lines

Ⓑ Point A

Ⓒ Parallel lines

Ⓓ Intersecting lines

Think about the relationship between the two lines.

Another Look!

 Triangles can be classified by their angle measures, side lengths, or both.

Equilateral triangle
All sides are the
same length.

Isosceles triangle
At least two sides
are the same length.

Scalene triangle
No sides are the
same length.

Right triangle
One angle is a
right angle.

Acute triangle
All three angles
are acute angles.

Obtuse triangle
One angle is an
obtuse angle.

r **1–6**, classify each triangle by its sides and then by its angles.

2.

3.

5.

6.

For **7–8**, use the figure at the right.

7. Hilary flew from Denver to Atlanta for business. From Atlanta, she flew to Chicago to visit her aunt. From Chicago, she flew back home to Denver. Classify the triangle made by her complete flight path.

8. How many miles complete the triangle made by Hilary's flight path?

9. **Algebra** The triangle shown is an equilateral triangle. Write an addition equation and a multiplication equation to show how to find the perimeter, *p*, of the triangle when *s* is the measure of one side.

10. **A-Z Vocabulary** Fill in the blanks to correctly complete the sentences:

A _____ triangle has no sides the same length.

A triangle with one 90° angle is called _____ triangle.

An isosceles triangle has _____ sides the same length.

11. **Critique Reasoning** Sylvia says a right triangle can have only one right angle. Joel says a right triangle can have more than one right angle. Who is correct? Explain.

12. **Higher Order Thinking** Dani measure the angles of a triangle as 120°, 36°, an 24°. Then, she measured the side lengt as 25.3 cm, 17.2 cm, and 11.8 cm. She said her triangle is an isosceles obtuse triangle. Do you agree? Explain.

Assessment ⊙ (ISTEP+ Ready)

13. Draw each triangle in its correct side classification.

Isosceles	Equilateral	Scalene

Help   Practice   Tools   Games
Buddy

Another Look!

Quadrilaterals can be named for their angles and sides.

Quadrilateral
A polygon with 4 sides.

Rectangle
There are four right angles and opposite sides are parallel.

Parallelogram
Opposite sides are parallel.

Square
There are four right angles. All sides are the same length.

Rhombus
Opposite sides are parallel and all sides are the same length.

Trapezoid
There is only one pair of parallel sides.

For **1–4**, write the most specific name for each quadrilateral.

1.

2.

3.

4.

For **5–7**, write all the names possible for each shape.

5.

6.

7.

8. The figure at the right is called an Escher cube. It is named after the Dutch artist M.C. Escher. Look at the 7 white shapes created by this drawing. Name each shape.

9. Be Precise Mr. Meyer draws a shape on the board. It has 4 sides of equal length and 4 right angles. List all of the names possible to describe the shape Mr. Meyer drew.

10. Generalize Why can a square never be a trapezoid?

11. Rick drew a rhombus. What names might describe the figure based on what you know about quadrilaterals? Explain.

12. Higher Order Thinking Hannah has 11 toothpicks that are the same length. Name the different types of triangles and quadrilaterals Hannah can make if she uses only one toothpick for each side of each figure.

13. Sasha draws a quadrilateral on her paper. She says, "My quadrilateral has 4 right angles, so it must be a square." Do you agree with Sasha? Write an explanation for how you would classify the shape Sasha drew.

Think about which types of quadrilaterals have 4 right angles.

ame _____

★ ☆ ★
Solve & Share

How many ways can you fold the square so one half fits exactly on top of the other half? How many ways can you fold the letter so one half fits exactly on top of the other half? *Solve this problem any way you choose.*

I can ...
recognize and draw lines of symmetry and identify line-symmetric figures.

Content Standard 4.G.2
Process Standards PS.2, PS.3, PS.5, PS.7

G

You can use appropriate tools. How can the edge of a ruler help you solve this problem?

Look Back! **Reasoning** What figures can you form when you fold a square in half?

A

A figure is line symmetric if it can be folded on a line to form two matching parts that fit exactly on top of each other. The fold line is called a line of symmetry. There is one line of symmetry drawn on the picture of the truck. How many lines of symmetry do the figures below have?

Count the lines of symmetry drawn on each figure below.

B A figure can have more than one line of symmetry.

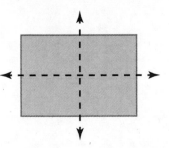

This figure is line symmetric. It has 2 lines of symmetry. It can be folded on each line of symmetry into matching parts.

C A figure can have many lines of symmetry.

This figure is line symmetric. It has 6 lines of symmetry. It can be folded on each line of symmetry into matching parts.

D A figure can have no lines of symmetry.

This figure is **NOT** line symmetric. It has 0 line of symmetry. It cannot be folded to have matching parts.

Convince Me! **Look for Relationships** Find two capital letters that have exactly one line of symmetry. Find two capital letters that have exactly two lines of symmetry.

Guided Practice*

Do You Understand?

1. How many lines of symmetry does the letter R have?

2. How many lines of symmetry does the figure below have?

3. **Construct Arguments** How many lines of symmetry can you find for a circle? Do you think you can count them?

Do You Know How?

For **4–5**, tell if each line is a line of symmetry.

4.

5.

For **6–7**, tell how many lines of symmetry each figure has.

6.

7.

Independent Practice

For **8–11**, tell if each line is a line of symmetry.

8.

9.

10.

11.

For **12–19**, decide if each figure is line symmetric. Draw and tell how many lines of symmetry each figure has.

12.

13.

14.

15.

16.

17.

18.

19.

Problem Solving

20. The Thomas Jefferson Memorial is located in Washington, D.C. Use the picture of the memorial at the right to decide whether the building is line symmetric. If so, describe where the line of symmetry is.

21. Name the type of triangle outlined in green on the picture of the memorial.

22. Construct Arguments How can you tell when a line is **NOT** a line of symmetry?

23. Higher Order Thinking How many lines of symmetry can a parallelogram have? Explain.

24. Which figure has six lines of symmetry? Draw lines as needed.

Ⓐ   Ⓒ

Ⓑ   Ⓓ

25. Which figure is **NOT** line symmetric?

Ⓐ   Ⓒ

Ⓑ   Ⓓ

Help Practice Buddy Tools Games

Another Look!

Line-symmetric figures are figures that can be folded to make matching parts.

How many lines of symmetry does a square have?

If you fold the square along any of the 4 dashed lines, the two matching parts will lie on top of each other.

A square has 4 lines of symmetry. It is a line-symmetric figure.

or **1–4**, tell if each line is a line of symmetry.

  2.   3.   4.

or **5–12**, decide if each figure is line symmetric. Draw and tell how many lines of symmetry ach figure has.

  6.   7.   8.

10.   11.   12.

13. Construct Arguments How many lines of symmetry does a scalene triangle have? Explain.

14. Reasoning Can an isosceles triangle have three lines of symmetry? Explain.

15. Reasoning How many lines of symmetry does the wagon wheel at the right have? Draw or explain where the lines of symmetry are located.

16. Number Sense Stuart has $23.75. He wants to buy 2 tickets that each cost $15.75. How much more money does Stuart need? Use coins and bills to solve.

17. Higher Order Thinking Regular polygons have sides that are all the sam length and angles that all have the sam measure. A regular pentagon has 5 line of symmetry and a regular hexagon ha 6 lines of symmetry. Make a conjecture about the number of lines of symmetry for a regular octagon. Draw a regular octagon to support your conjecture.

Assessment ⊙ (**ISTEP+ Ready**)

18. Which of the following numbers has exactly 2 lines of symmetry?

(A) 1

(B) 3

(C) 7

(D) 8

19. Which of the following letters is **NOT** line symmetric?

(A) W

(B) T

(C) S

(D) A

ame _____

Solve

Solve & Share

Craig and Julia are designing kites. A kite will fly well if the kite has line symmetry. Does Craig's or Julia's kite have line symmetry? Explain. Then, design your own kites. Design one kite with 2 lines of symmetry and another kite with 3 lines of symmetry. **Solve this problem any way you choose.**

I can ...
draw a figure that has line symmetry.

Content Standard Extends 4.G.2
Process Standards PS.1, PS.2, PS.3, PS.4

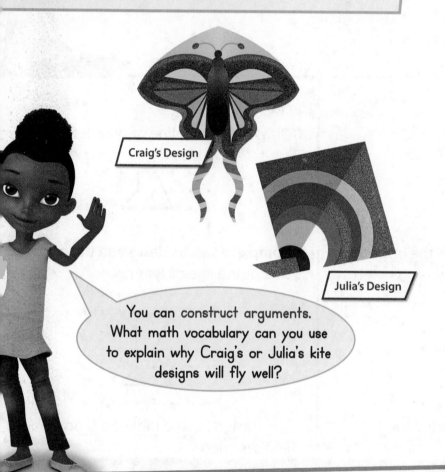

Craig's Design

Julia's Design

You can construct arguments. What math vocabulary can you use to explain why Craig's or Julia's kite designs will fly well?

Look Back! **Make Sense and Persevere** Can both Craig's and Julia's kites can be folded into matching parts? If one of the kites is not line symmetric, can it be changed so that it is? Explain.

Essential Question — How Can You Draw Figures with Line Symmetry?

A

Sarah wants to design a line-symmetric tabletop. She sketched half of the tabletop. What are two ways Sarah can complete her design?

The tabletop is line symmetric if the design can be folded along a line of symmetry into matching parts.

B **One Way**

Draw a line of symmetry.

Complete Sarah's design on the opposite side of the line of symmetry.

The design for the tabletop is now line symmetric.

C **Another Way**

Draw a different line of symmetry.

Complete Sarah's design on the opposite side of the line of symmetry.

The design for the tabletop is now line symmetric.

Convince Me! **Model with Math** Sarah sketched a different design for a smaller tabletop. Use the lines of symmetry to draw two ways Sarah can complete her design.

Homework & Practice 16-5

Draw Shapes with Line Symmetry

Another Look!

You can use dot paper to draw line-symmetric figures.

How to draw a line-symmetric figure:

Step 1

Draw a figure on dot paper.

Step 2

Draw a line of symmetry.

Step 3

Complete the figure on the opposite side of the line of symmetry.

or 1–6, use the line of symmetry to draw a line-symmetric figure.

1.

2.

3.

5.

6.

7. Reasoning Draw a quadrilateral that has no lines of symmetry.

8. Model with Math Draw a figure with exactly 2 lines of symmetry.

9. A storage compartment for a gym locker room can hold up to 7 folded towels. There are 22 compartments for towels. Katie has 150 towels to fold and put away. How many of the compartments will be filled? How many towels will be in a compartment that is not completely filled?

10. Model with Math James bought $175 in accessories for his video game conso He spent $15 on a new power cord and the rest of his money on 5 new video games. Each video game cost the same amount. Write two equations you could use to find the cost of each video game

11. Create a line symmetric figure. Draw half of a figure. Then draw a line of symmetry. Complete your figure on the opposite side of the line of symmetry.

12. **Vocabulary** Describe the difference between *parallel* and *intersecting* lines.

13. Higher Order Thinking Draw a figure that has both horizontal and vertical symmetry.

 ISTEP+ Ready

14. Which of the following figures has 4 lines of symmetry? Draw lines as needed.

Ⓐ   Ⓑ   Ⓒ   Ⓓ

ame _____

☆ ☆
Solve & Share

Nathan gave the answer shown to the following question. True or False? All right triangles have two sides the same length. How do you respond to Nathan's reasoning?

Nathan

That's true. Here are three different sizes of right triangles. In each, two sides are the same length.

2 cm   2 cm

3 in.

3 in.

4 mm
4 mm

I can ...
critique the reasoning of others by using what I know about two-dimensional shapes.

Process Standards PS.3 Also PS.1, PS.2, PS.6, PS.7
Content Standard 4.G.5

Thinking Habits
Be a good thinker!
These questions can help you.

- What questions can I ask to understand other people's thinking?

- Are there mistakes in other people's thinking?

- Can I improve other people's thinking?

Look Back! **Critique Reasoning** If Nathan had drawn even more triangles, would it show that the statement is true? Explain.

Learn   Glossary

Essential Question **How Can You Critique the Reasoning of Others?**

A

Abby gave the answer shown to the following question.

True or False? Every quadrilateral has at least one right angle.

Abby

True. Here are different quadrilaterals. They all have four sides and four right angles.

What is Abby's reasoning to support her statement?

Abby drew quadrilaterals that have right angles.

It only takes one example to show the statement is false.

Here's my thinking.

B **How can I critique the reasoning of others?**

I can

- ask questions about Abby's reasoning.

- look for flaws in her reasoning.

- decide whether all cases have been considered.

C

Abby's reasoning has flaws.

She used only special kinds of quadrilaterals in her argument. For these special cases, the statement is true.

Here is a quadrilateral that has no right angles. It shows the statement is not true about **every** quadrilateral.

The statement is false.

Convince Me! **Be Precise** Would Abby's reasoning be correct if the question was changed to: True or False? Some quadrilaterals have at least one right angle. Explain.

852   **Topic 16** | Lesson 16-6

Guided Practice

Critique Reasoning

Anthony said all multiples of 4 end in 2, 4 or 8. He gave 4, 8, 12, 24, and 28 as examples.

1. What is Anthony's argument? How does he support it?

2. Describe at least one thing you could do to critique Anthony's reasoning.

3. Does Anthony's reasoning make sense? Explain.

Independent Practice

Critique Reasoning

Marista said the polygons shown all have the same number of angles as they have sides.

Describe at least one thing you could do to critique Marista's reasoning.

Does Marista's reasoning make sense? Explain.

> When you critique reasoning, you decide whether or not another student's conclusion is logical.

Can you think of any examples that prove Marista wrong? Explain.

Problem Solving

Dog Pen

Caleb is designing a dog pen for the animal shelter. He has 16 feet of fence, including the gate. His designs and explanation are shown. Critique Caleb's reasoning.

Dog pens usually have right angles so I just used rectangles.

Both my pens used 16 feet of fence. I think the square one is better, because it has more area.

7. **Reasoning** What quantities are given in the problem and what do the numbers mean?

8. **Critique Reasoning** What can you do to critique Caleb's thinking?

9. **Be Precise** Did Caleb correctly calculate the perimeter of each fence? Explain.

When you critique reasoning, you ask questions to help understand someone's thinking.

10. **Critique Reasoning** Does Caleb's reasoning make sense? Explain.

11. **Reasoning** Explain how you know what units to use in your explanation.

Help   Practice   Tools   Games
       Buddy

Another Look!

Alisa said all obtuse triangles have acute angles because you cannot draw an obtuse triangle with all obtuse angles. Critique Alisa's reasoning.

Tell how you can critique the reasoning of others.

- I can look for flaws in her reasoning.

- I can decide whether all cases have been considered.

Decide whether or not you think Alisa's statement is true. Then, explain why.

> When you critique reasoning, you need to carefully consider all parts of an argument.

Alisa is correct. All obtuse triangles have one obtuse angle that is greater than 90°. The remaining angles are acute. An obtuse triangle cannot have a right angle.

tique Reasoning

nnie said that if all of the sides of a polygon have equal length, n all of the angles will have the same measure. He drew the ures shown.

Describe at least one thing you could do to critique Ronnie's reasoning.

Does Ronnie's reasoning make sense? Explain.

hel said the sum of three odd numbers is always d. She gave the examples shown.

Describe at least one thing you could do to critique Rachel's reasoning

Rachel

$5 + 3 + 7 = 15$

$21 + 33 + 45 = 99$

$127 + 901 + 65 = 1,093$

Does Rachel's reasoning make sense? Explain.

Designing a Logo

Tamara was asked to design a logo for the Writing Club. The logo needs to be a scalene triangle. Tamara reasons about how to draw the logo. Critique Tamara's reasoning.

Inspiration / Hard work / Writing Club

5. **Make Sense and Persevere** What do you know and what do you need to do?

Tamara's Reasoning
A scalene triangle has 3 side of differing lengths. Each of the angles is acute because I cannot draw a triangle wit 3 different right angles or 3 different obtuse angles.

6. **Critique Reasoning** Critique Tamara's reasoning. What can you do to improve her reasoning?

When you critique reasoning you carefully rea someone else's argument.

7. **Use Structure** Describe three possible logo designs Tamara could make using a scalene triangle and acute, right, or obtuse angles.

_____ ne

d a Match

Work with a partner. Point to a clue.
Read the clue.

Look below the clues to find a match. Write
the clue letter in the box next to the match.

Find a match for every clue.

I can ...
add multi-digit whole numbers

lues

A The sum is between 650 and 750.	**E** The sum is exactly 790.
B The sum is between 1,470 and 1,480.	**F** The sum is exactly 1,068.
C The sum is exactly 1,550.	**G** The sum is between 1,100 and 1,225.
D The sum is between 1,350 and 1,450.	**H** The sum is exactly 1,300.

☐
```
    510
    240
+   550
```

☐
```
    225
    350
+   125
```

☐
```
    400
    850
+   150
```

☐
```
      50
     390
+  1,110
```

☐
```
    125
    125
    225
+   315
```

☐
```
    475
    475
+   175
```

☐
```
    500
    425
    325
+   225
```

☐
```
    500
    250
    250
+    68
```

Word List

- acute triangle
- equilateral triangle
- intersecting lines
- isosceles triangle
- line of symmetry
- line symmetric
- obtuse triangle
- parallel lines
- parallelogram
- perpendicular line
- rectangle
- rhombus
- right triangle
- scalene triangle
- square
- trapezoid

Understand Vocabulary

Write T for *true* and F for *false*.

1. _____ An acute triangle is a triangle with one acute angle.

2. _____ An isosceles triangle has at least two equal sides.

3. _____ A figure is line symmetric if it has at least one line of symmetry.

4. _____ Perpendicular lines form obtuse angles where they intersect.

5. _____ A trapezoid has two pairs of parallel sides.

Write *always, sometimes,* or *never.*

6. An equilateral triangle _____ has three equal sides.

7. Parallel lines _____ intersect.

8. A scalene triangle _____ has equal sides.

9. A rectangle is _____ a square.

10. A rhombus _____ has opposite sides that are parallel.

Use Vocabulary in Writing

11. Rebecca drew a figure. Describe Rebecca's figure. Use at least 3 terms from the Word List in your description.

Danica incorrectly thinks a square is an example of a parallelogram, rectangle, rhombus, and trapezoid. Identify the shape that cannot be classified as a square. Explain.

[ ]

Which type of triangle has no equal side lengths?

Ⓐ Isosceles

Ⓑ Equilateral

Ⓒ Scalene

Ⓓ None of the above

Gavin drew different-colored lines. Draw a line that is parallel to $\overleftrightarrow{SR}$.

Marci described the light from the sun as a line that starts at the sun and continues on forever. Which geometric term best describes Marci's description of the sun's light?

[ ]

5. Four of Mrs. Cromwell's students decorated a bulletin board with the shapes shown below. Who made a shape with 8 lines of symmetry?

Ralph   Liza

Patricia   Dan

Ⓐ Ralph

Ⓑ Liza

Ⓒ Patricia

Ⓓ Dan

6. Are all intersecting lines perpendicular? Draw a picture to help explain your answer.

7. For questions 7a–7d, choose Yes or No to tell if each quadrilateral always has opposite sides that are parallel and right angles.

7a. Square ○ Yes ○ No

7b. Rhombus ○ Yes ○ No

7c. Parallelogram ○ Yes ○ No

7d. Rectangle ○ Yes ○ No

8. Fran drew an equilateral triangle and named it ABC. If Fran labeled one side of the triangle 4 inches, what are the lengths of each of the other two sides of the triangle? Explain.

9. Which set of angles could form a triangle?

Ⓐ Two right angles, one acute angle

Ⓑ One obtuse angle, one right angle, one acute angle

Ⓒ Two obtuse angles, one acute angle

Ⓓ One right angle, two acute angles

10. Lance named a figure that has one angle formed from a pair of perpendicular lines, one pair of parallel sides, and no sides with equal lengths. What geometric term did Lance use to name this figure?

11. Dina's teacher asks her to describe the top and bottom edges of her rule using a geometric term. What term c Dina use?

12. Tanner chose these shapes.

He said the following shapes did not belong with the ones he chose.

What generalization can be made abd the shapes Tanner chose?

13. Complete the drawing so the figure is line symmetric.

.oman Art

Ottoman Empire lasted from 1299 until 1922.
ch of the art from this period contained geometric shapes.

Use the **Ottoman Empire** figure to answer the following.

Part A

Name a pair of parallel lines and explain why the lines
are parallel.

Ottoman Empire

Part B

The enlarged part of the figure shows 4 triangles that
are all the same type. Classify these triangles by their
sides and by their angles. Explain.

Part C

Olivia said the 4 triangles were inside a square. When
asked other possible names for the square, she said it was
a quadrilateral, a parallelogram, and a rectangle. Critique
Olivia's reasoning.

2. The basic shape used in the **Ottoman Scarf** is a quadrilateral. Answer the following about this shape.

Ottoman Scarf

Part A

What are all the names you can use for this quadrilateral? Explain.

Part B

Corbin said the triangle named WXY is acute because it has acute angles. Critique Corbin's reasoning.

Part C

Draw all lines of symmetry on the **Decorative Plate**. How many lines of symmetry does the plate have? Explain why the plate is line symmetric.

Decorative Plate

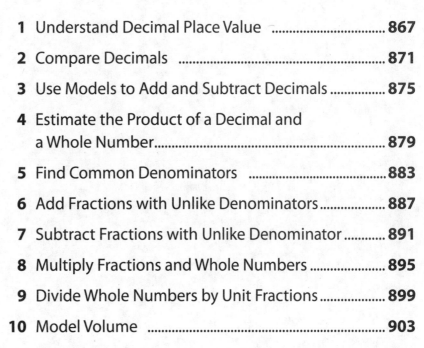

Step Up to Grade 5

Here's a preview of next year. These lessons help you step up to Grade 5.

Lessons

Name _____

☆ ☆
Solve & Share

Over the weekend, Eleni ate $\frac{1}{4}$ box of cereal, and Freddie ate $\frac{3}{8}$ of the same box. What portion of the box of cereal did they eat in all?

Step Up to Grade 5

Lesson 6
Add Fractions with Unlike Denominators

I can ...
add fractions with unlike denominators.

⚙ **Content Standard** 5.AT.2
Process Standards PS.1, PS.3, PS.4, PS.5

$\frac{3}{8}$

$\frac{1}{4}$

Use Appropriate Tools
You can use fraction strips to represent adding fractions. *Show your work!*

Look Back! **Make Sense and Persevere** What steps did you take to solve this problem?

Essential Question

How Can You Add Fractions with Unlike Denominators?

A

Alex rode his scooter from his house to the park. Later, he rode from the park to baseball practice. How far did Alex ride?

 You can add to find the total distance that Alex rode his scooter.

$\frac{1}{2}$ mile

$\frac{1}{3}$ mile

B ## Step 1

Change the fractions to equivalent fractions with a common, or like, denominator.

1

| $\frac{1}{2}$ | $\frac{1}{3}$ |

Multiples of 2: 2, 4, 6, 8, 10, 12, . . .

Multiples of 3: 3, 6, 9, 12, . . .

The number 6 is a common multiple of 2 and 3, so $\frac{1}{2}$ and $\frac{1}{3}$ can both be rewritten with a common denominator of 6.

C ## Step 2

Write equivalent fractions with a common denominator.

$\frac{1}{2} \times \frac{3}{3} = \frac{3}{6}$

$\frac{1}{3} \times \frac{2}{2} = \frac{2}{6}$

D ## Step 3

Add the fraction to find the total number of sixth

$$\frac{1}{2} = \frac{3}{6}$$
$$+ \frac{1}{3} = \frac{2}{6}$$
$$\overline{\frac{5}{6}}$$

Alex rode his scooter $\frac{5}{6}$ mile.

Convince Me! **Construct Arguments** In the example above, would you get the same sum if you used 12 as the common denominator? Explain.

nother Example

nd $\frac{5}{12} + \frac{1}{4}$.

$\frac{5}{12} + \frac{1}{4} = \frac{5}{12} + \frac{3}{12}$ Write equivalent fractions with common denominators.

$= \frac{5+3}{12} = \frac{8}{12}$ or $\frac{2}{3}$ Find the total number of twelfths by adding the numerators.

Guided Practice

o You Understand?

1. In the example at the top of page 888, if the park was $\frac{1}{8}$ mile from baseball practice instead of $\frac{1}{3}$ mile, how far would Alex ride his scooter in all?

2. **A-Z Vocabulary** Rico and Nita solved the same problem. Rico got $\frac{6}{8}$ for an answer, and Nita got $\frac{3}{4}$. Which answer is correct? Use the term *equivalent fraction* in your explanation.

Do You Know How?

For **3**, find the sum. Use fraction strips to help.

3. $\frac{1}{2} + \frac{2}{4} = \frac{\square}{\square} + \frac{\square}{\square} = \frac{\square}{\square}$

dependent Practice

r **4–5**, find each sum. Use fraction strips help.

Remember that you can use multiples to find a common denominator.

$\frac{1}{3} + \frac{1}{4} = \frac{\square}{\square} + \frac{\square}{\square} = \frac{\square}{\square}$

5. $\frac{1}{8} + \frac{1}{4} + \frac{1}{8} =$

$\frac{\square}{\square} + \frac{\square}{\square} + \frac{\square}{\square} = \frac{\square}{\square}$

Problem Solving

6. **Construct Arguments** Explain why the denominator 12 in $\frac{5}{12}$ is not changed when adding the fractions.

$$
\begin{array}{r}
\frac{5}{12} = \frac{5}{12} \\
+ \ \frac{1}{3} = \frac{4}{12} \\
\hline
\frac{9}{12}
\end{array}
$$

---

7. **Model with Math** To make juice, Cindy added $\frac{5}{8}$ cup of water to $\frac{1}{4}$ cup of juice concentrate. How much juice did Cindy make? Write and solve an equation.

8. **Math and Science** Of 36 chemical elements, 2 are named for women scientists and 25 are named for places. What fraction are named for women? Write two equivalent fractions.

---

9. **Higher Order Thinking** Alicia is making tropical punch for a picnic. What is the total amount of lemon juice and orange juice Alicia will need? Is this amount more than the amount of sugar she will need? Explain.

DATA

Tropical Punch Recipe	
Ingredient	**Amount**
Lemon Juice	$\frac{1}{3}$ cup
Water	4 cups
Sugar	$\frac{2}{3}$ cup
Orange Juice	$\frac{1}{2}$ cup

Assessment | **ISTEP+ Ready**

10. Choose Yes or No to tell if the fraction $\frac{1}{2}$ will make each equation true.

$\square + \frac{6}{6} = \frac{3}{2}$ ○ Yes ○ No

$\frac{1}{12} + \frac{2}{5} = \square$ ○ Yes ○ No

$\frac{1}{2} + \square = \frac{4}{4}$ ○ Yes ○ No

$\frac{1}{6} + \frac{2}{6} = \square$ ○ Yes ○ No

11. Choose Yes or No to tell if the fraction will make each equation true.

$\frac{12}{12} + \square = \frac{9}{6}$ ○ Yes ○ No

$\frac{1}{4} + \frac{2}{3} = \square$ ○ Yes ○ No

$\square + \frac{2}{8} = \frac{6}{8}$ ○ Yes ○ No

$\frac{1}{10} + \square = \frac{6}{10}$ ○ Yes ○ No

☆ ☆
Solve & Share

Rose bought the length of copper pipe shown below. She used $\frac{1}{2}$ yard to repair a water line in her house. How much pipe does she have left? **Solve this problem any way you choose.**

Solve

$\frac{4}{6}$ yard

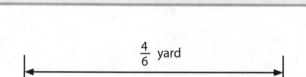

Lesson 7
Subtract Fractions with Unlike Denominators

I can ...
subtract fractions with unlike denominators.

Content Standard 5.AT.2
Process Standards PS.2, PS.3, PS.4, PS.7, PS.8

Use Structure You can use mental math to find equivalent fractions so that $\frac{1}{2}$ and $\frac{4}{6}$ will have like denominators. *Show your work!*

Look Back! **Generalize** How is subtracting fractions with unlike denominators similar to adding fractions with unlike denominators?

Essential Question

How Can You Subtract Fractions with Unlike Denominators?

A

Linda used $\frac{1}{4}$ yard of the fabric she bought for a sewing project. How much fabric did she have left?

You can use subtraction to find how much fabric was left.

$\frac{2}{3}$ yard

B ## Step 1

Find a common multiple of the denominators.

Multiples of 3: 3, 6, 9, 12, ...

Multiples of 4: 4, 8, 12, ...

The number 12 is a multiple of 3 and 4. Write equivalent fractions with a denominator of 12 for $\frac{2}{3}$ and $\frac{1}{4}$.

C ## Step 2

Use the Identity Property to rename the fractions with a common denominator.

$\frac{2}{3} \times \frac{4}{4} = \frac{8}{12}$

$\frac{2}{3} = \frac{8}{12}$

$\frac{1}{4} \times \frac{3}{3} = \frac{3}{12}$

$\frac{1}{4} \times \frac{3}{3} = \frac{3}{12}$

D ## Step 3

Subtract the numerators.

$\frac{2}{3} = \frac{8}{12}$
$-\frac{1}{4} = \frac{3}{12}$
$\phantom{-\frac{1}{4}} = \frac{5}{12}$

Linda has $\frac{5}{12}$ yard of fabric left.

Convince Me! **Critique Reasoning** Suppose Linda had $\frac{2}{3}$ of a yard of fabric and told Sandra that she used $\frac{3}{4}$ of a yard. Sandra says this is not possible. Do you agree? Explain your answer.

Guided Practice

Do You Understand?

1. Reasoning In the example on page 892, is it possible to use a common denominator greater than 12 and get the correct answer? Why or why not?

2. In the example on page 892, if Linda had started with 1 yard of fabric and used $\frac{5}{8}$ yard, how much fabric would be left?

Do You Know How?

For **3–6**, find each difference.

3.
$$\frac{3}{4} = \frac{9}{12}$$
$$-\frac{1}{3} = \frac{4}{12}$$

4.
$$\frac{5}{12} = \frac{10}{24}$$
$$-\frac{1}{8} = \frac{3}{24}$$

5.
$$\frac{2}{3}$$
$$-\frac{1}{6}$$

6.
$$\frac{7}{10}$$
$$-\frac{3}{8}$$

Independent Practice

Leveled Practice For **7–16**, find each difference.

7.
$$\frac{3}{5} = \frac{\square}{10}$$
$$-\frac{3}{10} = \frac{\square}{10}$$
$$\frac{\square}{\square}$$

8.
$$\frac{1}{2} = \frac{\square}{6}$$
$$-\frac{2}{6} = \frac{\square}{6}$$
$$\frac{\square}{\square}$$

9.
$$\frac{8}{9}$$
$$-\frac{5}{6}$$

10.
$$\frac{5}{6}$$
$$-\frac{1}{2}$$

11.
$$\frac{7}{8}$$
$$-\frac{2}{3}$$

12.
$$\frac{4}{5}$$
$$-\frac{3}{4}$$

13.
$$\frac{7}{10}$$
$$-\frac{1}{5}$$

14.
$$\frac{12}{16}$$
$$-\frac{2}{4}$$

15.
$$\frac{4}{9}$$
$$-\frac{2}{6}$$

16.
$$\frac{5}{5}$$
$$-\frac{2}{8}$$

Problem Solving

17. Model with Math Write and solve an equation to find the difference between the location of Point *A* and Point *B* on the ruler.

18. Algebra Write an addition and a subtraction equation for the diagram. Then find the missing value.

x	
$\frac{1}{6}$	$\frac{1}{3}$

19. Critique Reasoning Seth said, "Fractic need to have a common denominator before you can add or subtract them." Is Seth correct? Explain.

20. Number Sense What mistake was made in the problem? What is the correct answer?

$$\frac{7}{8} = \frac{7}{8}$$
$$-\frac{1}{4} = \frac{1}{8}$$
$$\overline{\qquad \frac{6}{8}}$$

21. Higher Order Thinking Find two fractions with a difference of $\frac{1}{2}$ but with neither denominator equal to 2.

22. Choose the correct fractions from the box below to complete the subtraction sentence that follows.

$\frac{5}{6}$	$\frac{2}{3}$	$\frac{1}{30}$	$\frac{6}{7}$	$\frac{3}{6}$

$$\boxed{} - \frac{1}{3} = \boxed{}$$

23. Choose the correct fractions from the box below to complete the subtraction sentence that follows.

$\frac{11}{12}$	$\frac{1}{6}$	$\frac{1}{4}$	$\frac{1}{2}$	$\frac{3}{4}$

$$\boxed{} - \boxed{} = \frac{9}{12}$$

Solve

Solve & Share

Julie has 10 yards of ribbon. She divides the ribbon into 3 equal pieces and uses 2 of the pieces on gifts. How much ribbon does she use? *Solve this problem any way you choose.*

I can ...
multiply fractions and whole numbers.

Content Standard 5.AT.3
Process Standards PS.2, PS.3, PS.4, PS.6

10 yd

Model with Math You can use words, pictures, and equations to solve the problem. *Show your work in the space above!*

Look Back! **Reasoning** Should the answer be less than or greater than 5? How do you know?

How Can You Multiply Fractions and Whole Numbers?

A

Hal spent $\frac{3}{4}$ hour reading each day for 7 days. How much total time did he spend reading?

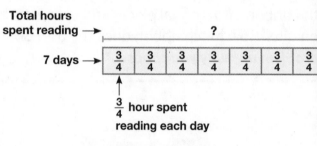

Total hours spent reading → | ? |

7 days → | $\frac{3}{4}$ | $\frac{3}{4}$ | $\frac{3}{4}$ | $\frac{3}{4}$ | $\frac{3}{4}$ | $\frac{3}{4}$ | $\frac{3}{4}$ |

$\frac{3}{4}$ hour spent reading each day

I need to find $7 \times \frac{3}{4}$.

B ## One Way

Multiply to find the number of fourths.

$7 \times \frac{3}{4} = 7 \times 3 \times \frac{1}{4}$

$= 21 \times \frac{1}{4}$

$= \frac{21}{4}$

To rename $\frac{21}{4}$, divide the numerator by the denominator.

Rewrite as a mixed number.

$\frac{21}{4} = 5\frac{1}{4}$

Hal spent $5\frac{1}{4}$ hours reading.

C ## Another Way

Rename the whole number as a fraction. Multiply the numerators, multiply the denominators, and then write the product as a mixed number.

$\frac{7}{1} \times \frac{3}{4} = \frac{7 \times 3}{1 \times 4} = \frac{21}{4} = 5\frac{1}{4}$

Hal spent $5\frac{1}{4}$ hours reading.

Every whole number can be written as a fraction with a denominator of 1.

Convince Me! **Be Precise** Find $6 \times \frac{4}{9}$. Then use repeated addition to justify your answer.

Guided Practice

Do You Understand?

1. Reasoning In the example at the top of the previous page, how can finding $\frac{1}{4}$ of 7 help you find $\frac{3}{4}$ of 7?

2. If Hal spent $\frac{2}{3}$ of an hour reading each day for 7 days, how much time, in all, did he spend reading? Show how you found your answer.

Do You Know How?

For **3–5**, find each product. Write the product as a mixed number.

3. $\frac{1}{3} \times 18 = \dfrac{\square \times \square}{\square} = \dfrac{\square}{\square} = \square$

4. $\frac{5}{6} \times 35 = \dfrac{\square \times \square}{\square} = \dfrac{\square}{\square} = \square\dfrac{\square}{\square}$

5. $\frac{2}{3} \times 26 = \dfrac{\square \times \square}{\square} = \dfrac{\square}{\square} = \square\dfrac{\square}{\square}$

Independent Practice

Leveled Practice For **6–16**, find each product. Write the product as a mixed number.

Remember: You can use division to rename a fraction as a mixed number.

6. $\frac{3}{5} \times 40 = \dfrac{\square \times \square}{\square}$
$= \dfrac{\square}{\square} = \square$

7. $\frac{7}{8} \times 56 = \dfrac{\square \times \square}{\square}$
$= \dfrac{\square}{\square} = \square$

8. $\frac{2}{3} \times 80 = \dfrac{\square \times \square}{\square}$
$= \dfrac{\square}{\square} = \square\dfrac{\square}{\square}$

9. $\frac{2}{5}$ of 35

10. $\frac{4}{7}$ of 45

11. $\frac{1}{4}$ of 28

12. $\frac{3}{7}$ of 63

13. $\frac{1}{6}$ of 205

14. $\frac{3}{4}$ of 100

15. $\frac{4}{5}$ of 231

16. $\frac{2}{3}$ of 204

Problem Solving

17. On Mars, your weight is about $\frac{1}{3}$ of your weight on Earth. If a fourth grader weighs 96 pounds on Earth, about how much would he or she weigh on Mars?

18. Number Sense How can you use men math to find $25 \times \frac{2}{10}$?

19. During a nature walk, Mary identified 24 species of animals and plants.

  a **Construct Arguments** Mary said $\frac{1}{5}$ of the species she identified were animals. Can this be correct? Explain.

  b If $\frac{1}{3}$ of the species Mary identified were animals, how many plants did Mary identify?

20. A rectangular painting is 3 feet long and $\frac{5}{6}$ foot wide. What is the area of the painting?

21. Higher Order Thinking One recipe calls for $\frac{1}{3}$ cup flour per batch and the other calls for $\frac{1}{2}$ cup flour per batch. How much flour will Marcy use if she makes 12 batches of each type of cookie?

22. Math and Science A water molecule is made up of 3 atoms. One third of the atoms are oxygen and the remaining atoms are hydrogen. If there are 125 water molecules, how many hydrogen atoms are there? Show your work.

Assessment ⊙ ISTEP+ Ready

23. Which is the product of 21 and $\frac{3}{7}$?

  Ⓐ $2\frac{3}{7}$

  Ⓑ 5

  Ⓒ 9

  Ⓓ $32\frac{2}{3}$

24. Which is the product of $\frac{11}{12}$ and 3?

  Ⓐ $1\frac{1}{4}$

  Ⓑ $2\frac{3}{4}$

  Ⓒ $4\frac{1}{3}$

  Ⓓ 33

ame_____

Solve & Share

One ball of dough can be stretched into a circle to make a pizza. After the pizza is cooked, it is cut into 8 equal slices. How many slices of pizza can you make with 3 balls of dough? **Solve this problem any way you choose.**

Lesson 9
Divide Whole Numbers by Unit Fractions

I can ...
divide a whole number by a unit fraction.

Content Standard 5.AT.4
Process Standards PS.1, PS.2, PS.4, PS.5

You can use appropriate tools to help find the answer. Show your work!

Look Back! **Reasoning** Into how many slices of pizza will each ball of dough be divided? What fraction of a whole pizza does 1 slice represent?

How Can You Divide by a Unit Fraction?

A

Joyce is making sushi rolls. She needs $\frac{1}{4}$ cup of rice for each sushi roll. How many sushi rolls can she make if she has 3 cups of rice?

$\frac{1}{4}$ is a unit fraction. A unit fraction is a fraction that describes one part of the whole. So, it has a numerator of 1.

B One Way

Use an area model to find how many $\frac{1}{4}$s are in 3.

There are four $\frac{1}{4}$s in 1 whole cup. So, there are twelve $\frac{1}{4}$s in three whole cups. So, Joyce can make 12 sushi rolls.

 You can also use a number line to represent this problem.

C Another Way

Use a number line to to find how many $\frac{1}{4}$s are in 3.

You can see that there are four $\frac{1}{4}$s between each whole number.

There are four $\frac{1}{4}$s in 1 whole, eight $\frac{1}{4}$s in 2 wholes, and twelve $\frac{1}{4}$s in 3 wholes.

So, $3 \div \frac{1}{4} = 12$.
Joyce can make 12 sushi rolls.

Convince Me! **Model with Math** Use the diagram below to find $4 \div \frac{1}{3}$.

$4 \div \frac{1}{3} =$ _____

900   **Step Up** | Lesson 9

Copyright © Savvas Learning Company LLC. All Rights Reserved.

Guided Practice

Do You Understand?

1. In the example at the top of page 900, if Joyce had 4 cups of rice, how many rolls could she make?

2. In the example at the top of page 900, how does the number line help to show that $3 \div \frac{1}{4}$ is equal to 3×4?

Do You Know How?

For **3–4**, use the picture below to find each quotient.

3. How many $\frac{1}{3}$s are in 2?

$2 \div \frac{1}{3} =$ _____

4. How many $\frac{1}{3}$s are in 3?

$3 \div \frac{1}{3} =$ _____

Independent Practice

Leveled Practice For **5–6**, use the picture to find each quotient.

5. How many $\frac{1}{6}$s are in 2?

$2 \div \frac{1}{6} =$ _____

6. How many $\frac{1}{6}$s are in 3?

$3 \div \frac{1}{6} =$ _____

For **7–14**, draw a picture or use a number line to find each quotient.

7. $2 \div \frac{1}{4}$

8. $15 \div \frac{1}{5}$

9. $5 \div \frac{1}{6}$

10. $21 \div \frac{1}{7}$

11. $16 \div \frac{1}{5}$

12. $25 \div \frac{1}{2}$

13. $3 \div \frac{1}{8}$

14. $10 \div \frac{1}{5}$

Problem Solving

15. Model with Math Sylvia made 3 loaves of bread. She gives each person $\frac{1}{6}$ of a loaf with dinner. How many people can Sylvia serve? Draw a picture to help answer the question.

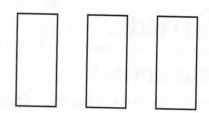

16. Higher Order Thinking Explain why dividing a whole number by a unit fraction results in a number greater than the whole number.

17. Number Sense The distance from Virginia Beach, VA, to San Jose, CA, is 2,990 miles. If you want to travel this distance in 3 months, about how many miles need to be traveled each month?

18. Make Sense and Persevere Carmen used one bag of flour. She baked three loaves of bread. Then she used the remaining flour to make 24 muffins. How much flour was in the bag to begin with?

DATA	Recipe	Amount of Flour Needed
	Bread	$2\frac{1}{4}$ cups per loaf
	Muffins	$3\frac{1}{4}$ cups per 24 muffins
	Pizza	$1\frac{1}{2}$ cups per pie

Assessment · **ISTEP+ Ready**

19. Alonso is making light-switch plates from pieces of wood. Each piece of wood is 6 feet long. How many light switch plates can Alonso make if he has 2 pieces of wood?

Ⓐ 12 light switch plates

Ⓑ 18 light switch plates

Ⓒ 36 light switch plates

Ⓓ 42 light switch plates

DATA	Wood Projects	
	Item	Length Needed for Each
	Cabinet Shelf	$\frac{3}{4}$ foot
	Light Switch Plate	$\frac{1}{3}$ foot
	Shingle	$\frac{2}{3}$ foot

ame _____

⭐ ⭐
Solve & Share

Gina is building a rectangular prism out of sugar cubes for her art class project. She started by drawing a diagram of the rectangular prism that is 4 cubes high and 4 cubes long. How many cubes does she use to make the prism? *Solve this problem any way you choose.*

I can ...
find the volume of solid figures.

Content Standard 5.M.4
Process Standards PS.2, PS.5

Use Appropriate Tools
You can draw a picture to find the number of cubes in a rectangular prism. *Show your work!*

Side View

Front View

Top View

Look Back! **Reasoning** Gina decided to change her art project and build a rectangular prism that is 3 cubes long, 4 cubes wide, and 2 cubes high. Use the picture to determine the number of cubes she used.

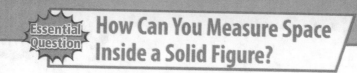
How Can You Measure Space Inside a Solid Figure?

A

Volume is the number of cubic units needed to pack a solid figure without gaps or overlaps. A cubic unit is the volume of a cube measuring 1 unit on each edge. What is the volume of this rectangular prism?

Each cube of a solid figure is 1 cubic unit.

unit cube

1 unit   1 unit

1 unit

B   Use unit cubes to make a model.

Count the number of cubes.

There are 15 unit cubes in the bottom layer. The volume of the bottom layer is 15 cubic units.

C   There are two layers.

second layer

Multiply the volume of the bottom layer by 2.

The volume of the prism is 2 × 15 or 30 cubic units.

Convince Me! **Reasoning**   In the picture below, how many unit cubes does it take to make the rectangular prism on the left without gaps or overlaps? How many 2-unit cubes does it take to make the rectangular prism?

2-unit cube

Tools Assessment

Guided Practice

Do You Understand?

1. Make a model of a rectangular prism with a bottom layer that is 4 cubes long by 3 cubes wide. Make a top layer that is the same as the bottom layer. Then draw a picture of your model. What is the volume?

2. **A-Z Vocabulary** Describe how to find the *volume* of a *rectangular prism*.

Do You Know How?

For **3–4**, use unit cubes to make a model of each rectangular prism. Find the volume.

3.

4.

Independent Practice

For **5–13**, find the volume of each solid. Use unit cubes to help.

5.

6.

7.

8.

9.

10.

11.

12.

13.

Problem Solving

For **14–18**, use the table.

Compare the volumes of the prisms.
Write >, <, or = for each ◯.

14. Prism A ◯ Prism B

15. Prism B ◯ Prism C

16. Prism C ◯ Prism A

Prism	Model
A	
B	
C	

17. If you added another layer of unit cubes on top of Prism C, what would its volume be in cubic units?

18. If you put Prism C on top of Prism A, wh would the volume of the new solid be ir cubic units?

19. **Reasoning** In an election, 15,392 people voted. Candidate B received 8,205 votes. Candidate A received the rest of the votes. Which candidate won the election? By how many votes?

20. **Higher Order Thinking** Ms. Smith's boxes are each 5 inches long, 5 inches wide, and 5 inches tall. How many of her boxes can she fit into a case that is 20 inches long, 20 inches wide, and 20 inches tall? Explain.

Assessment ▷◎ (ISTEP+ Ready)

21. Frank made the solid figures shown using unit cubes. Which statement about these models is true?

Model X   Model Y

Ⓐ Model X and Model Y have the same volume.

Ⓑ The volume of Model X is 7 cubic units greater than the volume of Model Y.

Ⓒ The volume of Model X is 15 cubic units greater than the volume of Model Y.

Ⓓ The volume of Model X and Model Y combined is 55 cubic units.

Glossary

A

acute angle An angle that is open less than a right angle.

acute triangle A triangle that has three acute angles.

addends The numbers that are added together to find a sum.
Example: $2 + 7 = 9$

Addends

algorithm A set of steps used to solve a math problem.

angle A figure formed by two rays that have the same endpoint.

angle measure The number of degrees in an angle.

area The number of square units needed to cover a region.

array A way of displaying objects in rows and columns.

Associative Property of Addition
Addends can be regrouped and the sum remains the same.

Associative Property of Multiplication Factors can be regrouped and the product stays the same.

B

bar diagram A tool used to help understand and solve word problems.

bar graph A graph using bars to show data.

benchmark fraction A known fraction that is commonly used for estimating.
Examples: $\frac{1}{4}, \frac{1}{3}, \frac{1}{2}, \frac{2}{3},$ and $\frac{3}{4}$.

billions A period of three places to the left of the millions period.

breaking apart Mental math method used to rewrite a number as the sum of numbers to form an easier problem.

C

capacity The amount a container can hold, measured in liquid units.

center A point within a circle that is the same distance from all points on a circle.

centimeter (cm) A metric unit used to measure length. 100 centimeters = 1 meter

century A unit of time equal to 100 years.

circle A closed plane figure in which all the points are the same distance from a point called the center.

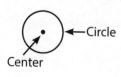
Circle
Center

common denominator A number that is the denominator of two or more fractions.

common factor A number that is a factor of two or more given numbers.

Commutative Property of Addition Numbers can be added in any order and the sum remains the same.

Commutative Property of Multiplication Factors can be multiplied in any order and the product stays the same.

compare Decide if one number is greater than, less than, or equal to another number.

compatible numbers Numbers that are easy to compute mentally.

compensation Choosing numbers close to the numbers in a problem to make the computation easier, and then adjusting the answer for the numbers chosen.

compose To combine parts.

composite number A whole number greater than 1 with more than two factors.

conjecture Statement that is believed to be true but has not been proven.

coordinate grid A grid used to show ordered pairs.

counting on Counting up from the lesser number to the greater number to find the difference of two numbers.

cube A solid figure with six identical squares as its faces.

cubic unit The volume of a cube that measures 1 unit on each edge.

cup (c) A customary unit of capacity. 1 cup = 8 fluid ounces

customary units of measure Units of measure that are used in the United States.

D

data Pieces of collected information.

day A unit of time equal to 24 hours.

decade A unit of time equal to 10 years.

decimal A number with one or more digits to the right of the decimal point.

decimal point A dot used to separate dollars from cents in money or to separate ones from tenths in a number.

decimeter (dm) A metric unit of length equal to 10 centimeters.

decompose To break into parts.

degree (°) A unit of measure for angles. $1° = \frac{1}{360}$ of a circle. Also a unit of measure for temperature.

denominator The number below the fraction bar in a fraction that represents the total number of equal parts in one whole.

difference The answer when subtracting two numbers.

digits The symbols used to write a number: 0, 1, 2, 3, 4, 5, 6, 7, 8, and 9.

Distributive Property Multiplying a sum (or difference) by a number is the same as multiplying each number in the sum (or difference) by that number and adding (or subtracting) the products. *Example:* $(3 \times 21) = (3 \times 20) + (3 \times 1)$

divide An operation to find the number in each group or the number of equal groups.

dividend The number to be divided.

divisibility rules The rules that state when a number is divisible by another number.

divisible Can be divided by another number without leaving a remainder. *Example:* 10 is divisible by 2

divisor The number by which another number is divided.
Example: $32 \div 4 = 8$
↑
Divisor

dot plot A type of line plot that uses dots to indicate the number of times a response occurred.

elapsed time The amount of time between the beginning of an event and the end of the event.

equation A number sentence that uses the equal sign ($=$) to show that two expressions have the same value. *Example:* $9 + 3 = 12$

equilateral triangle A triangle with three sides that are the same length.

equivalent Numbers that name the same amount.

equivalent fractions Fractions that name the same region, part of a set, or part of a segment.

estimate To give an approximate value rather than an exact answer.

expanded form A number written as the sum of the values of its digits. *Example:* $2,476 = 2,000 + 400 + 70 + 6$

expression A mathematical phrase. *Examples:* $x - 3$ or $2 + 7$

F

fact family A group of related facts using the same set of numbers.

factor pairs Numbers that when multiplied together give a certain product.

factors The numbers that are multiplied together to give a product.
Example: 3 × 6 = 18
↖ ↗
Factors

fluid ounce (fl oz) A customary unit of capacity. 1 fluid ounce = 2 tablespoons; 8 fluid ounces = 1 cup

foot (ft) A customary unit of length. 1 foot = 12 inches

formula An equation that uses symbols to relate two or more quantities.
Example: $A = \ell \times w$

fraction A symbol, such as $\frac{2}{3}, \frac{5}{1}$, or $\frac{8}{5}$, used to name a part of a whole, a part of a set, or a location on a number line.

frequency The number of times that a response occurs in a set of data.

frequency table A way to display data that shows how many times a response occurs in a set of data.

G

gallon (gal) A customary unit of capacity. 1 gallon = 4 quarts

generalize To make a general statement.

gram (g) A metric unit of mass. 1,000 grams = 1 kilogram

greater than symbol (>) A symbol that points away from a greater number or expression. *Example:* 450 > 449

H

hexagon A polygon with 6 sides.

hour A unit of time equal to 60 minutes.

hundredth One part of 100 equal parts of a whole.

I

Identity Property of Addition The sum of any number and zero is that number.

Identity Property of Multiplication The product of any number and one is that number.

inch (in.) A customary unit of length. 12 inches = 1 foot

inequality A number sentence that uses the greater than sign ($>$) or the less than sign ($<$) to show that two expressions do not have the same value. *Example:* 5 $>$ 3

intersecting lines Lines that pass through the same point.

interval A number which is the difference between two consecutive numbers on the scale of a graph.

inverse operations Operations that undo each other.
Examples: Adding 6 and subtracting 6; Multiplying by 4 and dividing by 4.

isosceles triangle A triangle with at least two equal sides.

key Part of a graph that tells what each symbol stands for.

kilogram (kg) A metric unit of mass equal to 1,000 grams. 1 kilogram = 1,000 grams

kilometer (km) A metric unit of length equal to 1,000 meters. 1 kilometer = 1,000 meters

leap year A calendar occurrence that happens every four years when an extra day is added to February. Leap years have 366 days.

less than symbol ($<$) A symbol that points towards a lesser number or expression. *Example:* 305 $<$ 320

line A straight path of points that goes on and on in opposite directions.

line of symmetry A line on which a figure can be folded so both halves are the same.

line plot A way to display data along a number line, where each dot represents one number in a set of data.

line segment A part of a line that has two endpoints.

line symmetric A figure that can be folded on a line to form two halves that fit exactly on top of each other.

liter (L) A metric unit of capacity. 1 liter = 1,000 milliliters

M

mass The amount of matter that something contains.

meter (m) A metric unit of length. 1 meter = 100 centimeters

metric units of measure Units of measure commonly used by scientists.

mile (mi) A customary unit of length. 1 mile = 5,280 feet

millennium (plural: millennia) A unit for measuring time equal to 1,000 years.

milligram (mg) A metric unit of mass. 1,000 milligrams = 1 gram

milliliter (mL) A metric unit of capacity. 1,000 milliliters = 1 liter

millimeter (mm) A metric unit of length. 1,000 millimeters = 1 meter

millions In a number, a period of three places to the left of the thousands period.

minute A unit of time equal to 60 seconds.

mixed number A number that has a whole number part and a fraction part.

month One of the 12 parts into which a year is divided.

multiple The product of a given whole number and any non-zero whole number.

N

number name A way to write a number in words. *Example:* Four thousand, six hundred thirty-two.

numerator In a fraction, the number above the fraction bar that represents the part of the whole.

numerical expression An expression that contains numbers and at least one operation. *Example:* 35 + 12

O

obtuse angle An angle that is open more than a right angle but less than a straight angle.

obtuse triangle A triangle that has one obtuse angle.

octagon A polygon with 8 sides.

ounce (oz) A customary unit of weight. 16 ounces = 1 pound

outlier Any number in a data set that is very different from the rest of the numbers.

overestimate An estimate that is greater than the exact answer.

parallel lines
Lines that never intersect.

parallelogram
A quadrilateral that has
two pairs of parallel sides.

partial products Products found by
breaking one factor in a multiplication
problem into ones, tens, hundreds, and so
on and then multiplying each of these by
the other factor.

partial quotients A way to divide
that finds quotients in parts until only
a remainder, if any, is left.

pentagon A plane figure with 5 sides.

perimeter The distance around a figure.

period In a number, a group of three
digits, separated by commas, starting
from the right.

perpendicular lines Intersecting
lines that form right angles.

pint (pt) A customary unit of capacity.
1 pint = 2 cups

place value The value given to a place a
digit has in a number.
Example: In 3,946, the 9 is in the hundreds
place. So, the 9 has a value of 900.

point An exact location in space.

polygon A closed plane figure made up
of line segments.

pound (lb) A customary unit of weight.
1 pound = 16 ounces

prime number A whole number greater
than 1 that has exactly two factors, itself
and 1.

product The answer to a
multiplication problem.

protractor A tool used to measure and
draw angles.

Q

quadrilateral A polygon with 4 sides.

quart (qt) A customary unit of capacity.
1 quart = 2 pints

quotient The answer to a
division problem.

ray A part of a line that has one endpoint and continues on forever in one direction.

rectangle A quadrilateral that has four right angles.

rectangular prism A solid figure with 6 rectangular faces.

regroup To name a whole number in a different way. *Example:* 32 = 2 tens 12 ones

remainder The number that remains after the division is complete.

repeated addition A way to write a multiplication expression as an addition expression. *Example:* 3 × 5 = 5 + 5 + 5

repeating pattern Made up of shapes or numbers that form a part that repeats.

rhombus A quadrilateral that has opposite sides that are parallel and all of its sides are the same length.

right angle An angle that forms a square corner.

right triangle A triangle that has one right angle.

rounding A process that determines which multiple of 10, 100, 1,000, and so on a number is closest to.

rule A mathematical phrase that tells how numbers in a table are related.

scale Numbers that show the units used on a graph.

scalene triangle A triangle with no sides that are the same length.

second A unit of time. 60 seconds = 1 minute

sequence A set of numbers that follows a pattern.

side Each of the line segments of a polygon.

solid figure A figure with three dimensions that has length, width, and height.

solution The value of the variable that makes an equation true.

solve an equation Find a solution to an equation.

square A quadrilateral that has four right angles and all sides are the same length.

square unit A square with sides one unit long used to measure area.

standard form A way to write a number showing only its digits. Commas separate groups of three digits starting from the right. *Example:* 613,095

straight angle An angle that forms a straight line.

sum The result of adding numbers together.

survey Collecting information by asking a number of people the same question and recording their answers.

T

tablespoon (tbsp) A customary unit of capacity. 1 tablespoon = 3 teaspoons

teaspoon (tsp) A customary unit of capacity. 3 teaspoons = 1 tablespoon

tenth One part of 10 equal parts of a whole.

terms Numbers in a sequence or variables, such as *x* and *y*, in an expression.

ton (T) A customary unit of weight. 1 ton = 2,000 pounds

trapezoid A quadrilateral with only one pair of parallel sides.

triangle A polygon with 3 sides.

U

underestimate An estimate that is less than the exact answer.

unit angle An angle that cuts off $\frac{1}{360}$ of a circle and measures 1°.

unit fraction A fraction with a numerator of 1. *Example:* $\frac{1}{2}$

unknown A symbol or letter, such as *x*, that represents a number in an expression or equation.

V

variable A symbol or letter that stands for a number.

vertex (plural: vertices) The point where two rays meet to form an angle.

volume The number of cubic units needed to fill a solid figure.

week A unit of time equal to 7 days.

weight A measure of how heavy an object is.

whole numbers The numbers 0, 1, 2, 3, 4, and so on.

yard (yd) A customary unit of length. 1 yard = 3 feet

year A unit of time equal to 365 days or 52 weeks or 12 months.

Zero Property of Multiplication The product of any number and zero is zero. *Examples:* $3 \times 0 = 0$; $5 \times 0 = 0$

enVisionmath® 2.0

Photographs

Photo locators denoted as follows: Top (T), Center (C), Bottom (B), Left (L), Right (R), Background (Bkgd)

001 MarclSchauer/Shutterstock; 032 petr84/Fotolia; 043 forkArt Photography/Fotolia; 060 Alexey Usachev/ Fotolia; 068 Digital Vision/Thinkstock; 091 John Hoffman/Shutterstock; 108 Stevanzz/Fotolia; 134CL Andreanita/Fotolia; 134CR Algre/Fotolia; 134L EcoView/Fotolia; 134R Eduardo Rivero/Fotolia; 138 Bork/Shutterstock; 152 Andrew Breeden/Fotolia; 167 Majeczka/Shutterstock; 204 Steve Byland/ Shutterstock; 210 2011/Photos To Go; 222 Rikke/ Fotolia; 224 Fotolia; 236L Neelsky/Shutterstock; 236R Serg64/Shutterstock; 249 Mark McClare/ Shutterstock; 325 ShutterStock; 340 Flashon Studio/ Shutterstock; 344 Cbpix/Shutterstock; 348L JackF/ Fotolia; 348R Smileus/Shutterstock; 365 ShutterStock; 378 Comstock Images/Jupiter Images; 382 Womue/ Fotolia; 407 Kletr/Shutterstock; 414 Hamik/Fotolia; 461 Adrio/Fotolia; 468 Oleksii Sagitov/Shutterstock; 470 Africa Studio/Fotolia; 516 Werner Dreblow/Fotolia; 520 Image Source/Jupiter Images; 524C Melinda Fawver/ Shutterstock; 524L Yaping/Shutterstock; 524R Undy/ Fotolia; 539 pk7comcastnet/Fotolia; 556 JLV Image Works/Fotolia; 587 NASA; 623 Bork/Shutterstock; 630 Hemera Technologies/ThinkStock; 648 Concept w/ Fotolia; 651 StockPhotosArt/Fotolia; 669CL Donfink/ Fotolia; 669CR Tim elliott/Fotolia; 669L Proedding/ Fotolia; 669R Petergyure/Fotolia; 670 Redwood/ Fotolia; 671 Katrina Brown/Fotolia; 690 CristinaMuraca/ Shutterstock; 694 Duncan Noakes/Fotolia; 696 Viorel Sima/Shutterstock; 706 Sergio Martínez/Fotolia; 708 Pascal Rateau/Fotolia; 728B LittleMiss/Shutterstock;

728T Margouillat photo/Shutterstock; 729 luchschen/ Shutterstock; 750 Justin Black/Shutterstock; 765 James Kingman/Shutterstock; 786 Tom Grundy/Shutterstock; 813 WitR/Shutterstock; 815 Dja65/Shutterstock; 822 Arina P Habich/Shutterstock; 842 Gary Blakeley/Fotolia; 863 EvrenKalinbacak/Shutterstock; 864B Orhan Cam/ Shutterstock; 864T Thampapon/Shutterstock.

IN6 Szasz-Fabian Erika/Fotolia; IN8 Zeng Wei Jun/ Shutterstock; IN54 speedygo/Shutterstock.

GRADE 4 LESSONS EXCLUSIVELY FOR INDIANA

You will use these lessons throughout the year.

Another Look!

Nick is painting blue and purple stripes on 2 walls. Write a mixed number and an improper fraction for the parts of the walls Nick has finished painting.

Each wall is divided into 10 equal parts. Nick has painted all of one wall and 7 out of 10 parts of the second wall.

Nick has finished painting $1\frac{7}{10}$, or $\frac{17}{10}$, walls.

A mixed number has a whole number part and a fraction part. A fraction is improper if its numerator is greater than or equal to its denominator.

For **1–2**, write a mixed number for each figure. Then, show how to use the drawing to write an equivalent improper fraction.

2.
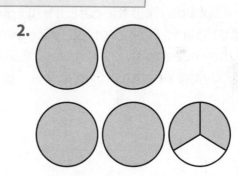

For **3–6**, write each whole number as an improper fraction.

$3 = \dfrac{\square}{10}$

4. $7 = \dfrac{\square}{1}$

5. $6 = \dfrac{\square}{2}$

6. $9 = \dfrac{\square}{6}$

For **7–10,** write each improper fraction as a mixed number.

$\dfrac{9}{4} =$

8. $\dfrac{24}{5} =$

9. $\dfrac{31}{2} =$

10. $\dfrac{38}{3} =$

For **11–13**, use the smoothie recipe at the right.

11. Jeremy used this recipe to make a smoothie. How many $\frac{1}{2}$-cups of ice does Jeremy need?

12. Write the amount of smoothie Jeremy made as an improper fraction.

13. Express the amount of bananas Jeremy used as a fraction with 2 as the denominator.

Smoothie Recipe	
Raspberry Tea	1 cup
Bananas	1 cup
Blueberries	$\frac{1}{2}$ cup
Lime juice	$\frac{1}{2}$ cup
Ice	$1\frac{1}{2}$ cups

The recipe makes $4\frac{1}{2}$ cups.

---

14. Higher Order Thinking Draw a picture to show that $3\frac{5}{8}$. Then write another mixed number that is equivalent to $3\frac{5}{8}$. Explain.

---

15. Make Sense and Persevere Ela and Darren's parents said they would pay half the cost of a 3D printer. Darren has saved $135 and Ela has saved twice as much. How much do they need to save each week to have enough money to buy the printer shown in 9 weeks? Explain your solution.

Half the cost of this 3D printer is $621.

Assessment ISTEP+ Ready

16. Which fractions are equivalent to 7? Select all that apply.

- ☐ $\frac{54}{6}$
- ☐ $\frac{63}{9}$
- ☐ $\frac{56}{7}$
- ☐ $\frac{84}{12}$
- ☐ $\frac{35}{5}$

17. Which equations are true? Select all that apply.

- ☐ $\frac{17}{6} = 2\frac{5}{6}$
- ☐ $\frac{35}{10} = 3$
- ☐ $5\frac{2}{3} = \frac{17}{3}$
- ☐ $3\frac{5}{8} = \frac{21}{8}$
- ☐ $\frac{13}{1} = \frac{1}{13}$

Select all of the fractions that are equivalent to 9.

☐ $\frac{45}{5}$

☐ $\frac{9}{9}$

☐ $\frac{18}{2}$

☐ $\frac{9}{1}$

☐ $\frac{53}{6}$

Tamika's family ate $2\frac{3}{4}$ of the pizza they ordered. Draw a picture. Use the circles to help find the equivalent improper fraction. Then, write the improper fraction.

3. Draw a line from each value on the left to its equivalent value on the right.

$\frac{8}{1}$	4
$7\frac{3}{4}$	$\frac{31}{4}$
$\frac{24}{6}$	1
5	8
$\frac{8}{8}$	$\frac{15}{3}$

Another Look!

Mr. Musial's fourth-grade class gets 10 minutes of free time in the computer lab each week.

Ben observed and recorded how many students were playing each type of computer game. Then he made a frequency table.

This question can be answered by collecting and analyzing data: Which type of computer game is most popular during free time?

Computer Games Played		
Game	Tallies	Number
Cards	III	3
Role Playing	ЖН IIII	9
Strategy	ЖН I	6

Based on the results shown in the frequency table, role-playing games are the most popular.

Jenna recorded the results of her survey. For **1–6**, use the tally chart.

1. Write a survey question that Jenna could have asked to get the results shown in the chart.

Pets Owned		
Pet	Tallies	Number
Dog	ЖН ЖН	
Cat	ЖН IIII	
Turtle	II	
Fish	ЖН III	
Bird	III	

2. Complete the last column of the tally chart to make a frequency table.

3. How many different types of pets do students own?

4. **Reasoning** Do more students own a dog or a cat than own each of the other 3 types of pets combined? Explain.

5. **Construct Arguments** Based on the data, can you say dogs are definitely the most popular pet? Explain.

6. **Reasoning** Three students own a fish and a dog, but in the survey, they only said "dog." Based on this information, which type of pet did most students own?

Thomas wants to know the best place to have his birthday party. He asked 18 friends this question:

Where is your favorite place to have a birthday party— in a bowling alley, a skating rink, or a museum?

Thomas got the answers shown.

Skating rink	Skating rink
Bowling alley	Museum
Skating rink	Skating rink
Museum	Bowling alley
Bowling alley	Skating rink
Skating rink	Museum
Skating rink	Museum
Bowling alley	Museum
Museum	Skating rink

7. Complete the frequency table to show the results.

8. **Reasoning** Based on the data, where should Thomas have his birthday party?

9. **Higher Order Thinking** Did more than half the students in the survey choose the skating rink? Explain.

Locations for a Party		
Location	Tallies	Numbe
Bowling alley		
Skating rink		
Museum		

10. **Construct Arguments** Is $\frac{27}{6}$ equivalent to a whole number or a mixed number? Explain.

11. **Model with Math** How much more does the cat eat than the parrot? Write and solve an equation to represent the problem.

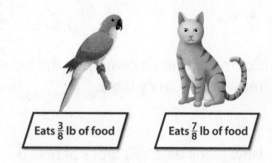

Eats $\frac{3}{8}$ lb of food   Eats $\frac{7}{8}$ lb of food

Assessment ⊙ ISTEP+ Ready

12. Write a question about vehicles, that could be answered by collecting and analyzing data.

13. Explain how you could collect and analy data to answer the question in Item 12.

Another Look!

You can make a bar graph to represent data. What does this bar graph tell about the results of a survey about students' favorite sport to watch?

- The longest bar shows that more students chose basketball than any other sport.

- The bar for soccer is shorter than the bar for baseball, so fewer students chose soccer than baseball.

- The bar for football is more than twice as long as the bar for baseball, so more than twice as many students chose football than baseball.

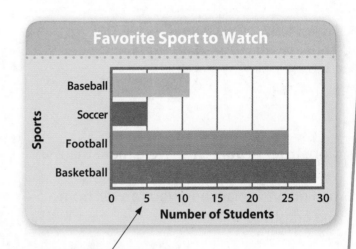

The scale is from 0 to 30.
The interval of the scale is 5.

---

ive students did an experiment to see how far they could fly paper airplane. The results are in the bar graph. For **1–5**, use e bar graph.

. What is the interval of the scale?

. Who had an airplane that flew the greatest distance?

. **Reasoning** Did Michelle's airplane or Owen's airplane fly farther? How much farther?

. **Reasoning** Which two students flew their airplanes close to the same distance?

. How many fewer feet did Reyna's airplane fly than Michelle's airplane?

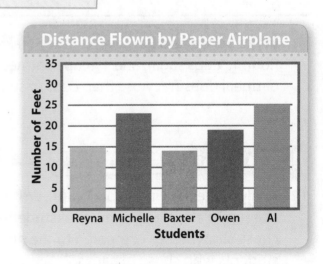

Isaac counted the number of coats left at school each day. The data he recorded are in the table.

Coats Left at School	
Day	**Number of Coats**
Monday	5
Tuesday	1
Wednesday	4
Thursday	7
Friday	2

6. **Model with Math** Make a bar graph of the data.

7. On which day were the fewest coats left at school? Explain how you can tell from the graph.

8. How many more coats were left on Thursday than Tuesday? Explain.

9. **Construct Arguments** Were more than twice as many coats left on Monday as on Friday? Explain how you can tell from the graph.

10. **Higher Order Thinking** How would the bar graph be different with intervals of 5 than intervals of 2?

11. **Make Sense and Persevere** Tracy makes her muffin recipe with $2\frac{1}{2}$ cups flour, $1\frac{1}{4}$ cups sugar, and $1\frac{3}{4}$ cups oatmeal. How many more cups of flour and oatmeal does Tracy use than cups of sugar? Explain.

Assessment ◑ (ISTEP+ Ready)

12. Analyze the data in the bar graph. Write a statement about the number of students who chose strawberries compared to the number of students who chose bananas.

Favorite Fruit

Name _____

Solve & Share

Ms. Hough's class took a survey to find how long it takes students to get home from school. The results are shown in the circle graph. What fraction of the students in the class get home in less than 30 minutes, between 15 and 30 minutes, and more than 30 minutes?

Indiana Lesson 5
Interpret Data in Circle Graphs

I can ...
interpret data given in a circle graph.

Content Standard 4.DA.3
Process Standards PS.1, PS.2, PS.3, PS.4

You can use reasoning to think about the parts of the circle.

Time It Takes Us to Get Home from School

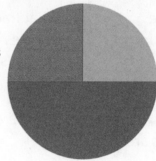

More than 30 minutes

Less than 15 minutes

15–30 minutes

Look Back! **Model with Math** What could you do to the circle graph to help you find the fraction of ...
each part? Expl...

10. Re...   rep...   of s...

Essential Question **How Can You Interpret Data in a Circle Graph?**

A

A graph in the shape of a circle that shows how a whole is broken into parts is a circle graph.

Roberto counted different types of vehicles in a parking lot. His results are shown in the circle graph. Use the circle graph to answer the questions below.

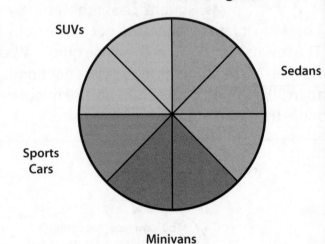

Vehicles in a Parking Lot

SUVs

Sedans

Sports Cars

Minivans

The circle graph is divided into 8 equal parts. Each part equals $\frac{1}{8}$.

B

What fraction of the vehicles in the parking lot are sports cars?

1 of the 8 parts represents sports cars.

So, $\frac{1}{8}$ of the vehicles are sports cars.

C

What fraction of the vehicles in the parking lot are SUVs?

2 of the 8 parts represent SUVs.

$\frac{2}{8} = \frac{1}{4}$

So, $\frac{2}{8}$ or $\frac{1}{4}$ of the vehicles are SUVs.

D

Which type of vehicle was $\frac{3}{8}$ of the cars Roberto counted?

The type of vehicle represented by 3 of the 8 parts is sedans.

Convince Me! **Reasoning** SUVs and minivans together made up what fraction of the vehicles in the parking lot? Explain.

Guided Practice

Do You Understand?

1. **Critique Reasoning** Use the circle graph on the previous page. Leah said that since there are 4 different colors in the graph, $\frac{1}{4}$ of each type of vehicle is in the parking lot. Is Leah correct? Explain.

2. If there were 16 vehicles in the parking lot, and 8 of the vehicles were SUVs what fraction of the circle graph would be shaded yellow? Explain.

Do You Know How?

For **3–4**, use the circle graph on the previous page.

3. What fraction of the vehicles are sedans and sports cars? Explain.

4. Which two types of cars combined equal $\frac{5}{8}$ of the vehicles? Explain.

Independent Practice

For **5–9**, use the circle graph.

5. How could the data have been collected?

6. What fraction of the people surveyed have blue eyes?

7. What eye color do half of the people have?

8. What fraction of the people have either brown or green eyes? Explain.

9. How much greater is the part for brown eyes than the part for green eyes? Explain.

Eye Color

Problem Solving

Maria took a survey and asked students how many glasses of water they drink a day. Her results are in the circle graph. For **10–14**, use the circle graph.

10. What fraction of students said they drink 4 to 5 glasses of water per day?

Glasses of Water Each D

6 to 8 glasses

1 to glas

4 to 5 glasse

11. How much water did $\frac{1}{5}$ of the students say they drink?

12. What fraction of students said they drink more than 3 glasses of water per day? Explain.

13. Higher Order Thinking If 20 students were surveyed, how many drink 4 to 5 glasses of water a day? Explain.

14. Make Sense and Persevere How muc greater is the part of students who said they drink either 1 to 3 glasses or 4 to 5 glasses than the part of students who said they drink 6 to 8 glasses? Explain.

15. Reasoning Name three common multiples of 3, 6, and 9.

16. How could you use mental math to find 4 × 23?

17. According to the circle graph, what part of Nick's budget does he spend on entertainment?

Ⓐ $\frac{1}{4}$

Ⓑ $\frac{1}{2}$

Ⓒ $\frac{2}{3}$

Ⓓ $\frac{4}{5}$

Nick's Budget

Clothes

Food

Entertainment

IN36   **Topic 11** | Indiana Lesson 5

Another Look!

The students in Mr. Murphy's class took a survey about their favorite school subjects. The results are shown in the circle graph.

What fraction of the students chose math?

2 of the 6 parts represent math.

$\frac{2}{6} = \frac{1}{3}$

So, $\frac{2}{6}$ or $\frac{1}{3}$ of the students chose math.

$\frac{1}{2}$ of the students chose which subject?

You can see that half of the students chose history.

A circle graph is in the shape of a circle and shows how a whole is broken into parts.

Our Favorite Subjects

Science

Math

History

or **1–6**, use the circle graph.

Construct Arguments How can you tell that more students play soccer than play softball?

Team Sports Students Play

Basketball   Softball

Soccer

What fraction of the students play softball?

What fraction of the students play basketball?

What sport do half of the students play?

What fraction of the students play either basketball or softball? Explain.

What survey question could the students have been asked?

Allan counted the number of daughters in families that each had
3 children. His results are in the circle graph. For **7–10**, use the circle graph.

7. How many daughters did $\frac{1}{8}$ of the families have?

8. What fraction of families have more than
1 daughter? Explain.

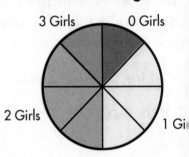

Number of Daughters

3 Girls 0 Girls

2 Girls

1 Gi...

9. **Higher Order Thinking** If 24 families
were surveyed, how many families have
1 girl? Explain how you decided.

10. **Make Sense and Persevere** How mu...
greater is the part of families with 1 o...
2 girls than with 0 or 3 girls? Explain.

For **11** and **12**, use the bar graph.

11. How many students have 7–9 letters in
their last names?

12. How many more students have 4–6
letters in their last names than have
more than 6 letters? Explain.

Number of Letters in Last Nam...

Number of Students

14
12
10
8
6
4
2
0

1–3 4–6 7–9 10–1...

Number of Letters

---

13. According to the circle graph, which part of
the books are either funny or scary?

Ⓐ $\frac{3}{8}$ Ⓒ $\frac{7}{10}$

Ⓑ $\frac{1}{2}$ Ⓓ $\frac{7}{8}$

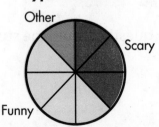

Types of Books

Other

Scary

Funny

1. Which can be answered by collecting and analyzing data? Select all that apply.

☐ How many floors are in our school?

☐ How many floors do you think a school should have?

☐ What is the best room in the school?

☐ How tall is that door?

☐ How many students are absent each day for 10 school days?

2. Ms. Smith's class took a survey to find out which science demonstration they would like to see. The results are below. Use the results to complete the frequency table. Analyze the results. Which demonstration would the students like to see?

Chemistry	Weather	Magnets	Weather
Chemistry	Chemistry	Weather	Weather
Weather	Magnets	Molecules	Weather
Chemistry	Magnets	Chemistry	Weather
Weather	Molecules	Chemistry	
Weather	Magnets	Chemistry	
Chemistry	Weather	Weather	

Favorite Science Demonstration		
Choice	Tallies	Number of Students
Chemistry		
Magnets		
Molecules		
Weather		

Mr. Curran's class voted for which animal they would like to see behind the scenes at the zoo. The results are in the table. Use the data for **3** and **4**.

Animals to See at the Zoo	
Animal	**Number of Students**
Elephant	9
Giraffe	6
Snake	7
Tiger	3

3. Complete the bar graph of the data in the table.

_____

_____

_____

_____

4. Which of the following statements is true?

Ⓐ More students choose the giraffe than the snake.

Ⓑ Four more students chose the snake than the tiger.

Ⓒ Twice as many students chose the elephant as chose the tiger.

Ⓓ Twice as many students chose the giraffe as chose the elephant.

Use the circle graph to answer **5** and **6**.

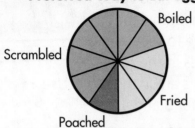

Preferred Way to Eat Eggs

5. What fraction of the students prefer to eat their eggs boiled?

Ⓐ $\frac{1}{10}$

Ⓑ $\frac{1}{5}$

Ⓒ $\frac{2}{5}$

Ⓓ $\frac{1}{2}$

6. What fraction of the students prefer to eat their eggs scrambled or fried? Explain.

ame _____

☆ ☆
Solve & Share

Measure the length of 4 different objects to the nearest inch and to the nearest $\frac{1}{4}$ inch. Record your measurements in the table.

I can ...
Measure length to the nearest $\frac{1}{4}$ inch, $\frac{1}{8}$ inch, or millimeter.

Content Standard 4.M.1
Process Standards PS.1, PS.2, PS.3, PS.5, PS.6

Object	Length to the Nearest Inch	Length to the Nearest $\frac{1}{4}$ Inch

You can be precise when you measure to the nearest inch and $\frac{1}{4}$ inch. Compare the length of the object to the halfway mark between inches and the halfway mark between $\frac{1}{4}$ inches.

Look Back! **Reasoning** The length of a pen is 6 inches to the nearest inch and $5\frac{3}{4}$ inches to the nearest $\frac{1}{4}$ inch. Could the length of this pen be a little less than $5\frac{3}{4}$ inches? Explain.

Essential Question

How Can You Measure to the Nearest Quarter Inch or Eighth Inch?

A

About how long is Greg's toy car?

You can use units on an inch ruler to measure. Measurements are always approximate.

B Measure to the nearest $\frac{1}{4}$ inch.

There are four $\frac{1}{4}$ inch marks in one inch.

The car is $2\frac{3}{4}$ inches long, to the nearest $\frac{1}{4}$ inch.

C Measure to the nearest $\frac{1}{8}$ inch.

The car is $2\frac{6}{8}$ inches long, to the nearest $\frac{1}{8}$ inch.

Convince Me! **Reasoning** When measuring to the nearest $\frac{1}{8}$ inch, could the length of an object be $2\frac{3}{4}$ inches? Explain your reasoning.

nother Example!

What is the body length of the beetle to he nearest millimeter?

Remember, 1 centimeter = 10 millimeters.

The beetle is 43 millimeters long.

CENTIMETERS

The tick marks are 1 mm apart.

Guided Practice

o You Understand?

1. **Construct Arguments** In the example on the previous page, how can Greg's car be $2\frac{3}{4}$ inches long and $2\frac{7}{8}$ inches long?

Do You Know How?

For **2**, use an inch ruler.

2. What is the length of the seashell to the nearest $\frac{1}{4}$ inch? Nearest $\frac{1}{8}$ inch?

dependent Practice

or **3–4**, use an inch ruler to find each length to the nearest $\frac{1}{4}$ inch and to the nearest $\frac{1}{8}$ inch.

4.

or **5–6**, use a centimeter ruler to find each length to the nearest millimeter.

6.

Problem Solving

7. Use Appropriate Tools What is the length of the snake to the nearest $\frac{1}{8}$ inch? How long will it be after it grows another $\frac{1}{8}$ inch?

8. Be Precise Measure the length of the red-eyed tree frog and the height of the seahorse to the nearest $\frac{1}{8}$ inch. What is the difference of these measures, in inches?

Ari collected data by measuring the lengths of different red-eyed tree frogs. She made a circle graph of the results.

Red-Eyed Tree Frogs Lengths in Inches

$2\frac{1}{2}$ to $2\frac{3}{4}$ $1\frac{1}{2}$ to $1\frac{5}{8}$

$2\frac{1}{4}$ to $2\frac{3}{8}$

$1\frac{3}{4}$ t

2 to $2\frac{1}{8}$

9. Write a question that could be answered with Ari's data.

10. What fraction of the tree frogs that Ari measured are from $1\frac{3}{4}$ to $1\frac{7}{8}$ inches long?

11. Reasoning What length are $\frac{1}{5}$ of the tree frogs?

12. Higher Order Thinking What fraction of the tree frogs Ari measured are 2 inches or longer? Explain.

13. What is the height of the acorn, to the nearest $\frac{1}{4}$ inch?

Ⓐ $\frac{3}{8}$ in. Ⓒ $\frac{3}{4}$ in.

Ⓑ $\frac{1}{2}$ in. Ⓓ $\frac{7}{8}$ in.

14. What is the length of the eraser to the nearest millimeter?

Ⓐ 4 mm Ⓒ 42 mm

Ⓑ 40 mm Ⓓ 50 mm

Help   Practice   Tools   Games
        Buddy

Another Look!

What is the length of the feather to the nearest millimeter?

Line up one end of the feather with the zero mark on the ruler.

Measure precisely by lining up one end of the feather with the zero mark on the ruler.

The feather is 141 millimeters long.

or **1–2**, use an inch ruler to find each length to the nearest $\frac{1}{4}$ inch and o the nearest $\frac{1}{8}$ inch.

2.

or **3–4**, use a centimeter ruler to find each length to the earest millimeter.

4.

For **5–7**, use the diagram of a plant's growth for 6 days.

| Day 1 | Day 2 | Day 3 | Day 4 | Day 5 | Day 6 |

Day	Height (In
1	
2	
3	
4	
5	
6	

5. **Use Appropriate Tools** Measure the heights of the plant to the nearest $\frac{1}{8}$ inch and record the heights in the table.

6. How much did the plant grow between Day 3 and Day 4?

7. How much did the plant grow between Day 1 and Day 6? Write this measure as a mixed number and as an improper fraction.

8. **Make Sense and Persevere** Regina is 115 centimeters tall and her father is 2 meters tall. How much taller is Regina's father? Explain.

9. **Higher Order Thinking** The length of a stamp is 36 millimeters. The width of the stamp is 28 millimeters. What is the perimeter of the stamp?

Assessment ISTEP+ Ready

10. What is the length of the praying mantis, to the nearest millimeter?

Ⓐ 30 mm   Ⓒ 38 mm

Ⓑ 35 mm   Ⓓ 40 mm

11. What is the length of the bead to the nearest $\frac{1}{8}$ inch?

Ⓐ $1\frac{2}{8}$ in.   Ⓒ 1 in.

Ⓑ $1\frac{1}{8}$ in.   Ⓓ $\frac{7}{8}$ in.

. Measure the length of the rock to the nearest $\frac{1}{4}$ inch and to the nearest $\frac{1}{8}$ inch. Select the measurements that apply.

☐ $1\frac{1}{4}$ inches

☐ $1\frac{2}{8}$ inches

☐ $1\frac{4}{8}$ inches

☐ $1\frac{2}{4}$ inches

☐ $1\frac{3}{4}$ inches

. Mindy said a pencil was $4\frac{1}{4}$ inches long to the nearest $\frac{1}{8}$ inch. When measuring to the nearest $\frac{1}{8}$ inch, can the length be $4\frac{1}{4}$ inches long? Explain.

3. The mascot for Nash's football team is a green hornet. What is the length of the green hornet to the nearest millimeter?

Ⓐ 40 mm

Ⓑ 44 mm

Ⓒ 50 mm

Ⓓ 52 mm

Solve

Indiana Lesson 7
Describe Relationships

★ ☆ ★
Solve & Share

Patty used the equation $P = 4s$ to find the perimeter of each of 3 square pictures.

What is the perimeter of the picture that has a side length of 8 inches? 9 inches? 10 inches? **Solve this problem any way you choose.**

I can ...
use an equation as a rule to generate a pattern.

Content Standard 4.AT.6
Process Standards PS.2, PS.3, PS.4, PS.8

You can generalize and use repeated reasoning to find the perimeter of the square picture for different side lengths.

Look Back! **Generalize** What is a pattern in the perimeter of the square picture for the 3 different side lengths?

How Can You Use An Equation as a Rule to Generate a Pattern?

A

An equation like $d = 3 + 7s$ is a rule. It can be used to find a second number when the first number is given.

Joel is completing the table for the equation $d = 3 + 7s$. What are the missing numbers?

s	d
2	
3	24
4	
5	
6	45

$7s$ is another way to write $7 \times s$.

B To find the value of d, when $s = 2$, replace the variable s in the equation with 2.

$d = 3 + 7s$
$d = 3 + (7 \times 2)$
$d = 3 + 14$
$d = 17$

Do the operation inside the parentheses first. Multiply before you add.

C Repeat the steps for the other two values of s.

When $s = 4$,

$d = 3 + (7 \times 4)$
$d = 3 + 28$
$d = 31$

When $s = 5$

$d = 3 + (7 \times 5)$
$d = 3 + 35$
$d = 38$

D Record the values in the table.

s	d
2	17
3	24
4	31
5	38
6	45

Convince Me! **Generalize** What patterns do you see in the table above?

Guided Practice

Do You Understand?

1. Harry can seat 4 people at each table. The equation $t = p \div 4$ represents the number of tables Harry needs to seat p people, where t is the number of tables. Explain how to find the number of tables Harry needs to seat 20 people.

2. Reasoning In the equation $t = p \div 4$, could you get the same value of t for two different values of p? Explain.

Do You Know How?

3. Complete the table for the equation $2c + 9 = d$.

c	d
9	
10	
11	
12	

4. What is the pattern in the table?

Independent Practice

Leveled Practice For **5–7**, complete each table for the equation given.

5. $k = 6j$

j	k
2	12
3	
4	
5	30
6	

6. $24 + m = n$

m	n
10	
20	
30	54
40	
50	

7. $n = 5m - 11$

m	n
3	4
4	
5	14
6	
7	

8. Nellie needs 4 minutes to run each lap. The equation $m = 4L$ represents the total time in minutes Nellie needs to run L laps, where m is the time in minutes. How many minutes does Nellie need to run 10, 20, or 30 laps?

9. Alvin is 5 years younger than his sister Mira. The equation $a = m - 5$ represents the relationship, where m is Mira's age and a is Alvin's age. How old is Alvin when Mira is 9, 10, or 11 years old?

Problem Solving

10. The equation $c = 2p$ represents a relationship between measurement units, where c is the number of cups and p is the number of pints. How many cups are in 6, 7, or 8 pints?

11. Construct Arguments Max says the value of r in the equation $r = 5s + 6$ is when $s = 4$. Is Max correct? Explain.

---

12. Congress consists of the House of Representatives and the Senate. Each state has 2 Senators. The number of representatives depends on the state's population. The equation $c = r + 2$ represents the members, where c is the total number of members from a state and r is the number of representatives the state has in the House. Complete the table for each state.

Members in Congress		
State	r	c
Illinois	18	
Indiana	9	
Kentucky	6	
Ohio	16	

13. Model with Math Complete the bar graph of the total number of members of congress for the four states in the table. What relationship can you see in the data from the graph easier than you can see in the table?

---

14. Higher Order Thinking What equation could represent the relationship between inches and feet, where i is the number of inches and f is the number of feet?

Assessment 🇮 ⊙ — ISTEP+ Ready

15. At a fair, ride tickets cost $5 each. The equation $c = 5t$ represents the cost, where c is the total cost and t is the number of ride tickets bought. Complete the table to find the cost when buying 4, 6, 8, or 10 ride tickets.

Cost of the Ride Tickets	
t	c
4	
6	
8	
10	

Another Look!

Jada is completing the table for the equation $d = 4c - 5$. What are the missing numbers?

An equation is a rule. It can be used to find a second number when the first number is given.

c	d
8	
9	31
10	35
11	
12	

To find the value of d, when $c = 8$, replace c in the equation with 8.

$d = 4c - 5$

$d = (4 \times 8) - 5$
$d = 32 - 5$

$d = 27$

Repeat the steps for the other two values of c.

When $c = 11$,

$d = (4 \times 11) - 5$
$d = 44 - 5$
$d = 39$

When $c = 12$,

$d = (4 \times 12) - 5$
$d = 48 - 5$
$d = 43$

Record the values in the table.

c	d
8	27
9	31
10	35
11	39
12	43

For **1–3**, complete each table for the equation g

1. $z \div 7 = y$

z	y
14	2
21	
28	4
35	
42	

2. $n = 40 + m$

m	
20	
25	
30	
35	75
40	

3. $7 + 4k = j$

k	j
5	
	31

4. A truck averages 20 miles per gallon. The equation $m = 20g$ represents the relationship, where m is the total miles a truck can go and g is the gallons of gas in the tank. How far can the truck go on 6, 8, or 10 gallons of gas?

5. A karate class has 2_ _ _ _ _ _ _ _e more sign up. The equation $p =$ _ _ _ _ resents the class, where p is the numb_ _ _ eople already in the class and n is the _ _ mber of new people who sign up. How many people are in the class if 4, 5, or 6 new people sign up?

6. Barry collects cups from different countries. He can buy cups in packages like the one shown. The equation $c = 2p$ represents Barry's cup collection, where c is the total number of cups and p is the number of packages Barry buys. How many cups will Barry have in his collection if he buys 8, 10, or 12 packages?

A package has 2 cups

7. Generalize Tacos cost $3 each. The equation $t = d \div 3$ represents how many tacos Kal can buy, where d is the money Kal has in dollars and t is the number of tacos he can buy. Complete the table to find how many tacos Kal can buy for each amount. What is the pattern?

Kal's Money	
d	t
$9	
$12	
$15	
$18	

Amy made a circle graph of the points her basketball team, the Lions, scored in games. For **8** and **9**, use Amy's graph.

8. In what fraction of the games did the Lions score 20 to 24 points?

9. Higher Order Thinking How much greater is the fraction of the games in which the Lions scored either 20 to 24 points or under 15 points than they scored 15 to 19 points? Explain.

Points Scored by the Lior

Over 24 Under 1

20 to 24

15 to 19

10. Leah's puppy weighed 9 ounces when it was born. The equation $z = 9 + w$ represents the puppy's weight, where z is the total weight in ounces and w is the weight the puppy has gained since birth. Complete the table to find the puppy's weight after it gains 8, 12, 16, and 20 ounces.

Puppy's Weight	
w	z
8	
12	
16	
20	

Name

ame

1. Draw a line to match each value of *n* on the left to a value of *m* on the right so that $m = 2n - 7$.

| $n = 8$ |
| $n = 10$ |
| $n = 7$ |
| $n = 9$ |
| $n = 6$ |

| $m = 13$ |
| $m = 11$ |
| $m = 5$ |
| $m = 9$ |
| $m = 7$ |

2. Anna bought some necklaces for $15 each. She had a coupon for $10 off. The equation $15n - 10 = c$ represents the relationship, where *c* is the total cost and *n* is number of necklaces Anna bought. What is the cost when Anna buys 3, 4, or 5 necklaces? Explain how you found each cost.

3. Which statements are true for the equation $3x + 5 = y$? Select all that apply.

- ☐ When $x = 6$, $y = 22$.
- ☐ When $x = 4$, $y = 17$.
- ☐ When $x = 8$, $y = 29$.
- ☐ When $x = 12$, $y = 40$.
- ☐ When $x = 10$, $y = 35$.

TOPIC 14

Assessment

ISTEP+ Ready